Mosques and Imams

Mosques and Imams

Everyday Islam in Eastern Indonesia

Edited by

Kathryn M. Robinson

NUS PRESS
SINGAPORE

Published by:

NUS Press
National University of Singapore
AS3-01-02, 3 Arts Link
Singapore 117569

Fax: (65) 6774-0652
E-mail: nusbooks@nus.edu.sg
Website: http://nuspress.nus.edu.sg

ISBN 978-981-325-120-5 (paper)

National Library Board, Singapore Cataloguing in Publication Data

Name(s): Robinson, Kathryn May, 1949– editor.
Title: Mosques and imams: everyday Islam in eastern Indonesia/edited by Kathryn M. Robinson.
Description: Singapore: NUS Press, [2021]|Includes index.
Identifier(s): OCN 1144122575|ISBN 978-981-32-5120-5 (paperback)
Subject(s): LCSH: Islam--Indonesia.|Muslims--Indonesia.|Imams (Mosque officers)--Indonesia.|Mosques--Indonesia.
Classification: DDC 297.09598--dc23

Cover image: The imam, H. Ahmad Djufri, calls the newborn baby to Islam by whispering the call to prayer in his right ear. Photo by Kathryn Robinson.

Printed by: Integrated Books International

Dedicated to

James J. Fox
Emeritus Professor of Anthropology
Australian National University

His innovative anthropological approach to studies of Islam in Java, and his ethnographic research in eastern Indonesia have been inspirational for the authors of this volume.

Contents

List of Illustrations

Maps

Table

Figures and Photographs

Acknowledgements

The research for the individual chapters in this volume was conducted by scholars who came together under the umbrella of the project "Being Muslim in Eastern Indonesia: Practice, Politics and Cultural Diversity". This was funded by an Australian Research Council Discovery Project (DP0881464). We acknowledge the vibrant research community of the College of Asia and the Pacific at the Australian National University, and would like to thank the following scholars who participated in our regular discussions and seminars and contributed to the development of the approaches to the study of local-level Islam: George Quinn, James J. Fox, Campbell Macknight, Wendy Mukherjee, Virginia Hooker, the late Merle Ricklefs, Luthfi Makhasin, Deni Hamdani and Safira Machrusah. We also acknowledge the contribution of Partner Investigator, Nurul Ilmi Idrus. Diana Glazebrook has provided invaluable research assistance including editing this manuscript. Maps are provided by CartoGIS services in the ANU College of Asia and the Pacific.

A Note on Non-English Words

Non-English words in this volume are Indonesian unless otherwise marked. Other Indonesian languages are indicated in the following ways: (Bim.) Bima; (Mak.) Makassarese; (Bug.) Bugis; (Sor.) Sorowako; (CC.) Cia-Cia; and Arabic is indicated thus (Ar.). Some religious phrases in Arabic are commonly used in Indonesia and in these cases we have presented them with Indonesian orthography.

In each chapter, non-English words that are used frequently will be italicised in the first instance and in roman font in subsequent mention.

Introduction

Kathryn M. Robinson

The Muslim communities of eastern Indonesia are, on the whole, far from centres of formal Islamic learning. It is notable that village imams (prayer leaders, local religious authorities)[1] have been the bearers of Islamic doctrine and practice. "Imam" (a term which in other Islamic societies can refer to the prayer leader in the mosque, a *primus inter pares*) have a distinctive role as religious authorities in local communities in the Indonesian archipelago. This regionally specific feature was noted by Ira M. Lapidus (2002: 390) in his grand historic sweep of Islamic societies. In eastern Indonesia, this title (for which there are also vernacular terms) is commonly conferred on a local mosque official who leads the congregational prayers in the mosque and authorises religious and ritual practices, including those that express local customs and norms. In many communities they have also assumed guardianship for ritual practices associated with "pre-Islamic" beliefs.

In spite of the critical influence these religious officials have on the quotidian religious practice of Muslim communities, the imam is an "understudied" figure in scholarship on Indonesian Islam. Indeed in general the Islamic peoples of eastern Indonesia have been understudied, compared to the populations of the western archipelago.

This volume asks: what can we learn about the processes and sociocultural impacts of Islam in the Indonesian archipelago, and the modes of local embrace of Islam through comparative ethnographic studies of contemporary Muslim communities? How do village imams execute Islamic authority, understood as "the right to impose rules that are deemed to be in consonance with the will of God...." in relation to "common values and rules of conduct" (Gaborieau 2010: 1).

The village imams of eastern Indonesia are significant as proselytisers; as exemplars and exponents of everyday Islamic practice; and as religious authorities whose influence extends beyond doctrinal interpretation and religiosity to life cycle rituals. Their performances of religious authority provide critical sites of accommodation between Islam and local cultural beliefs and practices. As religious and ritual leaders in many communities, they also assume authority in regard to magical practices and rituals derived from pre-Islamic traditions within the accommodative versions of everyday Islam (see for example Muhammad Adlin Sila, this volume).

The role of village imam is inherently linked to the institution of the mosque, which is a symbol of the Muslim identity of his community and also of his religious authority. The volume also focuses on mosques that provide the spatial anchoring of Muslim communities and local religious practices (see chapters by Adlin Sila, Phillip Winn and Eva Nisa, this volume). While most of the studies in this volume focus on majority-Muslim communities, in the easternmost parts of Indonesia Muslims can be a minority and the mosques figure importantly in the ways Muslims live as religious minorities (see Stella Aleida Hutagalung and Andrew McWilliam, this volume).

The comparative perspective of this volume is historically inflected and these contemporary studies illuminate the accommodative practices of conversion where especially Sufi-inflected Islam has melded to existing customs, giving rise to what Azyumadi Azra (2015) has termed the "colourful" or "flowery" Islam ("*Islam berbunga bunga*") of the Indonesian archipelago.

In this volume, chapters focus on forms of everyday Islam, and Islamic identities and religious authority, particularly in communities in South Sulawesi, but also communities that have come under its influence, like Bima in Sumbawa (chapter by Sila), and in Nusa Tenggara Timor (chapters by Hutagalung and McWilliam). The studies were conducted under the umbrella of the "Being Muslim in Eastern Indonesia" project in the Anthropology Department at the Australian National University.[2] This locally grounded, comparative approach takes inspiration from the body of work conducted by James J. Fox and students at the Australian National University, mainly in the 1980s and 1990s, which illuminate "religion and social life", the "multiple traditions" of Islam, even in a particular area (Fox 2002: 78) and involved "deep examination" of the complex traditions of Islam in particular areas of Indonesia (Fox 2002: 77). Like this previous generation of scholars, many of the authors have come to anthropology

Map 0.1 Locations of field studies and significant sites in the spread of Islam in eastern Indonesia

from religious studies. From their dual standpoint they can appreciate the "richness and variety of Islamic traditions" in Indonesia (Fox 2002: 81), such complex understanding and analysis providing a critical basis for understanding the complexities of the shifting landscape of contemporary Indonesian Islamic traditions.

Studying Everyday Islam

Traditions, as products of human creative endeavour, are by their nature constantly being remade: this volume considers the ongoing accommodations between Islam and the local cultural practices it encounters as it moves through the archipelago. As Christian Pelras (1993) concludes, Islamisation is not an event (even though popular histories often treat it as such), but a process. The religious and spiritual authority of imams are key to the accommodations between local communities and cultures and Islam. Fox (2002) notes in regard to Java, accommodations to Islam reflect local cultural practices and result in a kind of "patchwork".

Chapters in this volume interrogate the conceptual apparatus available to scholars for understanding religious transformation, for example building on the foundations of Abdul Ghoffir Muhaimin's (2004) critique of the concept of "syncretism", which is frequently employed by scholars and also by Muslims themselves to "explain" the relation between a religious tradition, that it is assumed can be grasped in a discrete and pure form, and social and cultural practices. In referring to "mixing" or "blending", syncretism can imply the existence of purer or more authentic—as well as monolithic—cultural and religious traditions. Muhaiman concludes, this approach manifests "confusion on how religion is distinguished from other governing values, codes of conduct and behaviour including, for example, adat or local traditions" (2004: 3). Religious practices are always the result of interaction and change, both past and present. The "flowery" Islam of the archipelago cannot be regarded as impure or lacking authenticity, or as merely a thin layer over authentic Indonesian selves.

A theme that emerges in many of the chapters is the shaping influence of the underlying cultural order or "cultural predilections" of eastern Indonesian societies in the diverse ways Islam lodges in place. Kathryn Robinson describes the ways that the hierarchical societies of South Sulawesi subsume Islam into the cultural principles of courtly power, while Adlin Sila and Andrew McWilliam analyse the manner in which the dyadic principles and structures that are characteristic of these Austronesian-speaking populations, inflect the accommodation between Islam and custom, and are expressed in everyday practices.

"Islamising" the Eastern Archipelago

Islam entered the Indonesian archipelago through trade routes linking India, Africa and the Middle East from across the Indian Ocean, to China. Beginning from at least the 8th century, the islands in the eastern part of the archipelago had global importance as sources of spices, especially cloves and nutmeg, which originated in the islands of Ternate and Banda respectively (Burnet 2011); and the sandalwood trade from Timor during the Srivijaya period (7th to 11th century) (Gunn 2016).

Much of the early China trade in the archipelago engaged societies of the eastern archipelago and in what is now the Philippines. There is early evidence of trade in spices from the eastern archipelago reaching Europe from early in the first millennium (Burnet 2011); Ferdinand Magellan's historic circumnavigation of the globe in the 1520s, which initiated European presence in the archipelago, was stimulated by his quest for the fabled "spice islands" (Burnet 2011). New commodities from the eastern islands were constantly entering global markets, including feathers, oils, turtle shell and resin.

Islam is a religion without a dedicated missionising priesthood, and every Muslim is a propagator of the faith. The earliest conversions are associated with traders, especially from India and China, presumed to initially occur through them marrying into local communities. There is evidence of beginnings of conversion by Muslim traders in coastal trading communities between the 13th and 15th centuries. The Islamising of the archipelago, began in earnest in the 14th century, however (Reid 1993: 151). Early historical accounts record Muslims of diverse national origins (including Chinese) in the coastal cities of north Java and also later Makassar. But it was only by the 16th century that conversion began on a mass societal scale (Reid 1993) involving proselytising Sufi preachers.

The "received" story of Islamisation in much of eastern Indonesia is commonly told as a series of conversions of the hereditary rulers of local polities whose legitimacy derived from origin myths asserting divine descent, and whose power and authority were bolstered by the political alliances forged with foreign traders. (An important exception to this is the origin story in Leihitu, discussed below.) The first historically recorded conversion in eastern Indonesia began with the profession of faith by the ruler (henceforth Sultan) of Ternate in the mid-15th century. This tiny island was the original source of cloves, and hence a critical node on the international spice trade.

The influence of this realm spread Islam inter alia to north Sulawesi, other parts of the Maluku islands and the east coast of Sulawesi. (The east coast Islamic polity of Bungku was recorded as part of Ternate's sphere of influence in the Bongaya treaty of 1667 [Andaya 1993].) Ternate's "twin" state, Tidore, was significant in Islamising the coastal areas and islands of New Guinea (now West Papua province).

Islamising South Sulawesi

South Sulawesi has been a particularly important node for the spread of Islam in the archipelago due to the Bugis traditions of sojourning and sailing. Many of the chapters in the volume address Muslim communities in South Sulawesi, or places elsewhere in the archipelago that now express its Islamic traditions.

The Sulawesi realms were relatively late among the pre-colonial polities of the archipelago to embrace Islam (Pelras 1993). The ruler of Gowa–Tallo who controlled the important entrepot of Makassar made the confession of faith in the first decade of the 17th century, as did the ruler of Luwu at the top of the Gulf of Bone (a gateway to inland trade). Both polities claim to have been "first". The conversion of the populace, it is said, followed soon after (see Pelras 1993; Reid 2006).

The "golden legend" (Pelras 1993: 135) credits the final "submission" to travelling religious scholars known as the Three Dato'. These Islamic preachers, allegedly from Minangkabau West Sumatra, converted the rulers of the coastal trading states of Gowa–Tallo and Luwu in the early 17th century.

The story goes that, initially not being successful in the powerful trading state of Gowa–Tallo, one of the Dato' went to Luwu, regarded as the originary Bugis polity and the cradle of the La Galigo traditions, the stories of the divine origins of the rulers that formed a core of the pre-Islamic religious tradition (see Pelras 1996).

The nature of authority in these polities—in particular the semi-divine power of the rulers—were critical elements in conversion. The Dato' are said to have been successful in Islamising Luwu because they found a way to present Islamic belief and authority in ways that did not challenge the spiritual basis of power: according to Pelras (1993) the rulers embraced Islam once they had a narrative that was not in conflict with the validation of their authority through belief in divine descent ("white blood") as the basis of legitimacy. They accepted Islam as it could be incorporated to bolster, not challenge the authority of the divinely descended rulers. That is, whereas many contemporary Islamic scholars will argue that Islamic values are inherently equitable, that all are equal before God, the South Sulawesi rulers were able to subsume Islam under existing beliefs and customs, so it became an arm of royal authority (see chapter by Kathryn Robinson, this volume).

Contemporary Muslim intellectuals in South Sulawesi like to credit the success of the Dato' to their Sufi style of Islam. In this telling of histories, the Dato' consciously urged people to embrace Islam without abandoning all aspects of the old beliefs (see also Pelras 1993: 142). It is commonly asserted by local Muslim intellectuals that the approach of the Dato' was to take some existing local belief or practice and interpret it in Islamic idiom, to say "You are already Islam". For example, in the island of Selayar where houses customarily have four rows of house pillars, I was told that this was interpreted as representing the prophet and his three companions.[3]

South Sulawesi is distinctive in the archipelago in that its polities had traditions of local historiography that document elite-centred accounts of the process of the subsumption of Islam by the courts and firmly locate Islam in their governing apparatus. Formal stories of Islamisation also survive in court chronicles in places under South Sulawesi influence, notably Bima in Sumbawa (Sila, this volume; Noorduyn 1987).

While the manuscript traditions have recorded elite-centric version of conversion, Pelras (1993: 135) considers important the one hundred-plus years of familiarisation with Islam through the presence of Muslims in port cities; and there are stories of earlier conversions, for example in Bira on the southern tip of Sulawesi, and nearby Selayar island (Pelras 1993: 137). There are some oral traditions (for example, in Wajo) of individual conversions prior to the court embrace of Islam.

The people of Leihitu in the north of Ambon have formalised conversion narratives that link back to named Javanese or Arabic preachers who converted their clans (see chapter by Winn; Kleinstuber and Maharadjo 2012).

Stella Hutagalung's chapter on a relatively recent Bugis migrant community in Kupang in Indonesia's eastern province of Nusa Tenggara Timor (NTT) describes the ways in which intermarriage of male sojourners with local women who convert to Islam becomes a way of embedding the faith. In parts of West Papua and Flores, interfaith marriage does not challenge the logics of the marriage system, based on formal principles of marriage exchange between clans. The district head in Kokas (West Papua) sang the praises of interfaith marriage as an aspect of affinal ties: the Muslims could cook for Christian relatives at Christmas, leaving them free to focus on worship and the favour would be reciprocated at Idul Fitri.

In South Sulawesi, once the rulers of Gowa–Tallo accepted Islam the neighbouring lowland polities of Sidenreng and Soppeng were forcibly Islamised in the *musu selleng* (Bug. religious war) by 1690; Wajo by 1610; and Bone by 1611. However the people in the mountainous interior of Sulawesi, often tributary peoples of Luwu (Schrauwers 1997), remained "pagan" headhunters, until the region was forcibly "pacified" by the Dutch in 1906 (see chapter by Robinson).

Adopting Islam

The common pattern of adoption of Islam in Bugis and Makassarese realms of South Sulawesi took the form of "subsumption" under the authority of the court. Islamic precepts and practice became incorporated as a strand of customary regulation. It is perhaps noteworthy that in South Sulawesi, the Sufi proselytisers are always referred to as Dato', the Malay title for noblemen, rather than as *ulama* or *kiai*.

Islam was formally incorporated into customary regulation (Bug. *panggaderreng*) of the realm. *Sara'* (Bug. matters pertaining to Islam) became one element alongside the pre-existing strands: *bicara* (Bug. jurisprudence/precedent); *rapang* (Bug. civil law) and *wari'* (Bug. rules concerning hierarchy by birth). Further, Islam was subsumed into the formal structures of the realm, reaching out from the centre and with its own officials. Religious matters were placed in the hands of a newly-created official, *kadi* (from *Ar. qaadiy* or judge)—known by titles of Daeng ta Kalia (Makassar) or Petta Kali (Bone)—which provided the formal mechanism to promote Islamic values.

Nobles monopolised these new Islamic offices (Pelras 1993: 147). The customary office of Daeng La Alakaya was retained to advise on mystical matters related to the religion of the La Galigo (the mythic corpus validating the divine ancestry and hence legitimacy of kings). This pattern of adoption, through subsumption of Islam and the enforcement of its regulations and practices through the office of the court, meant that the cultural logics of the court remained relatively unchanged. The power of Islamic precepts reinforced the existing forms of power. Islamic incantations "strengthened" the customary exhortations to ancestral and animistic spirits (Robinson 1998). Merle Ricklefs (2006) describes a protracted struggle in the previous century in Java between Islam and the pre-existing ruling culture and religion, to define the identity of the court. But he notes a similar accommodation in culture and belief.

Early conversions were under the auspices of the courts. Indeed, the initial profession of faith by the ruler's subjects was more a statement of loyalty to the ruler than a sign of devotion to the Islamic faith/statement of religious conviction (Mukhlis and Robinson 1985). In acting as a Muslim, the emphasis was on practices with social and ceremonial aspects. A person was a Muslim if he/she was given an Islamic name, circumcised, married and buried according to Islamic rites. Practices like drinking alcohol and gambling (associated with ritual and ceremonial events so critical to the exercise of courtly power) were not banned, and were still part of court practice. *Salat* (ritual prayer) and fasting in the holy month of Ramadan—both formally required of believers—were personal choice. But *not* eating pork quickly became a critical marker of social difference from non-Muslims, perhaps related to the precursor importance of commensality in expressing and performing social identity. In ritual practices there was substitution and addition of Islamic forms: for example Pelras (1993: 146) notes that recitation of *barzanji* (a set of poems celebrating the life of the Prophet) replaced the chanting of the sacred La Galigo texts at ritual events such as funerals (see chapters by Sila, Hutagalung and Robinson). Islamic life cycle rituals were grafted on to pre-existing rituals, for example the Islamic marriage contract added to the existing cycle of Bugis wedding celebrations (Alimi 2014b; Alimi, this volume; Robinson, this volume).

The Role of Village Imams as Cultural and Religious Mediators

In the formal bureaucracy of the Sulawesi realms, a local mosque-based official (imam) was an official position, a functionary of the court-centred hierarchy. Just as the ruler at the centre was represented in the villages by headmen as the furthest outreach of his power, the village imam was the lowest rung of the religious hierarchy. In the case of South Sulawesi polities, imams were appointed by the *kadi*. The position conferred high social status, and frequently became an inherited office, reflecting the ideas of authority based on descent (Mukhlis and Robinson 1985). Azyumardi Azra (2004) comments that hence many wandering preachers were attracted to settling down as court-appointed imams in local communities in Sulawesi. Sila's chapter focuses on the role of the *lebe*, the title given to mosque imams appointed by the royal court in the 24 mosques under their authority in the sultanate era in the period 1918–50.

Imam as an inherited office in South Sulawesi, and its cultural orbit, feature in several chapters in this book (see chapters by Robinson, Hutagalung and Faried F. Saenong). Collectively the chapters show local variations on the practices regarding the appointment of other mosque-based officials, such as *khatib* and *bilal* (chapters by Sila, Saenong, Winn and Hutagalung) but the presence and importance of the imam is constant.

The chapters describe how the imams are the bearers of religious authority in their communities, responsible for religious education and guidance in the modern world. They play key roles in religious practice in the social life of communities.

Dual Classification, Cultural Logics and Social Transformations

Dual classification is an intrinsic feature of social organisation and cultural expression in eastern Indonesia. This is a dynamic system in which binary categories (elder–younger; trunk–tip; male–female) are dynamic principles that underlie social and cultural reproduction and transformation. Such binary categories are not static but rather function as "symbolic operators" which are expressed in many contexts, and we can identify ways in which the dynamic principles of dualism conditions cultural responses and accommodations to Islam (see Fox 1989).

The characteristic dualism of eastern Indonesia is evident in Sila's discussion of Bima in Sumbawa. The Bima rulers were forced to embrace Islam under the influence of Makassar (Gowa–Tallo) after 1621 and it was grafted on to a binary form of political authority, a division between the authority of the ruler (who came to adopt the title Sultan) and the Raja Bicara ("Prime Minister"). This religious divide is also expressed in alternative sets of mosques, and appointment of *imam masjid* or, in the case of royal mosques, *lebe* (a Malay term for imam) (Prager 2010).

Andrew McWilliam's chapter discusses the dualistic basis of the incorporation of Islam in the Cia-Cia speaking community of Wabula on the island of Buton. "Cia-Cia speaking communities are socially and religiously focused on the twin structures of local tradition: the mosque (*mesjid*) and the central meeting house (*galampa*) which provide the locus for a range of adat ceremonies" (McWilliam, this volume, p. 232). These two structures are spatially separated with a cleared space (*kalia* [CC]—the field or yard) and the structural relationship between the mosque and the galampa is understood as a gendered unity, expressed through a metaphor of marriage between the male adat and female Islam. Unlike the other communities discussed in this book there is only one mosque in Wabula, because it symbolises the monogamous "marriage" between religion and adat.

Wabula people use an idiom of *masuk/keluar* (enter/go out) in regard to the relation between Islam and custom. When performing adat rituals in the ritual house (galampa) located across the public square from the mosque, the imam sits opposite the ritual specialist (*parabela* [CC]), near the sacred central pillar. When time approaches for the dawn prayers and they descend from the galampa (symbolically male, guarded by the *lingga*), cross the field and enter the mosque (marked by the *yoni*), they use the idiom "*keluar adat masuk agama*" (go out from culture and enter religion) (see also Yamaguchi 2011). This sharp distinction is not often heard in most of the places reported in this book; indeed in his chapter on Leihitu, Winn cites von Benda-Beckmanns' (1988) writing about the same community, reporting the local view that "*adat dibikin di mesjid*" (custom is made in the mosque). Islam is in most cases seamlessly interwoven with everyday ritual practices (such as life cycle rituals) to express Muslim identities.

And in many of the chapters, the imams provide critical leadership in the conduct of these rituals.

An underlying binary logic is also expressed in the spatial alignment of relationship between adat and Islam in a Bugis migrant village in Bantaeng district in South Sulawesi, reported in Saenong's chapter. He noticed a number of young women living at the imam's house. On investigation, it transpired that they were young unmarried women considered to have transgressed cultural religious norms in regard to personal conduct and links with the opposite sex; they are in a condition of transgression of *siri'* (Bug. honour) and have brought shame on their families—for which the punishment is death. The women run to the house of the imam where they are considered within his protection. In this community, the imam then takes responsibility for returning the situation to equilibrium, usually by organising a wedding for the young woman and most often with the man who is her partner in shame.[4]

Imams and Modern State Power

Just as imams were integrated into the formal structures of the Sulawesi sultanates, their contemporary roles are impacted by political forces of the modern state. Following Indonesia's achievement of independence, much of South Sulawesi (including areas now part of Southeast Sulawesi) was under the control of an Islamic rebellion led by Kahar Muzakkar, which aimed to have the new republic declared an Islamic State. This movement is known as Darul Islam (DI). It linked up with like-minded rebellions in West Java and Aceh. Robinson's chapter discusses the profound impacts this rebellion had on the way in which people in rural areas practised Islam, and how it transformed the role and responsibilities of the imam as their principal religious authority. DI state authority was based on a strict application of sharia and led to a transformation from a traditionalist to a modernist orientation, in the practice of Islam. It was intolerant of the mode of practising Islam that left intact the prerogatives of the Bugis nobility and practices associated with the La Galigo religion. This was a very disruptive period, which led to much population movement, including the migration of the predecessors of the Bugis villagers in Bantaeng that are the subject of Saenong's chapter. Robinson (this volume) discusses the crucial role of the imam in arbitrating these pressures on styles of religious conduct.

The impact of the so-called "traditionalist" and "modernist" tendencies in Indonesian Islam emerge as significantly dynamic in many of the chapters (see Hutagalung, Robinson and Sila). In Bima, Sila describes how its organisational form, the divide of mass religious organisations Nahdlatul Ulama and Muhammadiyah, was grafted onto the binary distinction of the religious authority associated with the Sultan mosques versus the power base of the Raja Bicara (see Prager 2010). The sultanate was dissolved in 1958, in the heady mood of nationalist politics and the religious bureaucracy with it. But the influence on practice remained. Sila shows how, at a practical level, the binary distinction is resolved in a tolerant manner in local mosques by allowing the practices of both streams in a single space, which he argues is unusual in Indonesia.

As Andrée Feillard and Rémy Madinier (2011) argue for Indonesia in general, the tensions of the Darul Islam period did not disappear with its defeat in the mid-1960s, and have emerged in Indonesia post-Reformasi, in the context of the politics of decentralisation. Moh Yasir Alimi (2014a; this volume) has investigated local attempts at the formalisation of Islam by way of district regulations based on sharia law (*perda syariah*) in Bulukumba, South Sulawesi. This district, and its *bupati* (district head) were the flag-bearers for the passage of sharia bylaws in the early years of Reformasi, after 2001. Distinctive local discourses, which could be argued express the "traditionalist" tolerance for "flowery" Islam operate in parallel with the discourses of formalisation. Local public discourses are expressed inter alia through what he terms "ritual paraphernalia"—the leaves and incense which are requisite in Islamic ritual prayer (Alimi 2014b). While not a confrontation, imams and other local ritual/religious practitioners who regard themselves as pious Muslims continue to assert their own forms of authentic Islamic practice in the face of formalisation efforts. In a curious move, the elements of purification that we see in the Bulukumba *perda syariah* include a requirement for Qur'anic literacy on the part of brides and grooms before marriage. This seems to be an instantiation of an Islamised practice that has been incorporated into the cycle of rituals accompanying Bugis and Makassarese weddings—the ritual of *mappatemme* (Bug. graduating in reading the Qur'an) which takes place in the days before the *akad nikah* (marriage contract) and the wedding reception. The village imam has hitherto overseen the practice of life cycle rituals and also Islamic education, so the aspirational formalisation through *perda syariah* is a direct challenge to the imam's authority.

Migration and the Spread of Islam

Several of the chapters discuss contemporary processes of religious conversions linked to economic migration. Trade networks through the archipelago have always been significant vectors of Islam. There has been migration out of South Sulawesi as a consequence of conflict, such as the conquest of Makassar in 1669 and the subsequent conflict between Sulawesi realms (see chapter by Saenong), and also in the Darul Islam period (chapters by Robinson and Hutagalung). Many of the Muslim populations of the eastern archipelago have strong traditions of migration and sojourning, linked to the vibrant inter-island trade dating centuries back. The contemporary processes described here give some insight into how Islamic proselytisation occurs as a concomitant of migration.

Analysis of the 2000 census data shows that two of Indonesia's principal sojourning/migratory groups, Bugis from South Sulawesi and Butonese from the contemporary province of Southeast Sulawesi, have a strong presence in the islands east of Sulawesi (although the Bugis are most likely to migrate westward, to Kalimantan, Sumatra and the Malay peninsula) (McWilliam, this volume).

Eastern Indonesian populations have been fluid and dynamic, especially along maritime routes. Studies of migrant populations reveal ways in which travelling communities are vehicles for the dissemination of Islam among ordinary folk. Hutagalung examines Muslims who form a minority in the majority-Christian town of Kupang, capital of the majority-Christian province of NTT. While Kupang contains some old Muslim communities whose migration from other islands dates from the colonial period (see chapter by McWilliam), Hutagalung focuses on a more recent Bugis migrant community in the urban village of Oesapa. The imam, haji Daeng Pawero, a founder of this community who exercises religious authority in the mosque he established, oversees religious practices that express the Aswaja (traditionalist) and Bugis traditions of his birthplace in Bone, South Sulawesi.

The contemporary practices of intermarriage give insight into the way that conversion associated with marriage of local non-Muslims to Muslim traders and other economic migrants has led to Islamisation. Many of the male migrants marry local women from the Christian groups of NTT. These women convert to marry and bear the identity of *mualaf* (convert). Haji Daeng Pawero's grandson organises religious instruction for this group (which includes his wife). But there are also modern forms of religious authority including the officials from the Department of Religious Affairs and preachers and mosque officials who have a higher level of formal religious education than the old imam, who has acquired his knowledge in traditional ways.

Wahyuddin Halim's chapter addresses the importance of Islamic education networks centred on South Sulawesi in sustaining links between the "homeland" and the Bugis diaspora. Many of the *santri* (students) from migrant families return to *pesantren* in South Sulawesi for Islamic education that has a strong Bugis inflection. The young educated graduates are in high demand as imams in the diasporic communities, signaling important shifts in local religious authority from past traditions.

Another important migration associated with the spread of Islam throughout the eastern archipelago is the movement of Hadhrami (migrants from what is now Yemen) especially from the 19th century (Slama 2011). These migrants also intermarried with local communities and have had a strong influence on forms of "everyday Islam". In general, their accommodative approach is more akin to the "traditionalist" Islam than contemporary Middle Eastern influence which is hostile to Indonesia's "flowery" Islam (see chapter by Nisa).

And of course Bugis in particular are very enthusiastic "short-term" migrants to make the haj pilgrimage to Mecca. Haj status is an important marker of social status, rivaling the "white blood" of people claiming aristocratic status.

New Forms of Religious Authority and Religious Networks

Islam in Java is firmly linked to the traditions of the pesantren and *kiai* and the ulama they produce. There are a number of significant pesantren networks in eastern Indonesia, several centred on the island of Sulawesi. These do not have the historic depth of the Javanese pesantren tradition but they have widespread influence in the eastern islands and are taking ever more important roles in producing and reproducing new kinds of religious authority. Halim's chapter discusses the very important As'adiyah pesantren in Wajo, established in 1930 by Mecca-born Bugis religious scholar Anregurutta Muhammad As'ad al-Bugis. It provides formal religious training for Bugis youth. The imam in the Bugis migrant village studied by Saenong is an As'adiyah alumnae. As'adiyah graduates have formed additional networks, perhaps the most important being Darud Da'wah wal Irsyad (DDI) founded by Ambo Dalle in 1938, which has branches in all Sulawesi provinces as well as Kalimantan and Papua. Another important pesantren network is Al Khairat Palu, Central Sulawesi, founded by Hadhrami scholar Al Habib Idrus ibn Salim Al Jufri (1889–1969) in 1930. Travelling around Central Sulawesi, I found there is a very strong presence of Al Khairat alumnae as imams and other religious leaders, and they have networks that extend to Maluku and Papua. All of these networks reach out to the diaspora but also draw the diasporic populations back into their "homelands" and their Islamic traditions. These Sulawesi-based networks align themselves with the traditionalist organisation Nahdlatul Ulama and participate in its national meetings.

The increasing importance of these networks of formal religious education is giving rise to new forms of religious authority grounded in formal education, rather than more customary forms such as inherited authority. The emerging new forms of religious authority of pesantren-educated imams challenge the pre-eminence of the traditional village imams in their communities.

Halim's chapter illustrates the processes by which the old forms of religious authority in villages are weakening in the modern world as the villagers hunger for connections to the skills produced through higher religious learning. He describes how the *hafiz* (memorisers of the Qur'an) in particular are in high demand as *imam tarawih*, leading the additional evening prayers during Ramadan. Many communities vie to keep these young men as local religious authorities. Robinson describes a similar shift to formally educated religious authority in Sorowako where the hereditary imam, once the source of all religious authority, is being challenged by a new generation of migrant preachers with high levels of formal religious education, who are being appointed through advertisement to local mosques that serve educated middle-class populations. The imam has lost his responsibility for religious instruction to the young, to afterschool classes (TPA, Taman Pendidikan Al-Qur'an) that use modern methods of instruction.

Mosques: Historical Traditions and Spatialising Religious Practice

In addition to the requirements for personal religious practice in regard to the five pillars of Islam, Muslim communities are obliged to build places for congregational worship. Mosques form the heart of Muslim communities. Islam does not prescribe a structural form for mosques: at base there must be a place for assembling for congregational prayer led by an imam (Wiryomartono 2009). Mosque construction accommodates vernacular architectural forms, in many cases developing from pre-existing community buildings in the places where Islam takes root. As part of the built environment, prayer houses (*musholla*) and mosques also exhibit structural features that express the history of the currents of Islamic influence as well as accommodations to vernacular built forms (Kleinstuber and Maharadjo 2012). In their review of historic mosques of the archipelago, Asti Kleinstuber and Syafri M. Maharadjo (2012) recount folk traditions around the diverse structural forms of these buildings. A common trope involves numerological claims about design features: the number of pillars (which show wide variation) are mnemonic devices for, or symbolically reflect aspects of Islamic doctrine. For example the fairly common four main pillars in the central hall can represent the prophet and his three companions, or even the four *mazhab* (schools of law).

As people of the archipelago adopted Islam, existing buildings like community halls were converted or their form adapted. Mosque forms (including their interior features) exemplify the "appropriation, preservation, and reinterpretation of pre-Islamic traditions" as a community engages with Islam (Feener 2017: 30). The Wapauwe mosque in Leihitu (Maluku), which sees itself as the gateway to Islam in the archipelago, was built in 1414. It is the oldest mosque that is still in its original form (although it mysteriously moved itself from its original location). Many mosques were originally made of wood, bamboo and other locally available (but perishable) materials. The Wapauwe mosque, like many of the historic mosques throughout eastern Indonesia, has the square shape and the multi-tiered roof associated with mosque-building traditions in Java. Winn (this volume) notes that particular roof shapes predominate as characterising regional designs.

Mosques are subject to reconstruction and renewal but some retain design elements that tell the story of the waves of Islamic influence, and the accommodation with local customs and practices, as well as material reflections of sociopolitical and religious trends. Mesjid Agung were often built close to royal palaces (as Sila describes for Bima in this volume) symbolising the joint authority of Islam and the ruler, the subsumption of Islam under the power of the Sultan. Royal graves are commonly located close by. In the colonial era, many Mesjid Raya (Grand Mosques in towns) were designed by Dutch architects incorporating European elements. Fashions in construction come and go and mosques are now often topped with domes, made of zinc. In South Sulawesi, minarets—once rare—are now common and mosques congregations compete to have the tallest mosques.

All mosques have a *mihrab* (niche) facing towards *kiblat* (the direction of Mecca) from where the imam leads the prayers, and a *mimbar* or elevated pulpit, often ornately carved, from where the khatib delivers the Friday sermon. When mosques are renovated, it is common for the original *mimbar* to be preserved. Another common feature is a *tongkat* (walking stick) kept in the *mimbar* which is held by the khatib signifying his authority when delivering the sermon. The *tongkat* or sometimes a metal-tipped spear are found in the *mimbar* of many mosques throughout the archipelago (Kleinstuber and Maharadjo 2012). It is an example of the "physical remnants … of pre-Islamic pasts" (Feener 2017: 24) that constitute Islamic heritage.

The prayer halls of old-style mosques are commonly accessed through a verandah where the *bedug* (drum) used to call the faithful to prayer is located (although these days there is likely to be a loud-speaker, and even a minaret to broadcast the *azan*). Kleinstuber and Maharadjo (2012) speculate that the *bedug*, found throughout the archipelago, may be the result of Chinese influence, as their form and positioning on the verandah mirrors that of Buddhist temples in China. Many of the old mosques in eastern Indonesia have *bedug*. These also accommodate symbolism: the *bedug* in the mosque inside the palace complex in Buton is 99 centimetres long, symbolising the 99 names of Allah (Kleinstuber and Maharadjo 2012).

Winn's chapter introduces us to the people of Leihitu in Maluku whose story of local conversion in the 16th century emphasised that they were Islamised by a proselytiser from Java, independent of the Sultanates of Ternate and Tidore. Some other local accounts credit preachers from the Middle East. Winn describes the manner in which local authority and relations between *soa* (social division of several clans) is reflected in the seating in the mosque. Much of his chapter focuses on the physical structure and spatial layout of the customary mosque form in this region. In particular he discusses the important ritual of periodic replacement of the distinctive Tiang Alif, a decorative tall wooden finial that sits at the apex of the mosque roof. This feature is characteristic of mosques in the Maluku region.

Congregations take enormous pride in their mosques and as communities become affluent the mosques can become more elaborate and ornate. Mosques are built by communities, or can be gifted by wealthy individuals, and this pious act is a way of acquiring religious merit even after death. During the Suharto era, in line with the trend to cultural sanitation and standardisation, the government built many mosques (for example, in schools) on a common design.

Bagoes Wiryomatono (2009) describes a contemporary trend in mosque building in which the once simple prayer hall becomes a multi-storey building which can accommodate a wide range of activities alongside prayer. The new buildings can accommodate administrative offices and places for educational activities and even for rituals. In urban environments, where families face difficulties in accommodating wedding rituals in a temporarily expanded house, hired halls provide the venues. In Sorowako, South Sulawesi, Robinson found that the village mosque (Masjid Jami or original mosque) has been magnificently expanded and renovated by a local businessman, using elegant white marble, and the old prayer hall is now such a space, for celebrations.

The mosque is not only a place for prayer but is also a community centre, and this latter function develops along with the character of urban populations. Nisa's chapter focuses on new kinds of Islamic movements that are attracting significant and growing followings through Indonesia, including among young university students. Campus mosques have become the site of contestation for space between followers of Salafi groups, Tarbiyah and Hizbut Tahrir, in the city of Makassar, South Sulawesi. The mosques thus become centres for the new forms of religious education, for *dakwah* (preaching, proselytising) and politics, as well as social interactions within and between groups. The mosques become sites for the development of new kinds of communities among the diverse urban population.

The presence of women in mosques has been contentious for some Muslim clerics and scholars from conservative religious movements, but Nisa argues that women are more active than men in the mosque-based campus groups. Further, she intimates that these young pious women are developing the basis of their own religious authority.

Mosques and churches mark out interfaith spatial relations but can symbolise religious harmony. For example, Hutagalung's chapter discusses the ways in which mosques express and symbolise historical religious co-operation between the minority Muslims and majority Christians in the town of Kupang. Muslim migrants have, since their original settlement, been provided with land and also often financial and labour support to build the mosque that is obligatory to a Muslim congregation. Imams, as religious leaders and authorities, are critical to such interfaith practices.

In contemporary Indonesia, places of worship have become flash-points for interreligious conflict and, in times of heightened religious tension, burning places of worship is a common expression of intolerance. Such conflict merged in the immediate post-Suharto era and, while its most heightened period is over, it still simmers in many multi-faith communities. However, the government response of formalising interfaith relations with a regulation requiring religious minorities to obtain permission from the majority before they are allowed to build new places of worship has merely provided a new weapon, not led to abatement (see chapter by Hutagalung).

Conclusion

This volume reports on the collective project of understanding Islamic traditions and the many ways of "being Muslim" in diverse communities in eastern Indonesia. South Sulawesi figures strongly in these accounts. The chapters highlight the significance of imams as religious and ritual authorities, and as community leaders. They also discuss the mosque as a key material element of a Muslim community, and a constantly transforming socio-religious space. The chapters emphasise the mutual interactions of Islam and preexisting cultural and social traditions, and also investigate historical processes of transformation, such as trade, conquest and the formation of the modern state.

Notes

1. Imam is used in Indonesia to mean leader or authority ("*pemimpin, penguasa atau ketua*" [Baiquni et al. 1996]) in the context of Islam. The office or position of imam can have slightly different meanings in other parts of the Islamic world (see Faried F. Saenong, this volume).
2. The studies were conducted as part of a research project entitled "Being Muslim in Eastern Indonesia: Practice, Politics and Diversity" (DP0881464). Chief Investigators were Kathryn Robinson and Andrew McWilliam (Australian National University) and Nurul Ilmi Idrus (Hasanuddin University) was Partner Investigator. Other contributors to this volume completed PhDs at ANU wholly or partly funded by the project. Phillip Winn was Senior Research Associate and Diana Glazebrook the Research Assistant.
3. This kind of numerological symbolism is common in regards to house and mosque construction. There are many examples in Kleinstuber and Maharadjo (2012).
4. I witnessed an event that involved honour killing in Makassar in 1996. A man was killed after his unmarried lover's brother found the pair in a "compromising situation"; people gathered around the house where the murder had occurred to threaten the perpetrator but backed off when they heard the circumstances. The woman was taken into protective custody by the police who attended the scene as she was in danger from her own family, endeavouring to recover their honour by killing her.

References

Alimi, Moh Yasir. 2014a. "Local Repertoires of Meaning and the Islamist Movement in Post-Authoritarian Indonesia." *Indonesia and the Malay World* 42 (122): 24–42.

———. 2014b. "Islam as Drama: Wedding Rituals and the Theatricality of Islam in South Sulawesi." *The Asia Pacific Journal of Anthropology* 15 (3): 265–85.

Andaya, Leonard. 1993. *The World of Maluku: Eastern Indonesia in the Early Modern Period.* Honolulu: University of Hawai'i Press.

Azra, Azyumardi. 2015. "Jaringan Ulama Nusantara" [Networks of Religious Scholars in the Archipelago]. In *Islam Nusantara: Dari Ushul Fiqh hingga Paham Kebangsaan*, ed. Akhmad Sahal and Munawir Aziz, 171–2. Bandung: Mizan.

Burnet, Ian. 2011. *Spice islands. The History, Romance and Adventure of the Spice Trade over 2000 Years.* Dural NSW: Rosenberg Publishing.

de Jonge, Huub and Nico Kaptein. 2002. *Transcending Borders. Arabs, Politics, Trade and Islam in Southeast Asia*. Leiden: KITLV Press.

Feener, Michael. 2017. "Muslim Cultures and the Pre-Islamic Past: Changing Perceptions of 'Heritage'." In *The Making of Islamic Heritage. Muslim Pasts and Heritage Presents*, ed. Trinidad Rico, 23–44. Singapore: Palgrave Macmillan.

Feillard, Andrée and Rémy Madinier. 2011. *The End of Innocence? Indonesian Islam and the Temptations of Radicalism*. Singapore: NUS Press.

Fox, James J. 1989. "Category and Complement: Binary Ideologies and the Organization of Dualism in Eastern Indonesia." In *The Attraction of Opposites: Thought and Society in a Dualistic Mode*, ed. D. Maybury-Lewis and U. Almagor, 33–56. Ann Arbor: University of Michigan Press.

______. 2002. "Toward a Social Anthropology of Islam in Indonesia." In *Islam in Indonesia: Islamic Studies and Social Transformation*, ed. Fu'ad Jabali and Jamhari, 73–81. Montreal; Jakarta: Indonesia-Canada Islamic Higher Education Project.

Gaborieau, Marc. 2010. "The Redefinition of Religious Authority among South Asian Muslims from 1919 to 1956." In *Varieties of Religious Authority: Changes and Challenges in 20th Century Indonesian Islam*, ed. Azyumardi Azra, Kees van Dijk, and Nico J.G. Kaptein, 1–16. Singapore: ISEAS.

Gunn, Geoffrey C. 2016. "The Timor-Macao Sandalwood Trade and the Asian Discovery of the Great South Land?" *Review of Culture* 53: 125–46.

Kleinstuber, Asti and Syafri M. Maharadjo. 2012. *Masjid-Masjid Kuno di Indonesia. Warisan Budaya dari Masa ke Masa* [Old Mosques in Indonesia. Cultural Heritage Through the Times]. Indonesia: PT AS productions.

Laffan, Michael. 2011. *The Makings of Indonesian Islam: Orientalism and the Narration of a Sufi Past*. Princeton, NJ: Princeton University Press.

Lapidus, Ira M. 2002. *A History of Islamic Societies*, 2nd ed. Cambridge: Cambridge University Press.

Muhaimin, A.G. 2006. *The Islamic Traditions of Cirebon. Ibadat and Adat Among Javanese Muslims*. Canberra: ANU Press.

Mukhlis [Mukhlis Paeni] and Kathryn Robinson, eds., 1985. *Agama dan Realitas Sosial* [Religion and Social Reality]. Ujung Pandang, Indonesia: Hasanuddin University Press for the Indonesian Social Science Foundation (YIIS).

Noorduyn, J. 1987. "Makassar and the Islamization of Bima." *Bijdragen tot de Taal-, Lande en Volkenkunde* 143 (2/3): 312–42.

Osella, Filipo and Caroline Osella. 2008. "Introduction: Islamic Reformism in South Asia." *Modern Asian Studies* 42 (2/3): 247–57.

Pelras, Christian. 1993. "Religion, Tradition and the Dynamics of Islamization in South Sulawesi." *Indonesia* 57: 133–54.

———. 1996. *The Bugis*. Cambridge, MA: Wiley Blackwell.

Prager, Michael. 2010. "Abandoning the 'Garden of Magic'." *Indonesia and the Malay World* 38 (110): 9–25.

Reid, Anthony. 1993. "Islamization and Christianization in Southeast Asia: the Critical Phase, 1550–1650." In *Southeast Asia in the Early Modern Phase: Trade Power, and Belief*, ed. Anthony Reid, 151–79. Ithaca, NY: Cornell University Press.

———. 2004 [1995]. "Continuity and Change in the Austronesian Transition to Islam and Christianity." In *The Austronesians: Historical and Comparative Perspectives*, ed. Peter Bellwood, James J. Fox, and Darrell Tryon, 333–50. Canberra: ANU Press.

Ricklefs, M.C. 2006. *Mystic Synthesis in Java: A History of Islamization from the Fourteenth to the Early Nineteenth Centuries*. Norwalk, CT: EastBridge Books.

Ricklefs, Merle. 2007. *Polarising Javanese Society: Islamic and Other Visions c. 1830–1930*. Singapore: NUS Press; Leiden: KITLV Press; Honolulu: University of Hawai'i Press.

Robinson, Kathryn. 1998. "Traditions of House-Building in South Sulawesi." In *Living Through Histories: Culture History and Social Life in South Sulawesi*, ed. Kathryn Robinson and Mukhlis Paeni, 168–95. Canberra and Jakarta: Anthropology ANU, in collaboration with the Indonesian National Archives.

Schrauwers, Albert. 1997. "Houses, Hierarchy, Headhunting and Exchange; Rethinking Political Relations in the Southeast Asian Realm of Luwu." *Bijdragen tot de Taal-, Land- en Volkenkunde* 153 (3): 356–80.

Slama, Martin. 2011. "Translocal Networks and Globalisation within Indonesia: Exploring the Hadhrami Diaspora from the Archipelago's North-East." *Asian Journal of Social Science* 39 (2): 238–57.

van Leur, J.C. 1955. *Indonesian Trade and Society. Essays in Asian Social and Economic History*. The Hague and Bandung: W. van Hoeve Ltd.

von Benda-Beckmann, Franz and Keebet von Benda-Beckmann. 1988. "Adat and Religion in Minangkabau and Ambon." In *Time Past, Time Present, Time Future: Perspectives on Indonesian Culture: Essays in Honour of Professor P.E. de Josselin de Jong*, ed. H.J.M. Claessen, 195–212. Dordrecht, Netherlands: Koninklijk Instituut voor Taal-, Land- en Volkenkunde.

Wiryomartono, Bagoes. 2009. "Postcard from the Field: A Historical View of Mosque Architecture in Indonesia." *The Asia Pacific Journal of Anthropology* 10 (1): 33–45.

Yamaguchi, Hiroko. 2011. "'True History' in Wabula, Buton Island." *The Asia Pacific Journal of Anthropology* 12 (5): 478–88.

1

Lebe and Sultan
Serving the Mosque and Sustaining Royal Authority

Muhammad Adlin Sila[1]

Introduction

This chapter focuses on the roles of imams in contemporary Bima mosques, in the context of the connection between Islam and political authority. Bima was Islamised from Gowa in South Sulawesi; and Islam has been intimately connected with the authority of the Bima Sultanate, since the period of the second Bima Sultan Abi'l Khair Sirajuddin (1640–82).

During the period of the second Bima Sultan, Islam began to penetrate the religious landscape of the local people. The second Bima Sultan Muhammad Abi'l Khair Sirajuddin constructed the Sultan mosque. This mosque is opposite the Bima Sultan's palace (Bim. *Asi Mbojo*): the mosque and the palace are historically paired and symbolise the heritage of the Bima Sultanate. According to the current religious leader of the mosque, Lebe Ishaka, its construction began on 25 July 1649 and was completed in 1770 during the reign of the eighth Sultan Abdul Kadim (1751–73).

The Sultanate under the second sultan created a religious council (Bim. *sara huku*, in Indonesian *majlis agama*) that recruited *lebe* (Bim. imam) who provided religious services in the mosque. Since that time, lebe have become the guardians of the religious lives of Bima Muslims. Following the activities of the contemporary figure, Lebe Ishaka of the Sultan mosque allowed me to understand the key role that lebe continue to play in Bima; they constantly create the identity of local Muslims through ritual performance and at the same time sustain the legacy of the royal authority.

The sultan appointed and paid the lebe, the Malay term adapted for the office of imam in the great mosques in Bima.[2] By observing imams (lebe) and mosque participants in the royal mosques in Bima (Masjid Sultan Muhammad Salahuddin and Masjid Baitul Hamid), I suggest that the distinctive ritual prayers of the mosque participants are deliberately constructed through the interplay between the authority of the imam and the royal court. In addition, differences in the choice of ritual prayers reflect different roles of imams and religious orientations in contemporary Bima—between traditionalist Muslims associated with the royal mosques, and reformist Muslims associated with the mosques of the *raja bicara*, the "prime minister". This office was created during the period of Sultan Abi'l Khair Sirajuddin (1640–82), the Second Bima Sultan. These differences in turn relate to sustaining the authority of the sultanate and also the legitimation of the political authority of its rivals in contemporary politics.

This chapter will first discuss the mosque as a field of study and then describe the nature of ritual prayer from the perspectives of local imams, and the differences in ritual prayers between traditionalist and reformist Muslims. Imams in Bima extend royal authority, and I also examine the roles of imam outside the mosque, particularly as practitioners of traditional healing and as guardians of customary rituals which are popularly associated with traditions of the royal legacy.

I follow the approach of John Bowen (2000) and David Parkin (2000) in first describing the way imams, also referred to as lebe in Bima, interpret and construct meanings of rituals inside and outside the mosque. Although Muslims in Bima observe ritual prayers from the same sources, the Qur'an and hadis, different interpretations result in different roles of imams observed in traditional and reformist Bima mosques. I argue that the imam affects the choice of ritual prayers among mosque participants.

Islamic ritual prayer (*salat*) has gained wide attention of scholars and historians: David Parkin and Stephen C. Headley (2000), Saba Mahmood (2001), and Heiko Henkel (2005) to mention a few.

Mahmood (2001: 828) postulated that the performance of ritual prayer among mosque participants was a way to construct their "intentions, emotions and desires in accord with orthodox standards of Islamic piety". By examining the difference between "formal (conventional) and spontaneous conduct", Mahmood (2001: 845) proposed the idea that, for the Egyptian mosque participants in her study, the ritual prayer is best analysed as a "disciplinary practice that complexly combines pragmatic action (i.e., day-to-day mundane activities) with formal and highly codified behavior".

Mahmood's emphasis on ritual prayer relies on her examination of liberal suppositions about the appropriate frontier between the religious and the secular, and agency and submission. Mahmood has acknowledged the impact of Talal Asad's essay "The idea of an Anthropology of Islam" (1986) on her work, and she has focused on the social elements of Muslim rituals, which result in differences in practices. This approach accords with that of Parkin and Headley (2000) who argue that ritual prayer for Muslims has different meanings in different locations.

The Mosque as an Anthropological Field Site

In Bima, the mosque is called *sigi*, derived from *masigi*, an Arabic word meaning a place of worship (also used in Makassar, the source of Islam in Bima). Local Muslims use the Malay-derived term lebe (rather than imam or *kiai*) to refer to an Islamic cleric or the person in charge of leading ritual prayer in a mosque, especially the Sultan mosques. In everyday conversation, *sigi* and *masjid* are used interchangeably to refer to the mosque. But local Muslims frequently use the term *sigi* in the local language. In written form, the term *masjid* is widely used, for example, Masjid Sultan Muhammad Salahuddin.

In conducting ethnographic research, my Muslim identity allowed me to take part in ritual prayers at local mosques. Participating in several mosques during the month of Ramadan enabled me to observe differences in the conduct of ritual prayer between members with different religious orientations.

My late father was known as an Islamic cleric and, during his lifetime, was called either imam or *kiai* by his audiences. This background, coupled with my Islamic education (I completed my first degree at IAIN Alauddin in Makassar) equips me to understand the formal meanings of terms such as *masjid*, imam, *kiai* and so forth as well as the forms of ritual prayer performed by mosque participants. However, in this chapter, my understanding of those terms relies on the meanings given by local Muslims—the understandings socially constructed by my interlocutors.

Lebe and the Royal Mosques

At dawn on Friday 26 August 2011, I met for the first time with a 60-year-old man, Haji Saleh Ishaka, at the grand mosque, Masjid Sultan Muhammad Salahuddin, located in the centre of Bima town. From the terrace of the mosque I could look across to the palace of the Sultan. Ishaka was leading the dawn prayer, *salat subuh*.[3] I noticed that he included a special supplication called *kunut*, a practice that differentiates the followers of the traditionalist organisation Nahdlatul Ulama (NU) from the followers of the modernist groups Muhammadiyah and Persis. *Kunut* requires a prayer leader to raise his palms above the waist while in the standing position in the last cycle of the prayer (Hooker 2003: 101, 237). Although at the time Ishaka was not yet a lebe, he frequently led the prayer in the mosque if the permanent lebe was absent. He officially became the lebe of the mosque in 2012.

That first observation of ritual dawn prayer in the grand mosque, Masjid Sultan Muhammad Salahuddin raised my curiosity to observe ritual prayers in other mosques across Bima. It was rebuilt after being destroyed during World War II by Japanese bombing in 1943 (see below). The *bupati* (district head) at the time built another mosque, Masjid Raya Al-Muwahidin located 100 metres from the original mosque, functioning as a substitute for Masjid Sultan Muhammad Salahuddin. In 1990, Siti Maryam, the daughter of the 14th Sultan, Muhammad Salahuddin (1915–51), finished the rebuilding of the original mosque and named it after her father, as Masjid Sultan Muhammad Salahuddin. As a result, Bima Muslims now have two dedicated Sultan mosques: Masjid Sultan Muhammad Salahuddin and Masjid Raya Al-Muwahidin. The two mosques each have their own lebe and are under the administration of a foundation, Yayasan Islam, known as YASIM, founded in 1968. Another important mosque administered by YASIM is Masjid Baitul Hamid, located in Raba sub-district east of Bima city. This mosque is dedicated to Raja Bicara

Abdul Hamid (deceased 1950), the last person to hold this office in the Bima Sultanate. YASIM also administers Masjid An-Nur Raba Dompu.

I also frequented the mosque located just across from my rented house in the village of Pane, Masjid Al-Muwahidin Pane. It bears a name similar to the grand mosque of Masjid Raya Al-Muwahidin noted above. The mosque in Pane is dedicated to Haji Abubakar Husain, whose body is buried in its grounds. He was a Muhammadiyah cadre, a prominent figure in Qur'anic recitation and, in the 1960s, a winner of the international competition for Qur'anic recitation held in Lahore. Whereas the sultan mosques, Masjid Sultan Muhammad Salahuddin and Masjid Raya Al-Muwahidin, follow the traditionalist Islam of NU (Nahdlatul Ulama), I noticed that Masjid Baitul Hamid and Masjid Al-Muwahidin Pane follow the so-called "reformist" model of ritual usually associated with Muhammadiyah.

Michael Prager (2010: 13–14) notes that the Bima Sultanate followed the general model of a Malay sultanate with an Islamised sultan as the spiritual authority complemented by that of a secular ruler, Raja Bicara, who was in charge of administration. This division is found in the South Sulawesi sultanates critical to the Islamisation of Bima. Reflecting the binary classification commonly found in the Indonesian archipelago, the sultan and the Raja Bicara thus formed a complementary pair. Collectively, they attempted to displace or subordinate the pre-Islamic local practices of Bima Muslims.

In the early 20th century, Sultan Muhammad Salahuddin and Raja Bicara Abdul Hamid had different religious orientations. Prager (2010: 14) argued that due to political support from the Raja Bicara (Abdul Hamid), Muhammadiyah clerics supported by returned haj pilgrims could present the "universal message" of Islam. The Sultan, through the Masjid Sultan, the institution of lebe, and the educational institution Madrasah Darululum, was associated with the traditions of the NU organisation. However, the Raja Bicara came to be linked to the reformist Muhammadiyah organisation through Masjid Baitul Hamid in Raba sub-district, Masjid Al-Muwahidin Pane and Madrasah Daruttarbiyah. These religious differences expressed political rivalry between the secular and spiritual power centres of the sultanate. Consequently, the sultan and his descendants, including Ferry Zulkarnaen (2005–15) the bupati of Bima district at the time of my fieldwork, are close to the followers of NU, while the descendants of the last Raja Bicara Abdul Hamid are commonly affiliated with Muhammadiyah.

Understanding Different Roles of *lebe*

Masjid Sultan Muhammad represents the focal symbol of identity-making of Islam in Bima. The lebe of the Sultan Mosque have been loyal to royal authority since the period of Sultan Abi'l Khair Sirajuddin (1640–82). Lebe receive compensation for their services, and there are various lebe roles: *lebedala* (Bim.) referring to those working inside the palace, and to the head of the religious court; *lebeNa'e*, prayer leaders in grand mosques located in the sub-districts (Bim. *jeneli*); and *cepelebe*, prayer leaders in grand mosques situated at village level (Bim. *gelarang*). This structural organisation was in place until the last Sultan Muhammad Salahuddin (1915–51). Muma Gani Masykur, who had been a lebe in the 1950s, said to me that at that time, the *lebe dalam* as the head of the religious court also took care of alms giving or tithing (*zakat*) and finances (see also Abdullah 2004: 171–4). In 1974, this court took a Malay name, Badan Hukum Syara', and was also responsible for managing Islamic schools (*madrasah*), and funding Islamic and social activism (*dakwah* and *tabligh*). The body also controlled the appointment of *lebeNa'e* and *cepelebe* at sub-districts (Bim. *jeneli*) and village level (Bim. *gelarang*) (Abdullah 2004).

Badan Hukum Syara' was dissolved by a former district head, so the royal family with the support of the government head of Bima district at the time, Soeharmadji, founded Yayasan Islam (YASIM) in 1968. This new organisation was given the responsibility for appointing lebe. Currently, YASIM has become a legal foundation that administers the appointment of lebe and the recruitment of teachers for Islamic schools, although limited to those built by the Bima Sultanate namely, Madrasah Darululum and Madrasah Daruttarbiyah.

Under the modern administration of YASIM, there are two types of lebe: *lebeNa'e* (or also called *lebeNae*) and *cepelebe*. The first type of lebe are employed in the district grand mosques, while *cepelebe* are appointed to the sub-district grand mosques. YASIM also recruits other mosque officials who assist lebe, namely *khatib* (sermon deliverer), *bilal* (a caller for prayer or *azan*) and *robo*, derived from the word *marbut* meaning mosque caretaker.[4]

In today's Bima municipality, *lebeNa'e* serve only in the following royal mosques: Masjid Sultan Muhammad Salahuddin, Masjid Raya Al-Muwahidin, Masjid An-Nur Raba Dompu and Masjid Baitul Hamid. The last mosque named is the largest in Raba sub-district located east of Bima city. This mosque is dedicated to Raja Bicara Abdul Hamid (1915–51), the last Raja Bicara of the Bima Sultanate.[5] In these grand mosques, I found the range of mosque officials numbered seven, consisting of *lebeNa'e*, *khatib* and *wakil khatib*, *bilal* and deputy, *robo* and deputy. In sub-district mosques, *cepelebe* are assisted by *khatib*, *bilal* and *robo* and their respective deputies.

Mosque officials referred to as imam are prayer leaders who provide services in smaller prayer houses called *langgar* (*musholla*), which are not used for Friday congregational prayer. But the term imam can also refer to prayer leaders in those mosques outside the control of YASIM, for example, Masjid Al-Muwahidin Pane, the Muhammadiyah mosque, or mosques built after the sultanate era, that is, after Indonesian independence. YASIM is currently responsible for administering 24 grand mosques, out of a total of around 500 mosques in Bima district and municipality. In practice, lebe function in a similar role to that of imam, as prayer leaders. To remind every Muslim about the five appointed times of prayer, Lebe Taufik explained that the role of *bilal* is important. The *bilal* is responsible for the call to prayer, which is broadcast with a loudspeaker from the minarets found in all Bima mosques.

During the Bima Sultanate, the Sultan used *dana paja kai* (Bim.) (royal tax)[6] to pay lebe and other mosque officials for their services to grand mosques. When Putra Kahir, the son of Sultan Muhammad Salahuddin, was elected as the head of the Swapraja (the Dutch era term referring to former sultanates regarded as self-governing units) in 1954, he resumed distributing the land to mosque officials. In 1968, when YASIM was founded, Sultan Putra Kahir put all these lands into religious endowments (*wakaf*) with YASIM as trustee (*nadzir*) in the provision of the land to lebe (Ar. *maukuf alaihi* literally the receiver) and other mosque officials. In fact, the portion of the farmed land given varies between lebe and other mosque officials, with lebe receiving the largest portion. In the era of the Bima Sultanate, lebe received around five hectares and *khatib* four hectares. As the amount of land owned by the Sultan was reduced in accord with the agrarian law (Undang-Undang Pokok Agraria or UUPA) in 1960, lebe now receive only one hectare of land, *khatib* are given 75 *are* (100 square metres), and bilal and *marbut* receive land ranging from 50 to 57 *are*.

In principle, the recruitment of lebe is open to candidates from all villages across Bima. Every village has the right to propose their candidates who must represent Muslim organisations in the village, such as NU and Muhammadiyah. The candidates must be well-educated and respectable persons and are not required to be hajis. In the initial phase of selection of lebe, for example, no more than three candidates may be proposed from every sub-district with the decision resting with a special committee of YASIM and the final decision made by the Sultanate family, previously led by Siti Maryam (the daughter of the 14th Sultan [see above] who died in 2017) during her lifetime. Officially, after the shortlisted candidates have been finalised, the committee advises all candidates to undergo oral and written examination. The examination mainly focuses on the mastery of Islamic tenets. Appointment is for life.

If a lebe retires due to ill health or dies in office, YASIM will set up an open recruitment process to appoint a successor. They will pass on the shortlisted candidates to the royal family to make a final decision. The process shows the significant role of YASIM, as the representative of the royal family, in the recruitment of mosque officials. This not only preserves traditional forms of ritual prayer in the Sultan mosque, but also sustains the authority of the royal family to the present day.

Between Traditionalist and Reformist Imams: Compromising Ritual Prayers

In this section, I will describe the different type of ritual prayers performed by different imam/lebe in mosques of differing religious orientations. Within Islam there are five canonical prayers to be conducted on a daily basis at times determined according to the sun's path through the sky, and these are universal elements of the religion (Bowen 1989, 2000; Parkin and Headley 2000; Mahmood 2001; Henkel 2005; Möller 2005; Muhaimin 2006). Each prayer has different numbers of cycles or prescribed postures and recitations (*rakaat*): at dawn (*salat subuh*) with two cycles, early afternoon (*salat zuhur*) with four cycles (but two cycles for Friday prayer), late afternoon (*salat asar*) with four cycles, sunset (*salat magrib*) three cycles and evening (*salat isya*) four cycles. Like other Muslims in Indonesia, Bima people understand that they are obliged to pray five times each day. Those who manage to perform these five prayers every single day are regarded as pious Muslims (Bim. *dou sale*, Ind. *orang saleh*).

I interviewed Lebe Taufik, the lebe of Masjid Al Muhawidin, regarding his understanding of ritual prayer. He explained that the term for Islamic ritual prayer, salat, is derived from an Arabic word meaning to sanctify, as opposed to spontaneous supplication to God (*doa*) or invocation (*zikir*) (see similar explanations of Islamic prayer in Bowen 1989, 2000; Parkin and Headley 2000; Mahmood 2001). Lebe Taufik advised that one should begin with an intention (*niat*), saying to yourself that you intend to offer this prayer to God alone.

> Then you recite *Allahu Akbar*, Allah is the greatest, and raise your hands to your ears in a standing position and place your right hand on the left, just below, above or on the navel, and start reciting Surat Al-Fatihah, the first chapter of the Qur'an, and then recite any other passage from the Qur'an—not always a long passage, a short one is acceptable.

Islamic ritual prayer consists of bodily movements and invocations. It begins in a standing position and the worshipper moves until he/she is kneeling; specified prayers are said in each posture: they concern the glorification of God, recitations of the Qur'an, and blessings on the Prophet. Prayer concludes with the greeting, "Peace be upon you", even when praying alone (Bowker 2000: 505). Lebe Taufik emphasised that performing prayer in the correct form is central to Islam. As Parkin (2000) noted in his study of Islam, the correct bodily postures during prayer are crucial to its success.

Prior to prayer, Muslims take ritual ablution (*air sembahyang*, Ar. *wudu*) by properly washing three times, their face, head to ears, hands to elbow, lower legs and feet. Prayer may be performed individually at home. But as Lebe Taufik explained, it carries special merit when undertaken with other Muslims or in congregation (*jemaah*) in a mosque (see also Bowen 1989, 2000; Möller 2005). This creates social relations between Muslims as a part of "Muslimness" (Henkel 2005: 489). The focal prayer of the week is the mid-day prayer at the mosque for Friday congregational prayer (*salat* Jumat).

Prayers can differ, according to the number of cycles and the accompanying invocations. These practices differentiate participants in Bima mosques affiliated to Muhammadiyah from those affiliated with NU.[7]

In regard to intention (*niat*) before prayer Lebe Taufik noted that followers of NU and Muhammadiyah disagree on whether it should be recited out loud or silently.[8] Members of these two groups also disagree on whether or not Muslims are permitted to murmur *bismillah* (full phrase "*Bismillah Ar-rahman Ar-rahim*", meaning "In the name of God, the Most Gracious, the Most Compassionate") loudly or silently before reciting Surat Al-Fatihah. Most followers of Muhammadiyah that I met in Bima said to me that one may not recite the *bismillah* aloud, as though it were a verse in Surat Al-Fatihah.

Muma Gani Masykur, the former *khatib karoto* (middle *khatib*) during the Bima Sultanate and the most prominent Muhammadiyah figure, cited a *hadis* on this matter, a report by one of the hadis narrators, Anas, saying: "I observed prayer along with the Messenger of Allah (may peace be upon him) and with Abu Bakr, Umar and Uthman (may Allah be pleased with all of them), but I never heard any one of them reciting *Bismillah Ar-rahman Ar-rahim* loudly." When I asked Lebe Taufik about this hadis, he replied: "the difference of opinion on this matter is valid as we both have evidence. We disputed whether it should be recited out loud or in silence and we both have our own proof." However, tension as a result of different versions of reciting *bismillah* between prayer leaders from NU and Muhammadiyah was not significant in the Bima mosques. I found Bima Muslims to be tolerant and able to accommodate differing religious views.

Most notably in this regard, on many occasions, I observed that the "Muhammadiyah mosque" gave the opportunity for NU-affiliated Lebe Taufik to lead the congregation at dawn prayer and pledge a special supplication (or *kunut*). But I witnessed on those occasions that Lebe Taufik did not raise his hands nor did he recite the *kunut* loudly in order to show respect to the differing views within the congregation.

I return to my description of Ramadan prayer in Masjid Sultan Muhammad Salahuddin. As my watch pointed to 7 pm, the bilal performed *azan*, calling congregants to prayer. As the people in the neighbourhood entered the mosque, they generally performed a welcoming prayer consisting of two cycles (*tahiyat masjid*). After that, they sat and chatted or quietly recited parts of the Qur'an. This was also a time that might be used for private supplications or chanting invocation (*zikir*) by counting *tasbih* (a string of beads counted with the right-hand fingers).

In my observation on several particular occasions, Lebe Ishaka and the bilal allowed a longer time than usual to lapse between the *azan* and the formal prayer. The bilal recited—or rather, sang—praise to the Prophet Muhammad (*selawat*) in order to fill the time. Once the bilal thought that prayer time had come, he called a shorter *azan* (*qomat*) through the microphone marking the imminent start of the evening prayer. Before starting the prayer, Lebe Ishaka led the congregants in the prayer of intention (*niat*). Next, Lebe Ishaka uttered *Allahu Akbar* (God is Great) while raising his hands. Some uttered the intent silently in Indonesian—mainly those who followed Muhammadiyah—but most recited this loudly. Then he recited aloud each cycle of the Qur'anic chapter of Surat Al-Fatihah, followed by an additional chapter.

After that, Lebe Ishaka bent forward (*ruku'*) then prostrated himself (*sujud*). The members of the congregation followed. The prayer concluded with the Arabic-derived greeting *salam*, and the congregants rested a while before the sermon. Some used this time to perform two additional cycles of optional prayer (*salat sunnat*). At the end of the sermon, which lasted half an hour, the bilal raised his voice again to say in Arabic, "Let us perform Ramadan prayer (*salat tarawih*) in congregation, in the hope that God will extend His Grace on you all." Some, but not all, replied by saying: there is no God but Allah, Muhammad is His Messenger. That was the sign that Ramadan prayer was about to begin and the entire congregation rose and started to murmur individually the prescribed intent for this: "*sunnata tarawī lillaahi ta'ala*" (the intention to perform the optional prayer of Ramadan prayer for God, the Exalted). Again, the Muhammadiyah-oriented congregants mostly prayed silently, and in Indonesian.

What struck me most about the Ramadan prayer in this mosque was that the prayer was conducted twice and led by two prayer leaders in sequence; the first consisted of 8 cycles and the second comprised 20 cycles. The first shorter type of Ramadan prayer is usually related to Muhammadiyah, whereas the second is traditionally the practice of NU followers.[9] The NU version of Ramadan prayer is locally referred to as *moda teo mboto* (*moda* meaning "ease in recalling the verses", *teo* referring to the lebe's recitation of short verses from the Qur'an, and *mboto* meaning many cycles).

I observed Lebe Ishaka lead the congregants in the second 20 cycles of Ramadan prayer: the Qur'anic verses he recited were mostly short, which made it easier for the congregants to remember and follow. In contrast, the imam from Muhammadiyah only led eight cycles of Ramadan prayer, but recited long Qur'anic verses. I also participated in Ramadan prayer in the mosque of Pesantren Al-Husainy, an Islamic boarding school known as the centre of Qur'anic memorisation. It is owned by Haji Ramli, the son-in-law of Haji Abubakar Husain, the late Muhammadiyah figure. Each night of Ramadan, the imam in the mosque recited one section of the Qur'an (*juz*) consisting of several chapters. The Qur'an contains 30 sections, hence the imam was able to recite the entire Qur'an in the holy month.[10] I spent almost four hours one night completing the entire eight cycles of Ramadan prayer. I learned that the Muhammadiyah version of Ramadan prayer may last longer than the NU version, even though the number of cycles performed is less.

The role of *bilal* in Masjid Sultan Muhammad Salahuddin is also important in determining the interval between these two types of Ramadan prayer. He is charged with ensuring that the respective congregations for the two versions of Ramadan prayer can exercise their chosen practice. Turning once more to Lebe Ishaka, he stood in front of the congregation before leading the prayer. After completing eight cycles, he sat to one side. The *bilal* stood up and uttered the invitation: "Come and join me to conclude Ramadan prayer" to those congregants joining eight cycles or following the Muhammadiyah model. Next, the imam from Muhammadiyah stepped forward to the prayer mat previously used by Lebe Ishaka, to lead the congregation. He added three cycles of extra evening prayer called *witir* (meaning *ganjil* or odd) to conclude Ramadan prayer according to the Muhammadiyah practice. The Muhammadiyah-oriented congregants left the mosque before Lebe Ishaka resumed the position of prayer leader and continued an additional 12 cycles in order to bring the total number of cycles to 20.

Just as in Masjid Sultan Muhammad Salahuddin and Masjid Raya Al-Muwahidin, the number of mosque participants who followed eight cycles of Ramadan prayer was larger than those who followed the longer NU version. I sought an explanation from a man who chose eight cycles and he answered: "I am not a Muhammadiyah follower, but I chose eight cycles because it has theological reasoning, and in fact is shorter so that I can go home earlier". Another stated that: "I chose eight cycles but have not yet concluded my Ramadan prayers because I prefer continuing the other twelve cycles at home". Similar differences in practice are found elsewhere in Indonesia. Möller (2005), for example, found in Java that NU followers who felt that the Ramadan prayer should be 20 cycles would perform an additional 12 cycles either at the mosque or at home. Muhammadiyah followers who agreed with the imam that the Ramadan prayer should only consist of eight cycles would return home after they concluded the eight cycles of prayer. Unlike Möller's (2005) findings for Java, however, I found that these two versions of Ramadan prayer were conducted in one mosque and led by two different prayer leaders: lebe and imam.

But to reiterate, the performance of the differing types of Ramadan prayer in one mosque is not common in other parts of Indonesia. The committee in Sultan Muhammad Salahuddin mosque decided to provide two prayer leaders—Lebe Ishaka and another imam from Muhammadiyah—to lead Ramadan prayer. This combination had become effective in the three years (2009–12) after a long period of tension. Lebe Ishaka commented that a high level of tension always existed between the proponents of the differing cycles in Ramadan prayer and other technicalities in ritual prayer. Previously, the Muhammadiyah imam was not permitted to perform eight cycles of Ramadan prayer in the mosque. Lebe Ishaka assumed that it might be that Muma Gani Masykur, the prominent figure of the Muhammadiyah organisation in Bima and a member of the advisory board of YASIM, was influential in allowing the Muhammadiyah imam to be accepted in the Sultan mosques. In many other parts of Indonesia, the followers of these two different versions of Ramadan prayer conduct their prayers at different mosques (see Möller 2005). There is no mosque membership: every mosque is open for every Muslim to pray regardless of religious orientation. But once a prayer leader is chosen, congregants should follow his preferred version of prayer, or find another mosque. That is, the political undertones to the identification of the Sultanate family with NU and the family of the political rival with Muhammadiyah (see Prager 2010) has not prevented a distinctive accommodation in theological differences about Islamic prayer.

Lebe Outside the Mosque: The Guardians of Villagers

Peter Just (2001: 32) described lowland Bima as the home of "Islamic fanaticism". Bima Muslims are ardent in performing their religious duties. This seemed to be the case in the early weeks of my fieldwork, as I arrived during the Ramadan month. I heard a local phrase, *mori ro made na Dou Mbojo ede kai hukum Islam-ku*, meaning "the life and death of Bima people should be based on Islam", also seemingly endorsing the view that Bima Muslims are indeed "fanatical" Muslims. As time went on, however, I found that many do not pray on a regular basis and are considered by others as less devout. Yet, they are proud to be Muslim and feel anger when they are called infidel (*kafir*). Lebe, *guru* (teacher) and imam or ordinary Muslims with a *haji* title are the most respected people in the community. Lebe are ritual leaders in life cycle rituals (Bim. *rawi rasa*) ranging from birth to death. They also become specialists in healing sick people assumed to have been possessed by harmful spirits.

Rahman (not his real name), a 35-year-old neighbour, for example, admitted to me that he rarely prayed and was often drunk. He expressed admiration for Lebe Taufik and when he conducted the circumcision ritual for his child, associated with a local rite of passage, he asked Lebe Taufik to lead it. Rahman and other Muslims in the village relied on the lebe as their religious authorities to lead life cycle and other village rituals. Local Muslims like Rahman show respect to Lebe Taufik and his ilk, both because of their religious expertise and their link to royal authority.

Rahman remembered when he was a child, he went to study Qur'anic recitation with a local lebe (in Bima, "*lao ngaji di uma guru*"). Although he was not particularly pious, Rahman's code of conduct always relied on a local phrase, "*na kanta ku ba ruma*", meaning "do not do anything that is forbidden by God" or "*wati taho na*", meaning "it is not good to commit wrongdoing".

Within the month of Ramadan, especially on Fridays, I noticed that more Muslims prayed in the mosque at sunset because more village life cycle rituals were conducted in that month. In fact, apart from his main duty of calling the faithful to prayer, the bilal was in charge of announcing through the mosque loudspeaker the invitations to congregants to attend village life cycle rituals soon after performing prayer. The bilal told me that people who did not come for sunset prayer or attend village life cycle rituals would be regarded as having no shame and fear (Bim. *tiwara maja labo dahu* [*malu dan takut*]).[11] I noticed that Rahman and others who rarely prayed, or did not pray at all, sat outside the room where the ritual was being completed when they came to a house hosting a life cycle event.

Some lebe also assist the villagers mediate their relations with *jin* (from *jinn* Ar.), ghosts and devils. Lebe are specialists in healing the victims of sorcery-related sickness and spirit possession. I will discuss one lebe who practises as a healer and cultivates personal relations with spirits through mediumship.[12] Bima's traditional healers are called *sando*. Some lebe are not automatically called *sando*. Some keep this power secret, while others like Haji Kasimu, popularly called as such, publicly announce it. He declared his healing power to surrounding villagers after he recovered from a severe illness. As I observed, Haji Kasimu's spiritual power enabled him to communicate with *jin* or spirits in his healing process even when fully conscious. Haji Kasimu was often called *dou maloa* (*orang pintar*), implying supernatural power in regard to his commitment to fight against sorcery and his ability to forecast the future. I often heard villagers say when they wanted to visit Haji Kasimu, "*lao aka dou maloa*", meaning "go to see a healer for the possessed".

The local name for ancestral spirits is *parafu* (Bim). *Parafu ro pambora* (the home of spirits) is the place where these ancestral spirits reside (Just 1986, 2001; Prager 2010: 17). Despite the practice being in decline (Prager 2010: 17), giving offerings to and taking water from the *parafu* prior to life cycle celebrations (particularly in circumcision rituals) was still in place among the villagers in my neighbourhood. Rahman told me that the descendants of the Sultan took sacred water from the Dara well (Bim. *temba ncuhi*), while those of Ruma Bicara drew water from another well Luwu Due, and the ordinary people took water from sacred springs such as Oi Monca (*air kuning*, a well with yellow water).

> The *sando* can use the sacred water for healing the sick. As I witnessed, every patient coming to visit Haji Kasimu brought a bottle of water. While some patients sourced water from *parafu ro pambora*, others carried water in *padasa* (Bim.), clay water containers mainly used for ritual ablutions. Others bought bottled spring water sold at nearby kiosks.

Lebe also lead a ritual called *doa dana* (Bim. prayer for the country) which seeks salvation for the whole village. At the ritual, a lebe invites all residents to eat porridge (Bim. *ngaha karedo*) made of rice and coconut milk, for five days—Monday to Friday. As I observed one

Friday morning and evening in 2011, two days before the first day of the month of Muharram, the first month in the Islamic calendar, residents were served rice porridge in banana leaves on the main village road. The households that made the porridge took turns almost every week, starting from the eastern to the western part of the village. *Doa dana* is performed over three consecutive days, Wednesday, Thursday and Friday, and adults are obliged to attend the event in the afternoon on these days, while the children are advised to attend the event on Friday morning before school hours (Friday being the most significant day in Islamic doctrine). "The reason is that the rice porridge is best served for children early in the morning", said Lebe Taufik.

On that Friday afternoon in 2011, I observed that villagers were advised to pray together before eating *karedo* at the main road, led by Lebe Taufik. At the event of *ngaha karedo*, the eldest of the children was told by an elder to begin by delivering prayers on behalf of the rest, since the prayer of the children is most welcomed by God. They recited Surat Al-Fatihah. After that, the children gathered to share *karedo* served on young banana leaves eaten with spoons made from pandanus leaves. The role of lebe in the ritual is important in enhancing the virtue of togetherness among villagers that can be seen in the acts of collecting rice, cooking and eating together.

In short, *doa dana* is a distinctive ritual aimed at giving spiritual and communal strength. The ritual is intended to protect the children and village from natural disasters and endemic disease. Although educated people in the region consider natural disasters as simply natural phenomena, the majority still maintain the central practices of the ritual even as it changes with contemporary Bima society. For example, in 2012, the district head celebrated Bima's Hari Jadi ("birthday") by conducting a *doa dana* ritual.

Conclusion

This chapter has described the relation between religious authority and the royal court in Bima. Bima is historically ruled by a dyadic arrangement of power represented by sultan and *raja bicara*. The differences in ritual prayer among mosque participants and the tolerant attitude in relation to mediating those differences is a concrete manifestation of this dyadic relationship. This relationship exemplifies Emile

Durkheim's (1964: 42) comment that when "an authority with power to govern is established its first and forever function is to ensure respect for beliefs, traditions and collective practices—namely to defend the common consciousness from all its enemies".

There are many interpretations of Islamic ritual prayers even within the same community (see Parkin and Headley 2000). Even though the local Muslims I observed reside in the same cultural settings and observe Islamic ritual prayer in the same mosque, they construct different meanings and observe different ritual prayers (see Bowen 1989). Different types of prayers and how they are perceived can become a tool to show distinction from the 'other' (Bell 1992: 74). This making of Muslim identity is not only in doctrinal but also political terms (Henkel 2005). At the same time, ritual prayer becomes a means of negotiating the understandings of authority, self and society.

It has been argued within the Sunni Muslim milieu that when religious authority is linked to power, it will marginalise, punish or exclude those who refuse to accept the doctrine of the royal authority (see Krämer and Schmidtke 2006: 10). But in Bima, modes of binary classification are linked to dynamic modes of resolving symbolic differences. In Bima, the lebe provide space in the Sultan mosques for Muslims of other religious orientations like members of the reformist Muhammadiyah, to practise their ritual prayers. This by no means lessens royal power. Lebe as embodied symbols of royal power have been able to authoritatively resolve conflict over the forms of ritual practice between NU and Muhammadiyah followers in the same religious space in ways that do not occur in other parts of Indonesia.

Lebe as royal-appointed prayer leaders play a key role in the lives of Bima Muslims inside and outside the Sultan mosques. In addition to leading Muslim prayer, Bima lebe also provide leadership in practices relating to the belief in supernatural beings and healing rituals for Muslims. They traditionally act as guardians, propagating and sustaining the legacy of royal authority both ritually and politically.

Notes

1. This study is based on 12 months' fieldwork in Bima for my doctoral dissertation (Sila 2015) from August 2011 to August 2012. My scholarship was funded by the Australian Research Council Discovery Project grant DP00881464 "Being Muslim in Eastern Indonesia: Practice, Politics

and Diversity", with Chief Investigators Kathryn Robinson and Andrew McWilliam (Anthropology, ANU College of Asia and the Pacific). I am grateful to Professor Kathryn Robinson, Professor James Jim Fox, Professor Andrew McWilliam and Dr Patrick Guinness for their comments on earlier drafts of the chapter.

2. Masjid Agung is translated as "Great Mosque", while Masjid Raya is translated as "Grand Mosque". Mesjid Keramat is translated as "Holy Mosque". Masjid Jami (Jami Mosque) refers to the village mosque where weekly Friday prayer takes place. According to a Ministerial Decree (Keputusan Menteri Agama or KMA) 394/2004, the title of the mosque is determined by its location: Masjid Negara or Masjid Istiqlal, meaning state mosque, is located in the capital city; Masjid Raya is located at the provincial level; Masjid Agung, for example, Masjid Muhammad Sultan Salahuddin in Bima district, is located at the district level; Masjid Besar is located at the sub-district level; and Masjid Jami is located at the village level.
3. I use salat, rather than *sembahyang* to refer to the act of Islamic ritual prayer conducted in Bima (see Mahmood 2001: 827).
4. *Bilal* is not derived from an Arabic word like the names of other mosque officials; the term was taken from the name of one of the Prophet Muhammad's companions who was a slave before he converted to Islam. The role of *bilal* as caller of *azan* relates to the man, Bilal, who was renowned for his beautiful voice in calling the *azan* during the lifetime of the Prophet.
5. Raja Bicara Abdul Hamid was the founder of the Muhammadiyah branch in Bima in 1937, but this mosque was formally affiliated to YASIM, not Muhammadiyah.
6. The Sultan serves as the ritual centre and source of prosperity of the domain in return for tribute in the form of harvest gifts from the subjects.
7. André Möller (2005) is among the few scholars who have comprehensively studied Islamic prayer in Java to find differences between what he called the "NU mosque" and the "Muhammadiyah mosque". Endang Turmudi (2006: 180–1) stated that the NU mosque would represent traditionalist beliefs and practices, while the Muhammadiyah mosque would promote "more purified Islamic beliefs and practices".
8. Muhammadiyah and Persis (two important reformist Muslim mass organisations) regard this practice as illegitimate as it is considered innovation, as are also the NU practices of audible recitation of intention (*niat*) and of *bismillah* (in the name of God) before performing ritual prayer.
9. Interestingly, I experienced the same thing when I visited Masjid Raya Al-Muwahidin on another night. There were also two prayer leaders in the mosque: Lebe Taufik and the mosque imam from Muhammadiyah.

10. The Qur'an consists of 114 chapters of varying lengths, each known as *surah*. Each chapter or *surah* consists of several verses, known as *ayat* (sign or evidence sent by God), and each chapter starts with the *bismillah* meaning "In the name of God".
11. This local phrase seems to be the main code of conduct in Bima and the local government officially erected a large poster headed "Maja Labo Dahu" (*malu dan takut*, literally, "shame and fear") at the front gate of Bima city.
12. They are best understood as spirit mediums, and not "shaman", the term used by Hitchcock (1996) and Just (2001).

References

Abdullah, Abdul Gani. 2004. *Peradilan Agama Dalam Pemerintahan Islam Di Kesultanan Bima (1947–1957)*. Yogyakarta: Lengge.

Asad, Talal. 1986. *The Idea of an Anthropology of Islam*, Occasional Papers Series. Center for Contemporary Arab Studies. Washington, DC: Georgetown University.

Bell, Catherine. 1992. *Ritual Theory, Ritual Practice*. New York: Oxford University Press.

Bowen, John R. 1989. "Salāt in Indonesia: The Social Meaning of an Islamic Ritual." *Man* 24 (4): 600–17.

______. 1998. "What is 'Universal' and 'Local' in Islam?" *Ethos* 26 (2): 258–61.

______. 2000. "Imputations of Faith and Allegiance: Islamic Prayer and Indonesian Politics Outside the Mosque." In *Islam Across the Indian Ocean: Inside and Outside the Mosque*, ed. David Parkin and Stephen Headley, 23–38. Richmond, UK: Curzon Press.

Durkheim, Emile. 1964 [1893]. *The Division of Labor in Society*. New York: Free Press.

Henkel, Heiko. 2005. "Between Belief and Unbelief Lies the Performance of *ṣalāt*': Meaning and Efficacy of a Muslim Ritual." *Journal of the Royal Anthropological Institute* 11 (3): 487–507.

Hitchcock, Michael. 1996. *Islam and Identity in Eastern Indonesia*. Hull: University of Hull Press.

Hooker, M.B. 2003. *Indonesian Islam: Social Change Through Contemporary Fatawa*. Honolulu: University of Hawai'i Press.

Ismail, M. Hilir. 2008. *Kebangkitan Islam di Dana Mbojo (Bima) (1540–1950)* [Emergence of Islam in Dana Mbojo (Bima) (1540–1950)]. Bogor, Indonesia: Penerbit CV Binasti.

Just, Peter. 1986. "Dou Donggo Social Organization: Ideology, Structure and Action in an Indonesian Society." PhD diss., University of Pennsylvania.

______. 2001. *Dou Donggo Justice: Conflict and Morality in an Indonesian Society*. Lanham, MD: Rowman & Littlefield Publishers, Inc.

Krämer, Gudrun and Sabine Schmidtke, eds. 2006. *Speaking for Islam: Religious Authorities in Muslim Societies*. Leiden, Boston: E.J. Brill.

Mahmood, Saba. 2001. "Rehearsed Spontaneity and the Conventionality of Ritual: Disciplines of *ṣalāt*." *American Ethnologist* 28 (4): 827–53.

Möller, André. 2005. "Islam and Traweh Prayers in Java: Unity, Diversity, and Cultural Smoothness." *Indonesia and the Malay World* 33 (95): 1–20.

Muhaimin, A.G. 2006. *The Islamic Traditions of Cirebon: Ibadat and Adat among Javanese Muslims*. Canberra: ANU E Press.

Parkin, David and Stephen C. Headley, eds. 2000. *Islamic Prayer across the Indian Ocean: Inside and Outside the Mosque*. Richmond: Curzon Press.

Parkin, David. 2000. "Inside and Outside the Mosque: A Master Trope." In *Islamic Prayer across the Indian Ocean. Inside and Outside the Mosque*, ed. David Parker and Stephen C. Headley, 1–22. Richmond: Curzon Press.

Prager, Michael. 2010. "Abandoning the 'Garden of Magic': Islamic Modernism and Contested Spirit Assertions in Bima." *Indonesia and the Malay World* 38 (110): 9–25.

Sila, Muhammad Adlin. 2015. "Being Muslims in Bima of Sumbawa, Indonesia: Practice, Politics and Cultural Diversity." PhD diss., The Australian National University.

Turmudi, Endang. 2006. *Struggling for the Umma: Changing Leadership Roles of Kiai in Jombang, East Java*. Canberra: ANU E Press.

2

Mediating Religious and Cultural Disputes

Imam Desa and Conflict Resolution in Rural Indonesia

Faried F. Saenong

Introduction

On my first visit to the house of Ustas Husain, an *imam desa* (village imam) of Ereng-Ereng in Bantaeng, South Sulawesi, I was intrigued by the sight of three girls drying coffee and cocoa beans in his yard. They picked up drying trays from the front yard of the mosque and took them up to the house. I knew that the imam had only a 11-year-old daughter and two sons; I assumed the three girls were not family members. I then discovered that they were *silariang* ([Mak.] run-away bride) cases. Although I knew about silariang, this was my first direct experience. It led me to think deeply about the role of imams in family conflicts in South Sulawesi life practices.

This chapter deals with the role of local imams or imam desa in serving Muslims in rural Indonesia, especially South Sulawesi. Taking the particular case of Ustas Husain, I scrutinise the role of imam desa in Bantaeng district, South Sulawesi. I address the conventional role of the imam as Muslim elite in rural areas; as a local reference for Islam; as marriage master; and as leader of religious rituals. In addition, this chapter observes his role as mediator of grassroots conflict in rural South Sulawesi.

Imam

The imam and officials of the Office for Religious Affairs (Kantor Urusan Agama, henceforth KUA) play similar roles in regard to marrying couples. People in South Sulawesi call them *pak imang* (Bug./Mak.) and *pak* KUA respectively, and both are considered as "*pak penghulu*" (an Indonesian term for officers tasked to marry couples). Both officials can serve Muslims intending to undergo an official (registered) marriage. However, sometimes an imam deals with those who are forced to have an "extraordinary", "unusual" or "unofficial" Islamic marriage, a role that cannot be undertaken by the KUA. "Unofficial" marriage can take place in remote areas, from where it is too hard to access the KUA, usually located in the *kecamatan* (sub-district). In such cases, an imam bridges the community and the KUA. Sometimes, a reputable imam may be licensed by the KUA to lead wedding ceremonies which the KUA officer attends as witness or invitee.

The respected position of the imam as religious figure in South Sulawesi has its roots in the history of local polities. In the power structure of the Makassar sultanate, for example, Islamic officials were structured as follows:

> Daengta' Kaliya (judge) working in the capital;
> Daengta' Imang (prayer leader or imam);
> Guruwa (ordinary teacher);
> Katte (preacher);
> Bidala (person in charge of *azan*, calling people to prayer); and
> Doja (mosque caretaker). (Sewang 2003: 134–7)

All villages in South Sulawesi have an imam, an assistant imam or other religious officers. These Islamic officers were added to the power structure after the 17th-century embrace of Islam by South Sulawesi kingdoms. This structure is commonly regarded as the legacy of "Three Dato'", the disseminators of Islam in South Sulawesi (see introduction to this volume).

Differing Roles of "Imam"

The role of imams in rural Indonesia, especially in South Sulawesi, is different from that of the imam in urban Muslim communities, especially in other parts of the world (see Saenong 2004, 2008). In many Muslim communities, especially in Western countries, the term imam is mainly used for the person responsible for leading Muslims in collective prayers in the mosque, or to deliver *khutbah* (sermons) each Friday in a particular mosque. Indeed this mosque imam (*imam masjid*) is the only individual who has the right to lead prayers and deliver khutbah and, while he is in good health, no other Muslim can replace him in these roles. He is not supposed to conduct other activities during collective prayer times (see for example, Haddad and Balz 2008; Shahid and van Koningsveld 2002). In addition, he is the person to consult on Islamic theological issues.

In Western countries, this kind of imam is often recruited from Middle East countries which provide professional training of imams. Mosques that request such imams usually have cultural ties with the sending country. A mosque that is built by the Saudi Muslim community, for example, will request imams from Saudi Arabia; if the major congregation is from Morocco, it will request an imam from that country. Usually, they are posted alone—without their family—to a particular mosque, for a certain period of time (for example, two to four years), and are provided with a room inside or close to the mosque. Generally, their activities focus on the mosque where they are posted. They are paid by the sending institution in the home country in most cases. But the Muslim community that uses the mosque and the imam's services also supports them financially. In some cases, however, imams are paid only by the Muslim community through charitable contributions to the mosque.[1]

If we look at imams across the Muslim world, some have additional roles within Muslim societies. Amitav Ghosh (1994) presents an ethnographic account of a village imam in Alexandria, Egypt, who also has a traditional, or alternative medical clinic. M. Rashiduzzaman (1997) shows how politicians use village imams to win elections in rural Bangladesh. David Shankland (1994) observes the role of a village imam in an Alevi (Alawi) village in Anatolia where the imam leads prayer and teaches Islam, but also conducts funerals and wedding rituals.

In Indonesia, the role of imam carries particular socio-cultural meaning; imams are not obliged to always lead prayers or deliver the Friday sermon. Being a mosque imam may not comprise a primary occupation; he may be a civil servant or have some other occupation. While leading the congregational prayers and delivering the khutbah comprises part of their duties, other proficient Muslims are allowed to do so, as long as they are able to recite the Qur'an competently and have sufficient knowledge of Islam. The current *imam besar* (great imam) of Istiqlal Mosque in central Jakarta, for example, is Professor Nasaruddin Umar. He is neither obliged to lead all collective prayers nor give khutbah. He manages his activities as lecturer, public intellectual and preacher, *pesantren* (religious residential school) teacher, and other religious duties. He also serves as a rector of the Institute of Qur'anic Studies in South Jakarta where he lives.

It is rare in Indonesia to find someone who has the title "imam besar" (great imam). Only those mosques classified as *masjid negara*, *masjid nasional*, *masjid raya*, *masjid agung*, *masjid besar*, and historical mosques at that level, have an imam besar.[2] The imam besar in these instances is elected from proficient local Muslims, not recruited from other areas. According to Jufri, a mosque caretaker in Makassar, this means that the imam possesses social and cultural awareness of his local Muslim community. Hence, an imam is supposed to have the local wisdom to solve any religious problems faced by his local community.

In Indonesia, the imam is not the only person who has the right to lead Muslims in the five daily collective prayers or to deliver the weekly Friday sermon in one particular mosque. He may deliver khutbah every Friday, in any mosque in his area. In Indonesia, the need for a *khatib* (preacher) every Friday is covered by khatib management committees established by Muslim organisations. Majelis Tabligh (MT), a section within Muhammadiyah, for example, runs the biggest khatib management operation in the city of Makassar, and is also in charge of *dakwah* (Islamic propagation), which includes Friday sermons. The MT annually circulates khatib—who become members of the MT—in mosques around Makassar. The analogous section of Nahdlatul Ulama (NU) also manages the circulation of khatib in Makassar, though in smaller numbers. Both khatib and mosques should be members of these organisations in order to benefit from its services.

Imams in Rural Indonesia

This chapter focuses on *imam desa* in rural areas who serve Muslim societies in the countryside. These imam deal with primary life cycle rituals related to birth, death and marriage. They are often appointed by *lurah* (village headmen) on the basis of competency, heredity (see Hutagalung, this volume), or for other reasons. The imam is not a civil servant or worker who signs a contract with the local government and is therefore paid a salary. However, some local authorities pay imams a monthly stipend. This may come from the budget of the *camat* (sub-district head), a civil servant under the Ministry of Home Affairs, or from the Kepala KUA (Head of Office of Religious Affairs) in the district, which is under the Ministry of Religious Affairs. Saenong Ibrahim, a former head of the Ministry of Religious Affairs in Selayar district, advised me that all KUA in that district pay a monthly stipend to imams varying from Rp. 50,000–100,000 ($4–10). But in some places, the imam is not paid at all. Additionally, there is no prescribed duration of service and an imam may work in that role for the term of his life. His house does not need to be located next to a mosque, and he is not obliged to lead all prayers or always deliver khutbah.

In the next section, I describe the profile of Ustas Husain, an imam in Desa Labbo, a village under Kelurahan Ereng-Ereng, Kecamatan Tompobulu in Bantaeng district.

Ustas Husain: An Authoritative Imam

Prior to fieldwork (2007–08), I already knew a large Bugis family in Tompobulu. Asnawi (aged 36) had been my friend since senior high school in Makassar. After graduating in 1994, we met again in Tompobulu when I came to do fieldwork, 14 years later. He became my host and a reliable informant. He was born in Tompobulu into a Bugis (Wajo) family whose parents had migrated to Bantaeng in the 1930s. It struck me the members of his extended family marry relatives, and that most of them play significant socio-cultural roles within their communities in Tompobulu (Saenong 2012). Asnawi's relatives include three respected members of the local elite.

Asnawi's parents, H. Zubairi and his wife Hj. Hadra are respected Bugis merchants, and have vast cocoa and coffee plantations in Tompobulu. H. Zubairi is a graduate of Pesantren As'adiyah in Sengkang, about 365 km north of Bantaeng (see Halim, this volume). Hj. Hadra is an independent merchant and operates shops in Tompobulu markets. The day before market day in Tompobulu, she goes alone to Makassar to buy her merchandise.

H. Syuaib is a local educator and preacher who supervises three Islamic schools in Tompobulu and Bantaeng. He is among the group of locally-respected people who founded the branch of Pesantren As'adiyah in Tompobulu. He is a graduate of As'adiyah in Sengkang, Wajo. At the time of fieldwork he was headmaster of Madrasah Aliyah As'adiyah in Desa Labbo in Tompobulu. Although having the same name, this school is not part of the Bantaeng branch of Pesantren As'adiyah which is headquartered in Sengkang. H. Syuaib delivers religious speeches (khutbah) in mosques, in Tompobulu and elsewhere in Bantaeng. In addition to this main job, he also runs business next to his house in Banyorang-Tompobulu, where he sells construction materials.

The third person noted above is Ustas Husain, the imam of Desa Labbo of Tompobulu. An esteemed and trusted Muslim scholar, he is responsible for Islamic-related matters in the village, such as marriage, birth, circumcision, death, rituals around building new houses and so forth. He also provides problem-solving and conflict resolution within families, including cases of elopement (Mak. silariang, *nilariang* or *erangkale*). I regard him as an authority on Islamic law. Also a graduate of Pesantren As'adiyah in Wajo, he is literate in Arabic and can therefore read conventional authoritative sources of Islamic law written in classical Arabic. As a result of the strong application of *adat* (customary) law, his house is upheld as a secure place for any eloping couples to seek refuge.

Ustas Husain is also a graduate of As'adiyah where he studied for many years beginning with Tsanawiyah (Islamic junior high school) and completing an undergraduate-level programme at the pesantren. His authority in Islamic law and theology is undisputed. His competency in Arabic language gives him access to classical sources and literature, especially concerning Islamic law. In classical Islamic studies, language and language sciences are called *'ilm al-aalat* ([Ar] lit. science of tools). In his personal library collection, I noted a number of authoritative classic *kitab kuning* (lit. yellow books) which are read in pesantren (van Bruinessen 1984, 1990), and a number of other collections written in Arabic, Indonesian and Bugis–Makassar languages and script: for example, the *kitab kuning al-Fiqh 'alā al-Madhāhib al-Arba'a* written by the Jurist al-Jazā'irī (1299–1360);[3] a well-known and trusted source among *santri* (students of Islam) of religious schools all over Indonesia, and indeed the Muslim world. Ustas Husain is married to Hj. Hadra and they have two sons and one daughter: Zainal Abidin (b. 1976); Syahrul Layali (b. 1981); and Fatimah (b. 1989).[4]

Ustas Husain's timber platform house (*rumah panggung*) is located just behind the village mosque, Nurul Yaqin, and there is no boundary fence between these buildings. Approaching his house, there is a small noticeboard headed "Imam Desa Labbo" to the right. When I visited him, the space underneath his house was being used for sawing timber. Asnawi told me that a neighbour was using the space to prepare timber for building a new house. Ustas Husain makes use of another part of the space underneath the house for sanitation. There is a *sumur* (well) made of bricks and cement, surrounded by a small bamboo fence. Here, a *timba* (pail) suspended on a rope is used to draw water from the well. A cement platform (about 3m × 3m) around the well is used for washing clothes and bathing. This platform also makes it easy for people to take *je'ne* (Mak., lit. water, but meaning *wudu*, ablution) before going to pray in the mosque. Next to the well is a small booth containing a toilet, facing north as prescribed in Islam. Ustas Husain confirmed to me that toilets should face north or south and not west (*kiblat*: the direction of the Ka'ba or Mecca) nor east, against kiblat. A small ladder on the side of the house allows access to the well.

Like other villagers in Tompobulu, Ustas Husain is also a coffee and cacao farmer. His plantation is located about six kilometres from his home. As he does not own a vehicle he walks to his coffee and cacao plantation every day, taking over an hour to do so. The plantation is situated on an extremely steep hill and no public transportation is available. If there is no agenda for socio-religious services in the morning (such as births, deaths or erecting new houses), he goes out to his plantation at around 7 am and returns home just before midday to take part in collective *zuhur* prayer in the mosque—which he sometimes leads.

Hj. Hadra, his wife, is occupied with domestic activities. In addition to raising their children and cooking at home, just like other women in the neighbourhood, she is busy with coffee and cacao production. Hj. Hadra and Ustas Husain work together to cultivate and process the coffee and cacao. Taking turns with other women in the neighbourhood, Hj. Hadra likes to dry the beans in the sun in the front yard of the mosque in front of her house. It is an open space, well exposed to sunlight. In the wet season, she must pay extra attention to the weather in order to collect the beans before rain. Wet beans mean extra work and can affect the quality of the coffee and cacao. She collects the beans in sacks in the afternoon or evening following sunset, and stores the sacks neatly in her house.

Another activity of Hj. Hadra involves accommodating and caring for girls who have run away and who come to her house seeking the imam's protection. She provides a room in her house for such girls (see below). In return, these girls assist Hj. Hadra in all domestic activities including cooking, weeding, drying and collecting coffee and cacao beans.

In Desa Labbo, Ustas Husain was appointed by the *kepala desa* (village headman who was elected in 1997). Ustas Husain informed me that there was no fixed period of assignment for an imam; he could be in the position for a lifetime. A new imam is installed when the incumbent dies or resigns. Ustas Husain's appointment in Desa Labbo was coloured by local-level politics. According to Ustas Husain, the previous imam—his uncle—resigned after the election of a new kepala desa. The previous imam had been the main supporter of the incumbent kepala desa who was defeated in the election.

In the early stages of his term as imam desa, Ustas Husain's zone of authority covered the vast area of Desa Labbo. Having faced difficulties with the distances, he proposed the appointment of assistant imam in particular *dusun* (neighbourhoods) including distant *dusun* such as Panjang and Bawah. Interestingly, these assistant imams were appointed by the KUA after being proposed by the imam desa, whereas Ustas Husain was appointed by the kepala desa. In practice, however, the assistant imams, usually called *imam dusun* (imam of small village) or *imam pembantu* (assistant imam), always seek Ustas Husain's approval or permission in advance of performing their duties.

How an imam is financially rewarded is not a big issue for an imam and his family, Ustas Husain told me; imams do not expect any regular salary from local authorities, although they are happy to receive support. The role of imams in rural South Sulawesi is a respected cultural position. As noted above in the era of South Sulawesi sultanates (pre-20th century), the imam was the second highest religious position after *kadi* (judge). In the past, imams received regular payment from political authorities. Nowadays an imam generally only receives voluntary contributions from people who use his services. An imam never determines a specific amount of money to be paid for a service. In many cases, after he leads a funeral service, for example, he will be given the belongings of the deceased (*mayit*) such as bed, mattress and clothes for his own use. This is in addition to any money gifted. According to Ustas Husain, in some other places, imams are regularly paid by district governments, although the amount is small compared to the pay of local public servants.

Ustas Husain himself never received money from either the kepala desa Labbo or the Kepala KUA of Tompobulu. He earned money for his family's living costs through his work as a cacao and coffee farmer. While he often received money from people who used his services, he never asked for it or set a standard fee. People gave an amount of money according to their financial situation. The more affluent, the more money they gave him. But sometimes people rewarded his service by giving daily necessities such as rice, sugar and oil.

Balla'na Imam: *A Place to Run Away to*

Apart from their routine activities throughout the year, *kawin lari* (elopement) comprises a significant focus for imams. Looking for his protection is usually enacted by a couple (man or woman), or either one of them, who ask the imam to marry them. The Bugis–Makassar use the general term "silariang" (lit. run away together) for such incidents. In Bugis–Makassar society, a family feels insulted, expressed as losing *siri'* (Bug./Mak. family dignity) (Abidin 1983), if their daughter runs away from home for the purpose of elopement, or because she has been sexually compromised by a man to whom she is not married. In order to regain their dignity, in a Bugis–Makassar tradition which is still widely accepted, the runaway daughter and the man who took her away or violated her chastity should be killed by the male members of her family. However, if the couple gain the sanctuary of an imam's house, according to Bugis–Makassar customary law, they are saved from any violence.

Among South Sulawesi communities, *balla'na imang* (Bug./Mak.), "the house of the imam", is widely respected as a place to seek protection, as a secure zone. And it is not only the house: people regard the back or front yards of the house also as integral parts of the imam's house. Fences surrounding the house mark the boundary and those who are hunted by people who want to kill them have thrown their clothes or bag into the yard of the imam's house, even before physically reaching it—this gives them protection. Bugis–Makassar children will often hear stories that someone is under the imam's protection, when he or she is at his house. According to local customary law, once under the imam's protection that person cannot be harmed.

Once the couple reaches the house of the imam, the family may not enter and forcibly take them away; this is considered a clear transgression of the customary law of Bugis–Makassar people. It is also taboo for the family to see the couple, for this would mean they would have to kill them. I have never heard of a family asking for the support of local police to pick up their daughter from the imam. If they pass by his house, they always look in the opposite direction in order to avoid breaking the taboo. In other words, they always avoid any opportunity where they might set eyes on their daughter as this would mean another more serious loss of siri'. Indeed, if their house is close to the imam's house, the family will look for a temporary place to stay, in order to not set eyes on their daughter. In some cases, an imam will take the initiative to transfer the couple to another imam in a different village, so that the family will have no access to them.

This avoidance works for both families: of the man and of the woman. Some techniques for avoidance have emerged. If both families know the risk of encounter in the village market, they will look for a different path or take a different direction to avoid this happening. In the past, the meeting of the families in public spaces would lead to physical conflict and might result in a death on one side or the other. Everyone in the village is aware of the runaway marriage case, so in public spaces, people will inform members of each family of the location of members of the other family, in order to avoid encounters.

The house of the imam therefore functions as a sanctuary and a fortress to prevent the couple from being killed. According to one imam I talked with, the imam has the right to report forcible removal of the girl from his house to the local police or authorities. In this case, a transgression of customary law is treated as an offence under national law. When I asked the imam to rationalise the relationship of customary and positive law, he had some difficulty. I suspect that although the imam cannot explain the relationship, the report of forcible removal to the police is a common strategy intended to avoid any killing.

The action of silariang results in loss of siri' or dignity for the woman's parents and extended family. Siri' means "shame", and it is used in everyday speech with a relatively bland meaning. For example, when a Bugis–Makassar says "*masiri'-siri'ka*" (Bug./Mak.; I am ashamed of) or "*de' gaga siri'na*" (Bug.) or "*tena siri'na*" (Mak.) meaning "he has no shame", it is common and an expression with no real consequences. In such cases, the expression has no social context. However, when a Bugis–Makassar person says, "return my siri'", it usually relates to family honour, and this is the expression which can invoke life and death consequences. This context is elaborated in the following section.

A number of scholars have introduced and explained siri' as a pivotal aspect of Bugis–Makassar values, including La Side (1977), Baharuddin Lopa (1984), M. Laica Marzuki (1995), Nurman Said (1983), Cornelius Salombe (1984), Abu Hamid (2003), Jawahir Thontowi (1997) and M. Afif Mahfud (2016). Shelley Errington (1977) links siri' to power and politics, while Hendrik Th. Chabot (1996) shows its significance in kinship and status relations. Ilmi Idrus (2005) and Faried F. Saenong (2012) demonstrate the importance of siri' in relations of marriage, gender and sexuality.

Siri' can simply be understood as dignity or stateliness of self and in this value Bugis–Makassar society is basically not different from other societies which acknowledge such values. The difference, or specificity of Bugis–Makassar, is the way they maintain siri' and deal with the consequence of losing it. Additionally, siri' in Bugis–Makassar society is enacted at the level of the family and not in terms of the individual. Family in this context is not just the conjugal or nuclear family but also the extended family (Saenong 2012).

When a case causes the loss of a family's siri', the men of that family will make every effort to restore it. Killing the perpetrator, the person who caused the loss, means that the family has restored its siri'.[5] The younger generation of Bugis–Makassar are usually told a story about *sitobo' lalang lipa'* (Bug.) which refers to a fight between two men enclosed in a sarong or cloth, in which each of them draws a *badik*, a traditional Bugis–Makassarese dagger. Although both sustain severe wounds, one dies and one lives.

People in Bugis–Makassar society are fully aware of the life-death consequences of losing (and taking back) siri' as a harsh or even barbaric practice. But in the avoidance behaviour described above, and through giving protective power to the imam, they have created social mechanisms which avoid or prevent murder. Here both Islam and Bugis–Makassar adat or custom play a significant role. They come together to prevent potentially fatal consequences and establish a traditional mechanism for restoring siri' that satisfies all sides involved in the social conflict.

Bugis–Makassar society recognises three kinds of *kawin lari* which traditionally have life-death consequences: silariang, *nilariang* and *erangkale* (Mak.). The first is a form of kawin lari which both the man and the woman agree to commit; while the second can be understood as "kidnap" of the woman by the man. The third kind refers to a situation where a woman ascends to the house of the imam because she has been sexually harassed or is pregnant. While these three kinds of kawin lari share the life-death consequence of loss of family siri', each leads to different processes of resolution.

In cases of silariang in the past, my host told me that a couple usually approached the imam's house at night as their journey was less likely to be obstructed. The couple might pre-arrange how and when to elope. The man would come to the woman's house and give a signal (by whistling or clapping hands for example). He sometimes asked for help from his friends to accompany him to the imam's house and they could help distract the woman's family if the plan was discovered. If the family of the woman discovered the plan, the man might be set upon.

Abbaji': *Conflict Resolution*

When a couple or a woman enters the house of the imam, the case is in his hands. He will investigate, assess, and even advocate the case. He will ask many questions of the couple or woman to determine the type of elopement (that is, silariang, nilariang, or erangkale). Each type of elopement requires a different approach, treatment and solution. On the following day, the imam will make an official report to the village head (kepala desa) about the arrival of the couple or woman seeking refuge. The imam then contacts the respective families to determine how to resolve the problem. If the case involves a family who lives in another village, the imam will co-ordinate with his counterpart there. If both families agree to a way to solve the problem, the case is regarded as closed, and the couple or the woman who sought refuge in the house of the imam can return to their community as ordinary members of society.

The term silariang is used for cases in which both man and woman agree to run away to the house of the imam, in order to seek refuge and ask him to marry them. The couple ascends to the imam's house and engaging in some discussion, the man subsequently departs. A sign of a case of silariang is that the woman brings her emergency possessions in a bag. This means that the couple had planned to carry out silariang. In cases where the woman does not bring any possessions, she may have been kidnapped, sexually abused or raped, or brought to the imam's house involuntarily. By this indicator, the imam will determine the case to be nilariang. After being sexually abused, the woman, perceiving her loss of siri', will be compelled to join the man to go to an imam. In other cases, if a woman comes up to the imam's house alone, it can be regarded as erangkale. While in the case of nilariang, the man may admit his guilt in kidnapping the woman, in the case of erangkale, the man has usually fled or it is not possible for him to marry the woman either because of a family relationship (he may be the woman's uncle, for example), or because he is already married. That is why the woman comes alone to the house of the imam.

While all cases oblige the imam to follow a standard procedure of assessing, reporting, connecting both families and then marrying the couple, each type of case may take different paths to this end. In nilariang cases, the imam will work extra hard, especially to obtain agreement from the woman's family. Many nilariang cases ended up in a cul de sac with the woman's parents rejecting the imam's efforts to marry them. In cases where the woman's family gives their agreement to a wedding, they usually ask for a higher marriage payment, important for the restoration of their family's honour.

An imam faces a number of technical obstacles (easy and difficult) in solving the cases of runaway marriages. Many village imams have no vehicle, not even a motorcycle. They might have to walk far to reach the office of the kepala desa or the houses of the families in conflict. Sometimes an imam will use public transportation at his own expense in their effort to solve the case as soon as possible. The area of the village—the range of authority of an imam—is greater than that of the *kelurahan* (suburb) in urban areas. Sometimes, the imam can only send letters to the house of the family and has no idea when they will respond.

The period of time required to resolve cases of runaway marriage varies. The fastest resolution might take just one month, whereas some unique cases take from three months up to a year, or even more. If the case involves families who live in the same village as the imam, resolution may take a relatively short time. However, if the case involves families in other villages, or other *kabupaten* (districts)—and this frequently happens—considerably more time is needed.

Silariang in all forms transgresses customary law. Further, it results in the loss of siri' for the woman's family. Therefore, another action must be undertaken to restore the family's honour. If the family is happy to marry their daughter with her desired man, they should perform another ritual called *abbaji'* (Mak.), lit. making peace and good relations. Proposing abbaji' or the peace process is the main task of an imam once a couple have come to his house and asked for refuge. The imam will try his best to obtain the agreement of the woman's family for abbaji'. He may wait for anger to subside, then after a while, he may contact several key persons to help him in convincing the family. He may ask people who the woman's family respects. The imam needs to deliberate on the best strategy to approach the woman's family.

After preparing the abbaji', the eloping couple, wearing their wedding clothes, come to her parent's house to ask for blessing. This peace process proceeds to the wedding ceremony. The couple then ask for the blessing of the extended family by greeting them one by one. They may need to visit other families also for blessing. After the conclusion of these rituals, the couple is regarded as having been released from customary law sanction. By this, the woman's family regain their lost siri'.

The additional requirement of having abbaji' is that the man should pay *doe passala'* (Mak.), which is money for abbaji' and wedding necessities, instead of *doe panai* (Bug./Mak.) or money for the wedding party that is usually the case. As it is an extraordinary situation, the former is in many cases higher than the latter. A problem may arise for those who elope for financial reasons. Some couples elope because the man and his family cannot raise the amount of money for wedding payments requested by the woman's family. In this situation, an imam is required to make concerted effort to convince the woman's family to undertake abbaji'. Without it, the sanction of customary law—killing—is still in force.

Sometimes, an imam fails to convince the woman's family to have abbaji'. If this is the case, the imam has no sanction, and the couple still faces the prospect of being killed at any time. If the woman's family refuses abbaji', they will make a public announcement through the mosque or by word of mouth. The announcement notifies that they no longer uphold a familial relationship with the eloping woman (their daughter). The announcement is called *nimateangi* (Mak.), meaning that the daughter is regarded as dead. Some expressions (in the Makassar language) used for this announcement are, for example, "*tenamo anakku ri lino na ri ahera*" (I don't have any daughter in this world and hereafter). Other people sometimes would say "*natallaki ana'na*", that the family has divorced their daughter, or "*nasassala ri manggena*", that her father has left her, or "*nipapisabbiyangi ri Nabiyya*", that the family invokes the Prophet as witness of the announcement. In the case of a family announcing nimateangi, this means that the eloping woman becomes free from customary sanction, which is killing. It also means that she no longer has any rights in her parents' inheritance. However, if the family does not make any announcement of nimateangi, the sanction of death persists.

The Indonesian legal system, to an extent, acknowledges customary law (adat) and Islamic law in addition to national law. Legal pluralism has varying applications in different parts of Indonesia. The national criminal law regards killing as an offence that warrants a jail sentence of up to 15 years (Article 338 Kitab Undang-Undangan Hukum Pidana-KUHP). In addition, KUHP contains another article on pre-meditated murder (Pasal 340 KUHP). Most siri'-related killing is regarded as pre-meditated murder as the killer had a clear intention to kill.

In South Sulawesi, however, siri'-related killings that have been brought to court often receive special treatment (Thontowi 1997) as many judges consider siri' as a mitigating factor. Many defendants in siri'-related murder cases are sentenced to between five and seven years in prison. However, when a case is brought to a higher-level court, a defendant may face a longer jail term.

Anthropologists use the term "culture of honour" or "honour/ shame" complex to identify societies that individually, institutionally and socially allow violent retribution when honour is violated. This complex is based on patriarchal traditions and culture where male members of society prescribe "the rules of the game" in the social arena and delimit that arena to men. In many social arenas (politics, economics, religion, arts, science and so forth), women are used as objects in order to reflect the ideal selves of men. Masculinity in this sense cannot be constructed without women participating as objects. In this regard, Pierre Bourdieu (2001) and Carol Delaney (1987) argue that honour is a male—not female—attribute. In his 1966 paper "Sentiment of Honour", Bourdieu once asked the Kabyles which objects of honour required protection and defence, and they replied: "house, woman and gun" (Bourdieu 1966: 193).

The culture of honour occurs in many places, but in the contemporary world it is most prevalent in Middle Eastern and Mediterranean societies (Peristiany 1966; Pitt-Rivers 1963). Arab societies acknowledge the concepts of *sharaf/şeref* ([Ar.] dignity or honour) and *'ird* or *namus* ([Ar.] chastity or purity).

The former concept deals with the honour of social units: the failure of members to maintain honour will result in the degradation of the social status of the family or the tribal unit. The latter concept by contrast has much to do with the honour of female members of the family.

Muslims in many places have endeavoured to distinguish honour killing as a cultural practice from Islam as a religion. This chapter has demonstrated how Muslims in Bantaeng have found a way to use the Islamic office of imam as a way to manage the negative consequences of concepts of honour and seek a solution that preserves dignity and life.

Concluding Remarks

This chapter has shown how the imam assumes key social, cultural and religious roles in Tompobulu, and how his religious authority gives him the ability and responsibility to resolve social conflict. While on a daily basis Ustas Husain deals more with Islamic matters, in the case of elopement, he has also the important task to prevent murder ordained by custom. The eloping man who has taken the siri' from the woman's family has been the main target for killing. The eloping woman was also formerly a target of killing by her family. Nowadays, when it is considered that there is no means of resolution, the daughter is regarded as "dead". But although women are not the main target of killing, they are central to these violent practices among Bugis–Makassar peoples, as it is women who embody the dignity of the family. Muslims in South Sulawesi have creatively established socio-religious mechanisms to integrate local customary law, national law and Islamic law, in order to avoid killing. The imam plays a significant role in resolving conflict that has its roots in cultural beliefs and social practices in rural areas in South Sulawesi.

Notes

1. Because the imam is the only one permitted to lead prayers and give khutbah, the transfer of knowledge to Muslim community becomes a reiteration of the knowledge and perspective of the posted imam. This has led authorities in some European and American mosques in Western countries to intervene in managing the imams (see among others, Haddad and Balz 2008; Shahid and van Koningsveld 2002).
2. The Department of Religious Affairs has a classification system for mosques: for example the *masjid negara* or national mosque (Istiqlal Mosque in Jakarta); *masjid nasional* at provincial level; *masjid raya* in provincial capitals; *masjid agung* in district capitals; *masjid besar* in sub-district (kecamatan) capitals, that is, *masjid jami* at neighbourhood or village level. There are also the categories of *masjid bersejarah* or historical mosque, *masjid di tempat umum* or public mosque, and *musholla* (prayer house or small mosque). See Ministry of Religious Affairs Decree No. DJ.II./802/2014 on the Standard of Mosque Management. Other community-based great mosques may also have an imam besar.
3. This book has been a respected classic source of Islamic law covering Islamic law according to four leading Islamic schools of law or *mazhab*: Shafi'i, Maliki, Hanafi and Hanbali. Other Arabic-language collections of Islamic law in his collection are *Kifāya al-Akhyār* by Taqiy al-Dīn al-Dimashqī (d. 829/1426); *Bidāya al-Mujtahid* by Ibn Rushd (520/1126–595/1198); *Bulūgh al-Marām* by Ibn Hajar al-'Asqalānī (1372–1449); *Riyād al-Sālihīn* by Muhy al-Dīn al-Nawawī (1234–78).
4. I know Zainal very well; we were classmates for three years (1991–94) in MAPK, an Islamic Senior High School in Ujung Pandang (now Makassar). While I continued my studies in Jakarta in 1994, he went to study at

al-Azhar in Cairo. Four years later, in 1999, we met again in Cairo where I worked until 2002.

5. The practice of honour killing in South Sulawesi is different from similar murders in Mediterranean society. In South Sulawesi, the man is the main object of killing, whereas the woman becomes the main object of killing in Mediterranean society (Peristiany 1966).

References

Abidin, A.Z. 1983. *Persepsi Orang Bugis Makassar tentang Hukum, Negara dan Dunia Luar* [The Perception of Bugis Makasaar People Concerning Law, Nation and the World Outside]. Bandung: Alumni.

Bourdieu, Pierre. 1966. "The Sentiment of Honour in Kabyle Society." In *Honour and Shame: The Values of Mediterranean Society*, ed. Jean G. Peristiany, 192–241. Chicago: University of Chicago Press.

———. 2001. *Masculine Domination*. Stanford: Stanford University Press.

Chabot, H. Th. 1996. *Kinship, Status and Gender in South Sulawesi*. Leiden: KITLV Press.

Delaney, Carol. 1987. "Seeds of Honor, Fields of Shame." In *Honor and Shame and the Unity of the Mediterranean*, ed. D. Gilmore, 35–48. Washington: American Anthropological Association.

Errington, S. 1977. "Siri', Darah dan Kekuasaan Politik di dalam Kerajaan Luwu' Zaman Dulu" [Siri', Blood and Political Power in the Luwu Polity in the Past]. Paper presented in the seminar "Siri' and Its Problems in South Sulawesi" organised by the Regional Police of South Sulawesi and Southeast Sulawesi, and Hasanuddin University, Ujung Pandang, 11–13 July.

Ghosh, Amitav. 1994. "The Imam and the Indian." In *Displacement: Cultural Identities in Questions*, ed. Angelika Bammer, 47–56. Bloomington and Indianapolis: Indiana University Press.

Haddad, Y.Y. and M.J. Balz. 2008. "Taming the Imams: European Governments and Islamic Preachers since 9/11." *Islam and Christian-Muslim Relations* 19 (2): 215–35.

Hamid, A. 2003. *Siri' Dan Pesse: Harga Diri Orang Bugis, Makassar, Mandar, Toraja* [Siri' and Pesse: Pride of the Bugis, Makassar, Mandar, Toraja]. Makassar: Pustaka Refleksi.

Idrus, Nurul Ilmi. 2005. "Siri', Gender, and Sexuality among the Bugis in South Sulawesi." *Antropologi Indonesia* 29 (1): 38–55.

La Side. 1977. "Beberapa Keterangan dan Petunjuk Tentang Pengertian dan Perkembangan Siri' Pada Suku Bugis" [Some Explanations and Pointers Concerning Siri' among the Bugis People]. Paper presented in the seminar "Siri' and Its Problems in South Sulawesi" organised by the Regional Police of South Sulawesi and Southeast Sulawesi, and Hasanuddin University, Ujung Pandang, 11–13 July.

Lopa, B. 1984. "Siri' dalam Masyarakat Mandar dan Pemanfaatannya dalam Pembangunan di Sulawesi Selatan" [Siri' Among the Mandar People and its Use in National Development]. Ujung Pandang: P3K Hasanuddin University.

Mahfud, M. Afif. 2016. "The Implementation of Local Wisdom: *Siri' na Pacce* as an Effort of Corruption Eradication in Indonesia." Paper presented at the 2nd Proceedings, Indonesia Clean of Corruption in 2020, Comparative Law System of Procurement of Goods and Services around Countries in Asia, Australia, and Europe. Semarang, Indonesia, 9 December.

Marzuki, L. 1995. *Siri', Bagian Kesadaran Hukum Rakyat Bugis-Makassar: Sebuah Telaah Filsafat Hukum* [Siri', An Aspect of People's Law: Some Legal Research]. Ujung Pandang: Hasanuddin University Press.

Peristiany, J.G. 1966. *Honour and Shame: The Values of Mediterranean Society*. Chicago: University of Chicago Press.

Pitt-Rivers, Julian, ed., 1963. *Mediterranean Countrymen: Essays in the Social Anthropology of Mediterranean*. Paris: Mouton.

Rashiduzzaman, M. 1997. "The Dichotomy of Islam and Development: NGOs, Women's Development, and Fatawa in Bangladesh." *Contemporary South Asia* 6 (3): 239–46.

Saenong, Faried, F. 2004. "Change and Continuity: Religious Marriage among Muslims in the Netherlands." Masters thesis, Universiteit Leiden, The Netherlands.

______. 2008. "In Search of *Barakka'* and Authenticity: Local and International Network of Pesantren and 'Ulmâ' in Contemporary South Sulawesi (Indonesia)." Paper presented at the International Conference on Inter-Asia Connections organised by the Social Sciences Research Council (SSRC New York), Dubai, 22–25 February.

______. 2012. "Kindred Endogamy in a Bugis Migrant Community." *Intersections: Gender and Sexuality in Asia and the Pacific*, Issue 30. www.intersections.anu.edu.au/issue30/saenong1.htm.

Said, N. 1983. "Siri' sebagai Suatu Nilai Dasar atau Pedoman Bertingkah Laku (Norma-Norma) dalam Tertib Sosial di Sul-Sel" [Siri' as a Basic Value or a Basis for Behaviour (Norms) in Social Regulation in Sul-Sel]. Ujung Pandang: P3K Hasanuddin University.

Salombe, C. 1984. "Siri' dalam Hidup Kemasyarakatn Suku Toraja" [Siri' in the Social Life of the Toraja People]. Ujung Pandang: P3K Hasanuddin University.

Sewang, Ahmad. 2003. *Islamisasi Kerajaan Gowa (abad XVI sampai abad XVII)* [The Islamisation of the Gowa Kingdom]. Jakarta: Obor.

Shadid, W. and P.S. van Koningsveld. 2002. "Religious Authorities of Muslims in the West: Their Views on Political Participation." In *Intercultural Relations and Religious Authorities: Muslims in the European Union*, ed. W. Shadid and P.S. van Koningsveld, 149–70. Leuven/Paris/Sterling, VA: Peeters.

Shankland, David. 1994. "Social Change and Culture: Responses to Modernization in an Alevi Village in Anatolia." In *When History Accelerates: Essays in Rapid Social Change, Complexity and Creativity*, ed. C.M. Hann, 238–54. London: Bloomsbury.

Thontowi, Jawahir. 1997. "Law and Custom in Makassar Society: The Interaction of Local Custom and the Indonesian Legal System in Dispute Resolution." PhD Diss., University of Western Australia.

Tika, Syam. 2005. *Silariang* [Run-away Marriage]. Makassar: Pustaka Refleksi.

van Bruinessen, Martin. 1984. "Pesantren and Kitab Kuning: Continuity and Change in a Tradition of Religious Learning." In *Texts from the Islands: Oral and Written Traditions of Indonesia and the Malay World*, ed. Wolfgang Marschall, 121–46. Berne: The University of Berne Institute of Ethnology.

______. 1990. "Kitab Kuning: Books in Arabic Script Used in Pesantren Milieu; Comments on a New Collection in KITLV Library." *Bijdragen tot de Tal-. Land- en Volkenkunde* 146 (2/3): 226–69.

3

Shariaisation, Wedding Rituals and the Role of Imams in South Sulawesi[1]

Moh Yasir Alimi

Introduction

Two important features of Islam in the social life of South Sulawesi are the centrality of the imam (religious leader at the village level) and the significance of the rituals accompanying marriage. Here, the village imam has greater importance in wedding rituals than his counterparts in Java where marriage rites are the responsibility of the head of the sub-district religious office (KUA, Kantor Urusan Agama). Moreover, in Java, the role of the village imam, known as *modin,* is limited to ceremonies associated with death, including religious gatherings locally termed *tahlilan* that commemorate the deceased. This chapter explores the role of the imam and the significance of wedding rituals, thus highlighting the particularity of Islam in South Sulawesi. It draws on a year's fieldwork in Kindang village in the district of Bulukumba, South Sulawesi in 2006–07. During this period, the formalisation of sharia in religious bylaws (*perda syariah*) was being intensively debated, including bylaws relating to the conduct of Muslim weddings.

After the collapse of the Suharto regime and the decentralisation of political authority to the district level, the Bulukumba district government was one of the first to formalise some aspects of sharia (Alimi 2011, 2014). The four sharia-inspired regulations introduced in Bulukumba in 1999 were: requirement for Qur'anic literacy for marriage regulation; Muslim dress regulation; alms and charity regulation; and alcohol consumption regulation. Several of these affected wedding rites and related imam practices.

The four Islamic bylaws introduced by the administrative government of Bulukumba in 1999 were shaped by and, in turn, shaped wedding rituals. For example, Muslim dress bylaws responded to the practice that had developed of singers at wedding rituals wearing tight and short dresses. Similarly, alcohol consumption bylaws were created in response to drinking parties associated with wedding rites. Hence, the forms of sharia bylaws in regard to marriage were as much informed by customary wedding practices as by the normative discourse of sharia. I argue that ordinary Muslims challenged the formalisation initiative through their practice of marriage rites rather than through discursive argumentation.

South Sulawesi Muslim life is characterised by contradictory tendencies—to cling to hierarchy on the one hand and seek equality on the other. South Sulawesi Muslims display both fixity and change in social life; and express customary beliefs and practices as well as commitment to a universal faith (Reid 2009). Reid (2000: 56) has noted their social practices are "at once marked ... by a tenacious clinging to old belief and rituals and openness to change". These apparent contradictions in the life of South Sulawesi Muslims have attracted the attention of many scholars including Pelras (1996), Friberg (1993), and Reid (2000).

Customary Wedding Rituals in South Sulawesi

Wedding rituals are the most important social rituals for the people of South Sulawesi. Their centrality renders them spaces for contestation between new and old ideas, and as sites for social and personal transformation. Through wedding rites, Muslims both reproduce and transform personhood and social relations and express public morality. They absorb and subvert new ideas and practices introduced by the radical social changes taking place in their lives. Examining the practice of Bugis weddings in Soppeng, north of Bulukumba, during the 1980s, Susan Millar notes their centrality: "First, weddings celebrate the most important of Bugis life-crisis events.... Second, weddings are structured in a manner that allows elaborate display of social hierarchies.... Third, weddings integrate the Bugis past, associated with the present realities of the villages, with the culture emerging on the provincial and national levels" (Millar 1989: 185).

In many senses wedding rites exhibit liminality. The concept of liminality refers to a "betwixt-and-between" situation in the context of rites of passage, a site of a "fructile chaos ... a storehouse of possibilities, not by any means a random assemblage but a striving after new forms" (Turner 1990: 11–12). In the state of liminality, ritual participants have left behind their prior status but have not yet transitioned to the status they will hold upon completion of the ritual. They "stand at the threshold" between their previous way of structuring their identity, time or community, and a new way established by the ritual. The wedding rituals discussed here transform relationships—they are located on the "threshold" of hierarchy and equality, fixity and change, tradition and global faith that characterise the social life of South Sulawesi Muslims.

At such times, Turner (1990) argues that people look to concrete individuals for guidance. In the wedding rites addressed here, such guidance is found in the role of the village imam who occupies a central role in the social life of South Sulawesi. Of particular focus in this chapter is the role of imams during the "shariaisation" of Bulukumba where the desire to "shariaise" wedding rituals was considered by many to be in opposition to the customary wedding rites.

Many other ethnographic studies of South Sulawesi have noted the centrality of wedding rituals (Acciaioli 1985; Chabot 1996; de Jong 1996; Idrus 2004; Millar 1989; Robinson 1986), tending to emphasis their importance as spectacles of adat (custom). In this mode of interpretation, only two Islamic elements are contained in the wedding: the partners' religion as Islam (Idrus 2004) and the importance of the contract or *akad* (Ind.) (Chabot 1996; de Jong 1996; Idrus 2004; Millar 1989). While ethnographies of weddings can segregate Islam and custom, for the Islamic peoples of South Sulawesi, Islam and adat are seamlessly integrated in the wedding rites as an expression of their sociocultural identity. The "Islamic" elements of a wedding can seem to be invariant or place-transcendent, while elements that display uniquely what it means to be local can be seen as extraneous to the religion.

Distinctions between what is Islamic and what is not have exercised Islamic reformists. Many modernist Muslims regard the *akad* as the only truly Islamic aspect of the wedding ceremony, while all other ritual embellishments are dismissed as pre-Islamic or unacceptable innovations. Such views were the basis of revolutionary attempts in the 1950s and 1960s under the radical Islamic rule of the Darul Islam rebels to drastically simplify wedding rites in South Sulawesi (see Robinson, this volume) as well as of the contemporary calls to bring local wedding rites into line with sharia law, through local regulation.

South Sulawesi is thus the site of both highly elaborate and theatrical rituals and of equally dramatic attempts to sweep them away. But ritualism and custom in South Sulawesi are not necessarily antithetical to Islam or un-Islamic. In contradiction to the austere interpretations of Islam associated with reformist movements, Muslims in South Sulawesi embody Islam through their distinctive rites, performances, architecture and storytelling. Islam in South Sulawesi can be approached as performance, as embodied identity and as material culture, which contrasts with views of Islam as an austere, inner, interpretive or discursive religious phenomenon.

From this perspective, wedding rites are a local form of Islamic expression, as well as spaces to display adat, social location, memory and local cultural identity. Complex wedding rituals in this region can be regarded as "Islamic traditions", an approach that is in line with the understanding of most Bugis and Makassar Muslims.

Looking at wedding rites as spectacles of Islam may resolve the apparent contradiction between the elaborate attention to hierarchy and performative ritualism in this region and its notoriety as a site for some of the most spectacular and uncompromising instances of Islamic purification.

In South Sulawesi, wedding rites are central to the production of Islamic identity, but also to the transformation of this Islamic society and its public sphere. These elaborate ritual forms enable Muslims to display, perform and overcome the contradictions between the inclination to embrace the fixity of faith on the one hand and the dynamics of social life on the other. A wedding ritual is an enduring public expression which reproduces Islamic identity.

And everything public is vulnerable to government interests (Bowen 1993). In pre-modern South Sulawesi, for example, the Gowa ruler changed wedding practice in order to change religious practice. The ruler replaced *bissu* (the pre-Islamic priests) with *kadi* (Bug./Mak. jurist in Islamic kingdom) and imam—kadi at the state level and imams at the village level—one of whose main tasks was to lead the wedding ceremony (Pelras 1996). The recitation on ritual occasions of the Bugis pre-Islamic literary tradition (La Galigo) was often replaced with the literary tradition of Islam such as reciting *barzanji* (Pelras 1996). In modern South Sulawesi, the wedding still prevails as a site for social transformation. For example, in recent years there has been a transformation of wedding dress—the adoption of Muslim head-covering expressing Islamisation in South Sulawesi. The performance of wedding rituals focuses our attention on the way Islam is expressed and displayed in material forms and corporeal movements and the ways in which these show both constancy and change.

The Elaborate Wedding of Karaeng Butung's Daughter

The elaborate wedding of the daughter of nobleman Karaeng Butung occurred during my fieldwork. Wedding rituals in Kindang share characteristics that Millar (1989) outlined for Bugis communities (which are also shared with Makassarese and Konjo[2] populations). Three kinds of gifts—wedding expense money, rank price and the groom's compulsory wedding gift to the bride are characteristic of weddings in South Sulawesi. Social stratification is clearly marked, with high and low ranks differentiated by the amount of wedding expense money (*uang belanja*[3]); rank price (Mak. *sunrang*[4]); number and status of invited guests at the wedding feast; the number of animals slaughtered; the scale of the entertainment; ornaments worn by bride and groom, and even the text chanted during the wedding.[5] These different kinds of gifts are so important that imams and KUA officers in South Sulawesi receive training about them and their relation to social rank.

Wedding Payments

Of the three gifts mentioned above, the most dynamic wedding gifts are the wedding ritual expense money and *mahar* (bridewealth). While the amount and forms of the marriage payments noted above have changed over time, *sunrang* remains fixed at historical levels. In contemporary Kindang it is no longer common to pay wedding expenses with animals. The difficulty of transporting large animals such as horses, cows or buffalos has led people to use money, which is portable and flexible. The amount of wedding expense money varies across time and geographical setting.[6] The *mahar* also takes many forms: clove trees, rice fields or, increasingly popular, prayer paraphernalia such as *rukuh* (prayer dress), *sajadah* (prayer mat) and the Qur'an. The gifting of prayer goods is a recent phenomenon that has emerged in tandem with the upsurge of Islamic awareness and expressions of piety that have swept Indonesia since the 1990s.

In Kindang, as in all of Muslim South Sulawesi, after completing the pilgrimage to Mecca women raise their status and therefore can demand more "spending money" (*uang belanja*). An imam explained that women who have already acquired *hajja* status command a high price because the husband will not be required to pay the cost of pilgrimage after marriage. This reveals one of the reasons that cohorts of pilgrims from South Sulawesi include large numbers of young and unmarried women, which is not the case for other parts of Indonesia where pilgrims are more likely to be male and older.[7] Older women *hajja* command respect at weddings and are commonly invited to sit with other high-ranking guests in a "higher" place.[8]

Renewal and reproduction of hierarchy are reflected in the different types of wedding gift—wedding expense money, rank price (in *reyal*), *mahar*—and their presentation. The first two are bundled in a metal pan and covered with a white cloth, while *mahar* is usually packed in a decorated basket. At the beginning phase of a wedding ritual, when the groom arrives at the house of the bride, an administrative official and the imam of the village examine the white cloth bundle—and this is regarded as an important adat component. In a public ceremony, the imam removes the white cloth, symbolising the mutual attraction of the bride and groom and their desire to remain together. Then the imam reads out a letter of agreement made during wedding negotiations between the two families and witnessed by the village administration.

It is the role of the imam to ensure the proper conduct of the rituals. In this meeting at the bride's house, he is tasked to check the contents of the metal pan against the agreement, in regard to the total wedding expense money and the amount of *reyal*. On many occasions, I witnessed an imam pick up the money and then drop it in the pan creating a sharp clanging sound. This sound is the confirmation and reproduction of social status, evoking the confidence and the robustness of South Sulawesi Muslims' social imagination. Through weddings, they internalise and embody Islam and accentuate their particular forms of Islam. The continued practice of this most significant socio-religious ritual has remained a challenge to the increasingly "shariaised" public sphere.

The Wedding Feast

Three vital accessories for a noble family wedding—*tuka* (Kon. bamboo ladder), *rumah pengantin* (bridal house) and *campaniga* (Kon. decorative cloth symbolising royal heritage)—were installed in the bride's house three months prior to the wedding. The bamboo ladder (*tuka*) was installed near the everyday wooden steps and used in this period by guests to go in and out of the elevated wooden house. A miniature bamboo house (*rumah pengantin*) was constructed in the corner of the living room. Karaeng Butung and his wife stood in front of the *rumah pengantin* to welcome guests. The *rumah pengantin* was enveloped in the strong aroma of burned ground candlenut. The lower parts of the miniature house were plastered with bamboo decorations (Kon. *halasuji*) and shrouded in white cloth normally used to cover the body of deceased Muslims prior to burial (*kafan*). Karaeng Butung explained that white cloth is used as a reminder that all of us will die: "All of us will wear that white dress ... the white cloth is the eternal reminder of this message."

Campaniga, a pink and white antique cloth hung majestically at the centre of the bamboo house, was the most auspicious accessory—symbolising royalty. Karaeng Butung's brother, who kept this cloth, explained that *campaniga* may only be borrowed and must be returned to the keeper.

A large *gong* (a traditional music instrument) covered with a white cloth dominated the front of the miniature house. Next to it was another musical instrument, a set of rusty cymbals (Kon. *anak bacin*), each about 5 cm by 30 cm, also covered with a white cloth. The *gong* and the cymbals are significant not only as decorations; they are heirlooms from the Kindang kingdom that survived until the time of Dutch rule, established in the early 20th century. Three days before a wedding the *gong* is played—normally in the late afternoon when the setting sun signifies *magrib* (the evening prayer)—creating the soundscape of a royal court.

These elements—*campaniga*, *tuka* and *gong*—were only used by high-ranking people to display their status. Karaeng Butung elaborated that when his grandmother and grandfather were alive, if they thought people were not entitled to use these accessories, they would confidently break the *tuka* and rip the *campaniga* without the owner's consent.

Sharia and Wedding Rites

Below I will describe several threshold cases where tensions emerged in wedding rituals as a result of the introduction of sharia bylaws. These incidents also illustrate the crucial role played by the imam in wedding rituals.

Qur'anic Reading Ritual

The ritual of "graduating" in reading the Qur'an known as *mappatemme* (Bug./Mak.) is an important part of wedding ritual conducted along with *barzanji* chanting and the purification ritual *mapacci* (Bug.) on the night before the wedding party. During a *mappatemme* ritual that I observed in Kindang, the bride sat in front of an imam, flanked by her grandmother and aunts. As the imam read, the bride listened and pointed to the corresponding Arabic lines. The imam read chapter by chapter, beginning at *ad-Dzhuha* (The Morning) until *Fatihah* (Opening). When he had finished each chapter, the bride's grandmother, sitting on the floor behind her, placed a *sarung* (wrapped skirt) on the bride's back and scattered rice from a small container. She did this repeatedly until nine *sarung* had been put on the bride's back. The *sarung* is an expression of Islamic identity.

The *mappatemme* is the ceremonial celebration of Qur'anic literacy. I was informed that in former times it was organised after a student finished their Qur'anic training but, since the 1980s, for economic reasons, most people in Kindang have organised this ritual in tandem with a wedding party. Most of the weddings I attended featured *mappatemme* followed by barzanji chanting on the night before the wedding.

The Qur'anic literacy regulation enacted in Bulukumba makes it compulsory for prospective brides and grooms to be literate in the Qur'an. It recommends that the bride and groom learn to read the Qur'an before they decide to marry. Indeed, the regulation affects the procedures of wedding registration.

A bride and groom request letters from the village head attesting to their ability to read the Qur'an which they take to the KUA office where their ability is tested; the officer randomly selects a page in the Qur'an and then requests the groom to read that page. The imam then decides whether or not he will lead the wedding rituals based upon the recommendation of the KUA. However, imams have normally only required the bride or groom to recite the *Al-Fatihah* (first *sura* of the Qur'an) or short verses of the Qur'an. In one case in Kindang where an imam refused to marry a bride and groom due to their failure of the test required by the regulation, villagers' reactions against his decision caused him to relent and agree to conduct the ceremony.

Barzanji Rituals

The recitation of barzanji occurs during the *mapacci* ceremony, the night before the wedding party. Originally called *'iqd al-jawahir* (Ar. gem necklace), barzanji is a poetic text written by Syaikh Ja'far al-Barzanjiy in 1184 (580 H). It describes the Prophet's attributes as reflecting those of God because of the purity of his heart. I found that in Bulukumba this text is chanted on many occasions: entering a newly-built house, during a wedding ceremony, birth ritual (*akekah*), and to express gratitude (*syukuran*). As Puang Saleng told me "If there is a gathering there should be the burning of incense and the chanting of barzanji."

However, not all Muslims approve of barzanji. Modernist Muslims regard it as an unacceptable religious innovation. Muhammad, the Prophet, they argue, never conducted this practice in his lifetime. When the newly-appointed imam to Benteng Palioi village refused to lead the barzanji because of his understanding of Islam, the village community complained to the Head of the KUA. He, in turn, advised the new imam that he was an imam for all people: those who recited barzanji and those who disapproved. "You should respect them", he advised. The imam eventually followed the KUA's suggestion, even accompanying in chanting barzanji when requested by the host family. The *paccing* (Bug.) rite that involves writing on the palm with a finger is conducted when the chanters arrive at the line "My love, my greeting to you", and stand up to respect the spiritual presence of Muhammad. After *paccing* is finished and the barzanji chanters have resumed their seats, the barzanji ends, drawing to a close the long process of the first day of the wedding rites.

Entertainment

While South Sulawesi Muslims inculcate Islam through wedding rites, weddings also provide a place to contest new ideas and new practices. This tension between values can be observed in the dynamics of *elekton*—the musical performance involving an electronic organ used for entertainment during wedding rituals. Musical performances are integral to weddings in South Sulawesi. People aspire to lavish wedding celebrations and, as a result, the industry providing entertainment for weddings has burgeoned. Elekton performance is a relatively new phenomenon that emerged with the rise of *dangdut* (a genre of Indonesian popular music with roots in Hindustani, Malay and Arabic music) replacing performances such as *rebana* (tambourine, played by a group singing devotional songs), *kecapi* (traditional two-string lute) and even the projection of videos—popular in the 1980s. Twenty out of the 25 wedding rituals I attended included elekton music. During the show, a singer performs the most popular *dangdut* and Bugis or Makassar songs while young men in the audience dance to the rhythm of the songs. Of the many activities at a wedding, the elekton performance is the most optional, the most dynamic and the most controversial. In many cases, family members debate its necessity. In the case of the wedding of Karaeng Butung's daughter, while his children wanted elekton he argued that it often ended up with youth fighting each other. In Kindang, young people often drink alcohol while watching elekton and may touch each other unintentionally when they dance during the *dangdut* performance. Drunk, they are quick to anger and become involved in fighting. As one man put it:

> Elekton music turns young men into sand brains. Instead of causing conflicts, it is better to leave out the elekton. In the beginning, my children encouraged me to have elekton. But after I explained, they understood. Some are still unsatisfied, but that is normal. For the elders in my family, the imperative is that the royal paraphernalia should not be left out.

Elekton has become a source of contestation and a marker of difference in religious orientation. Followers of the modernist Islamic organisations Muhammadiah and Istiqamah tend to refuse to use elekton performance at weddings, preferring instead religious preaching.

With the current increased concern for public expression of piety, in many cases elekton has given way to *simponi* shows in which performers chant religious songs, wearing modest Muslim dress including headscarves. According to a leader of a *simponi* group, this genre grew in popularity because of concerns about lewd *cadoleng-doleng* (a kind of stripping) performances. In 2003 in the districts of Sidrap, Pare and Pangkep, elekton became further transformed into *cadoleng-doleng*. The singers exposed their bodies, parts of their breasts and, occasionally, their genitals in front of the wedding audience. The transformation of elekton into *cadoleng-doleng* illustrates how unfamiliar ideas or practices can be accepted so long as they do not question hierarchy. Many districts have imposed rules to regulate public musical performances. In Bulukumba, for example, elekton singers are targetted by a regulation requiring that female entertainers should wear Muslim dress.[9]

Weddings in South Sulawesi express the constancy of traditions but also social and religious dynamism. On the one hand the wedding stabilises hierarchy; on the other it can embrace extreme practices such as *cadoleng-doleng*. The resonant voices promoting Islamic regulation exist and so, too, the voices promoting *cadoleng-doleng*. Weddings integrate Muslim society and Islamic culture with secular pop-culture. This polyvalent character of the wedding ceremony was a factor that provoked government efforts to regulate weddings through bylaws.

Reformist Criticism of Wedding Rituals

Wedding rituals are sites of religious contestation, as the most important rituals for South Sulawesi Muslims. Religious criticism of South Sulawesi wedding rituals date back to at least 1926 when Muhammadiyah—the Java-originated reformist movement—was established in the region. Criticism of local traditions was initially focused on alcohol consumption, gambling, cockfighting, barzanji recitations, celebration of Maulid (the birth of the Prophet) and the cult of royal ancestors. By 1937, the organisation had 16 branches; in 1941, it had 7,000 members and 30,000 sympathisers (Gibson 2007: 170; Pelras 1994: 127). Only in the 1940s, after Muhammadiyah had expanded its influence and recruited more local followers, did local scholars begin to seriously attack the wedding rituals as un-Islamic (as "innovation").

New forms of attack against wedding rites commenced when Kahar Muzakkar controlled large areas of South Sulawesi in his struggle for the proclamation of an Islamic state (1951–65) (see also Robinson, this volume). Kahar regarded wedding rites as feudalistic and religious innovation, and his constitution for the Islamic State of Eastern Indonesia (Makalua Charter) imposed regulations on weddings. It restricted *uang belanja* to a set amount, restricted wedding feast celebrations to no more than one day[10] and prohibited the use of hierarchical titles (such as Puang and Karaeng) or ritual passages in the wedding ritual. No less controversial was the regulation that every wedding proposal should be accepted unless one or more of the following conditions was present: age below 15-years-old, impotency, contagious disease and bad behaviour. Further, men were required to marry women widowed as a result of the armed struggle for an Islamic state (Mattalioe 1994).

In addition to these regulations, there were other instructions relating to wedding feasts: people were not permitted to slaughter their own animals for wedding feasts as the Darul Islam armies accused them of not slaughtering in the name of Allah. Some people reported that eating horse meat (popular with Makassarese) was prohibited, reflecting the Bugis disinclination to consume horse meat. Soon after the death of Kahar Muzakkar in 1965, which brought the rebellion to a close, the old wedding rites were resurrected in Kindang.

Religious-based contestation around weddings again came to the fore as a result of the revival of sharia discourse in South Sulawesi in the 1990s that culminated in the adoption of sharia bylaws in Bulukumba in 2003. Critiques of the wedding rituals were launched by preachers from the provincial capital, Makassar, affiliated either with Istiqamah or other reformist schools. Reformists argued that many aspects of South Sulawesi wedding rituals were not in accordance with Islamic teachings. Traditionalist Muslims[11] of South Sulawesi responded with religious arguments, anecdotes and continued practice of traditional rituals (such as weddings) as a mode of resistance. In South Sulawesi, the imam—whose role it is to arrange wedding rituals—is caught up in these critiques.

While Istiqamah focuses on the *akad* (contract) as the most important element of a wedding, the Ahli Sunnah Wal-Jamaah followers emphasise the series of events in wedding rituals that express social exchange, status, kinship and Islamic mysticism, as reflecting the Islamic identity of Bugis and Makassar Muslims.

In response to modernist criticism, those Muslims who have persisted in following traditional marriage rituals claim that they are indeed grounded in Islam. The former head of KUA in Kindang told me the following story. A couple came to his office complaining that they felt they were not yet married since the traditional rituals had not been followed. This, in spite of the fact that an imam in a mosque declared them to be husband and wife, a ritual they described as "Istiqamah" (that is, according to Islam). (However Istiqamah leaders did not recognise this as an Islamic procedure; that is one exemplified by the Prophet.[12])

In Java, contestation between the traditionalists and modernists centres on normative practice—such as the number of *rakaat* (standing, sitting, bowing, prostrating) in Ramadhan prayers or *tarawih* (cf. Sila, this volume); the use of *kunut* (special recitation made at the second part [*rakaat*] of the morning prayer); the death ritual; and other readings such as barzanji and *tahlilan* (ritual prayers to commemorate the deceased) during a *kenduri* (ritual feast). In South Sulawesi, however, the wedding is a key marker of religious difference. While religious contestation in Java is highly discursive, in South Sulawesi it is dispositional. That is, distinctive Islamic religious orientations in South Sulawesi are largely marked by differences in style, stance, body performance and clothing. In the case of the wedding discussed above, Karaeng Butung understood the attacks on traditional rituals in the context of the "shariaisation" of the district's public sphere, but he continued to practise them as a particular form of Islam that he accepted and defended, in the public sphere.

Istiqamah Wedding Rituals

In modern South Sulawesi, in addition to Muhammadiyah, the modernist Darul Istiqamah has many followers. Muslims in Kindang refer to the followers of Darul Istiqamah as "Istiqamah". It began with a school founded by a religious cleric (K.H. Muzdakir Ali) in Kahar Muzakkar's Islamic state, dedicated to purifying Islam in South Sulawesi in response to the founder's dissatisfaction with Muhammadiyah. While the first branch was established in Maros, north of Makassar, there are now many branches including in Bulukumba district. Istiqamah seeks to identify particular forms of Islam different from the Ahli Sunnah Wal-Jamaah style. The quest of Istiqamah followers to develop a "more Islamic" wedding procedure is discussed below through the marriage of Puang Bahang's daughter, which follows a different pattern from the wedding hosted by Karaeng Butung, discussed above.

Istiqamah followers call for a return to the Qur'an and *sunnah* (precedents established by the Prophet) as a way to purify Islam from local elements. They do not use the elements discussed above—welcoming house (*sarappo*), *mappatemme*, barzanji, *mapacci* or *pattahara* (see below)—as they allege these are unacceptable innovations.

Puang Bahang converted to Istiqamah in 1982 after frequent visits to his family in Pambambaeng, the main enclave of Istiqamah in Bulukumba. This community sustains its own mosque, style of clothing and religious practices. Puang Bahang followed traditional rituals for his own wedding in 1979, but following his conversion, he adopted Istiqamah procedures for his daughter's wedding in 2000. Below is his story:

> In 2000, I organised the wedding for my daughter. Like other people, I still invited a wedding ritual specialist [Bug. *indo botting*; literally, wedding mother], who happened to be my cousin, to decorate my house. However, I did not build the welcoming house [*sarappo*], nor rent the wedding seat [for *duduk bersanding*] and the bride and groom remained in the house after the prescribed ritual [for the marriage contract or *akad*]. In Kindang, the bride and groom usually sit down on the wedding seat located outside the house and this can last a long time. This stage is called "sitting side-by-side" [*duduk bersanding*]; I did not use this ritual in my daughter's wedding. *Mapacci*, barzanji and Qur'anic reading were also not performed. The bride and groom also only wore their customary wedding dress (sarong and *baju bodo*) for a short time. For most of the time, the bride wore a Muslim headscarf and the groom a suit [in everyday life, Puang Bahar's daughter did not usually wear a headscarf]. Only one letter of invitation was sent to each family. Usually invitations are sent to each family member. Most importantly, male and female guests were separated. Men sat on chairs set up outside and women sat inside the house. Following the wedding ceremony, during the evening, I rented a video player and screened Indonesian karate movies, which were popular at that time. Now the popular performance is elekton—*dangdut* music and electronic

> organ shows. After the wedding in my house, we went to the groom's house. His family are strong Khalwatiah[13] followers. They insisted on using traditional wedding rituals and it was up to them because they organised the rituals in their house whereas I consider Istiqamah procedures to be more sincere [*ikhlas*].

I attended a few weddings of Muhammadiyah and Istiqamah followers. Like Puang Bahang's wedding, they usually omitted the *sarappo*, dazzling decorations and elekton, and male and female guests were separated, either inside and outside the house or between the upstairs and the ground level. Elekton performances were replaced by religious speeches (*ceramah*) in an effort to challenge traditional wedding practices as well as to recruit new followers. Indeed, Puang Bahang had been recruited in 1982 after hearing speeches at a wedding. However, the leader of Istiqamah explained that in Kindang the tradition of seeking the costs of wedding and *mahar* (but not *sunrang*) from the groom's family is still practised.

Pattahara and Duduk Bersanding

In South Sulawesi, the three important wedding rituals, in order of importance, are the *akad nikah* (marriage contract, henceforth *akad*) led by the imam; the *pattahara* (the inner marriage or *nikah batin*); and the bride and groom sitting side-by-side on the wedding chairs (*duduk bersanding*). These stages are imperative to the legitimacy of the wedding. In contrast, the legitimacy of marriage in Javanese Muslim communities is confirmed by the contract which is read before the imam, recitation of the *shahada* by the imam and groom, and the spoken phrase contained within the contract: "I marry [full name] with [full name] with wedding gift paid." For Kindang Muslims the legitimacy of the marriage is demonstrated by both *pattahara* (Bug.) and *duduk bersanding*.

Chabot (1996) explains *pattahara* as a ritualised touching in the context of the wedding. Some Kindang people explained *pattahara* as the "inner wedding" conducted by an authorised person. This stage was regarded by some Kindang Muslims as the real marriage, "the wedding of the soul" or "inner wedding". This is in contrast to *akad* which is regarded as engaging two families and the public. In *pattahara*, either the imam or a man or woman authorised by the groom's family, takes the groom to the room where the bride waits on a bed with female senior members of her family and the *indo botting*.

Sitting face-to-face, the groom and the bride then touch each other, guided by the imam or other senior figure, who then takes each party's breath in his/her hand and gives it to the other partner for them to inhale. While the wedding contract (*akad nikah*) led by the imam engages the two families in the act of marriage and is regarded as a public announcement, the *pattahara* determines the relative roles of the bride and groom as wife and husband. *Duduk bersanding* signifies that a bride and groom has entered into a new phase and status in their life, and this new status has been accepted by the community in accord with village adat. While the emergence of *perda syariah* has raised the intensity of religious criticism towards the traditional elements and practices of wedding rites in South Sulawesi, the regulations have not had significant impact (Alimi 2017). The elaborate rituals and decoration in wedding rites persist. Muslims are familiar with the critics, and the imams serve as effective state apparatus to challenge the reforming influence. The imams and Muslim communities had experienced greater pressure during the Darul Islam rebellion, so they are not surprised by the new challenge. The strength of wedding rites in the face of modernist criticism lies in the fact that the wedding is the organising principle in the social and cultural life of South Sulawesi Muslims. It is the most important ritual to overcome many contradictions in their life—their aspiration for social status, their practice of Islam and their cultural identity as Bugis–Makassar Muslims.

Conclusion

The wedding has become the most important icon of identity and hence of Islam in South Sulawesi, where it is not only integrated through the prescribed Islamic ritual *akad* but also enacted through other numerous wedding rites including: the Qur'anic reading ritual; display of *sarung*; role of the imam; barzanji chanting; bride and groom sitting side-by-side (*duduk bersanding*) and in the display of *sunrang* (customary bridewealth). This enactment is paramount to the construction of social identity and, through which, the Islamic social world is imprinted on the bodies of Bugis–Makassar Muslims.

The introduction of *perda syariah* in South Sulawesi has posed particular challenges to the role of imams in maintaining the continuity of traditional Islamic rituals. Wedding rites are sites of in-betweenness where new ideas and practices are introduced, and the imam mediates between old and new, and between competing new ideas. The ethnographic cases in this chapter illustrate thresholds that occur in wedding rites, and the role of the imam in relation to these. Imams are guardians of Islamic identity, the bridge between state and society and a symbol of equality and change. The introduction of sharia bylaws in South Sulawesi has posed particular challenges to the role of imams in maintaining the continuity of traditional Islamic rituals.

The vibrancy of wedding rituals in South Sulawesi cannot be explained in terms of normative prescriptions of Islamic marriage only. Islamic elements cannot be reduced to the *akad* or selection of the bride. Nor can adat be reduced to elements such as "dispositions" or bodily movements, style and performance. While it is through wedding rites that Muslims inculcate and transform Islam, and achieve Islamic personhood, these rites also provide a site for Kindang traditionalist Muslims to differentiate themselves from Muslims with other religious orientations.

Notes

1. This chapter is derived, in part, from an article published in *The Asia Pacific Journal of Anthropology* on June 2014, available online: http://www.tandfonline.com/DOI:10.1080/14442213.2014.915875
2. The Muslims in Kindang are Konjo speakers—a Makassar dialect spoken by those living in villages bordering Makassar and Bugis-speaking communities.
3. *Uang belanja* refers to the wedding costs paid by the groom's family to the bride's family. For high-ranking people, at the time of fieldwork, it ranged from 20 million rupiah (around AU$3,000) to 40 million (around AU$5,000) and for ordinary people between 7 million (around AU$1,000) to 15 million (around AU$2,000). Because of its importance as a marker of social status, if the groom's family is unable to pay much, it is not rare that the amount will be exaggerated during the public examination by adat figures comprising the village head and imam.
4. *Sunrang* is the amount of Dutch guilders and *reyal* (Ar.) money paid to the groom's family as regulated by customary law. It is calculated in *guilder*, the currency of the Dutch colonial period, or in *reyal*, the currency used by the Arab residents of Makassar during the 15th century. Nobles generally receive 88 or 44 *reyal* and ordinary people 22 or 12 *reyal*. In Kindang, these traditional prescriptions are strictly applied. In one case where a groom's family was unable to provide sufficient *reyal* for

the wedding festival, it may not have taken place if not for the efforts made by the bride's family and other community members to contribute money. These currencies (coins) are no longer in general circulation, but must be purchased locally to provide *sunrang*.

5. In Java by contrast, the only gift is *mahar*; which is also the only gift regulated in Islamic prescriptions of wedding.
6. De Jong's (1996) note offers a detailed account of the 1960s and 1970s: In Selayar the high status pay 2 buffaloes, 300 litres of rice and Rp. 25,000; commoners pay one buffalo, 100 litres of rice and Rp. 5,000; the poor pay the amount they can afford. In Gowa a young noble paid two buffalo, 700 litres of rice and Rp. 50,000; a commoner paid one buffalo, 500 litres of rice and Rp. 25,000; the poor paid one buffalo or horse. In Soppeng the amount ranged between Rp. 5,000 and 15,000. The rank price paid by Selayar noblemen in the 1930s was f. 160 (= 80 rial; 1 rial = 20 gram of gold); in the 1970s it was 88, 44 and 22 rial and in Gowa 30, 28 and 14 rial for the commoners (1906: 44, 22 and 12 rial); 1 rial is equivalent to 2 gulden. In addition to buffalo, rice or money, the people can also pay with rice fields, boats, plantations (gardens), coconut trees, slaves, or horses.
7. When asked about pilgrimage, South Sulawesi Muslims routinely made fun of the age of Javanese pilgrims saying, "They are ready to go to the grave."
8. The greeting *naik ki* literally means "Go up, Sir or Madam!" but socially means "Sit in the first ranks with other respected people."
9. Cianjur, West Java produced a similar local regulation, but this was a response to the prevalence of sex tourism.
10. Traditionally, the ceremony could last for up to seven days depending on the social status of the family. The modernists alleged such celebrations to be a waste of money and served no purpose.
11. In this context, traditionalists Muslims are those who follow a sufistic style of Islam and adopt Bugis Makassar traditional wedding rituals. They are normally called *ahlus sunnah* (Ahli Sunnah Wal-Jamaah or ASWAJA) and are culturally affiliated with Nahdlatul Ulama.
12. Interview with Ustad Haris, a teacher who graduated from an Istiqamah *pesantren* before building an enclave in Kindang (12 August 2007).
13. Khalwatiyah is a traditionalist-oriented Sufi group (*tarekat*).

References

Alimi, M.Y. 2011. "Inculcating Islam: The Public Sphere and the Islamic Traditions of South Sulawesi". PhD diss., The Australian National University.

———. 2012. "Head Covering to Live By: Cipo'-Cipo', Shari'ah and Women's Experience of Clothing in South Sulawesi." *Intersections: Gender and Sexuality in Asia and the Pacific*, 30 (November). http://intersections.anu.edu.au/issue30/alimi.htm.

———. 2014. "Local Repertoires of Meaning and the Islamist Movement in Post-Authoritarian Indonesia." *Indonesia and the Malay World* 42 (122): 24–42.

———. 2017. "Rethinking Anthropology of Shari'a: Contestation Over the Meanings and Uses of Shari'a in South Sulawesi, Indonesia." *Contemporary Islam* 12: 123–51. https://doi.org/10.1007/s11562-017-0410-x.

Bowen, J.R. 1993. "Modernist Muslim Poetic: Irony and Social Critique in Gayo Islamic Verse." *Journal of Asian Studies* 52 (3): 629–46. doi:10.2307/2058857.

Chabot, H. Th. 1996. *Kinship, Status and Gender in South Sulawesi.* Leiden: KITLV Press.

de Jong, Chris G.F. 1996. *Ilalang Arenna: Sejarah Zending Belanda di antara Umat Bugis Makassar Sulawesi Selatan* [Ilalang Arenna: The History of Dutch Zending among the Bugis Makassar in South Sulawesi]. Jakarta: PT BPK Gunung Mulia.

Friberg, B. 1993. "Ritual in South Sulawesi." In *Ritual, Belief and Kinship in South Sulawesi*, ed. M. Gregerson, 20–35. Dallas: International Museum of Cultures.

Gibson, T. 2007. *Islamic Narrative and Authority in Southeast Asia: From the 16th to the 21st Century.* New York: Palgrave MacMillan.

Idrus, N.I. 2004. "Behind the Notion of Siala: Marriage, Adat and Islam among the Bugis in South Sulawesi." *Intersections: Gender and Sexuality in Asia and the Pacific*, 10 (August). http://intersections.anu.edu.au/issue10/idrus.html.

Millar, S.B. 1989. *Bugis Weddings: Rituals of Social Location in Modern Indonesia.* Berkeley: Center for South and Southeast Asia Studies, University of California at Berkeley.

Pelras, C. 1994. "Religion, Tradition and the Dynamics of Islamization in South Sulawesi." *Indonesia* 57: 133–54. doi:10.2307/3351245.

Reid, A. 2009. "Pluralism and Progress in Seventeenth-Century Makassar." In *Authority and Enterprise among the People in South Sulawesi*, ed. G. Acciaioli, K. van Dijk, and R. Tol, 55–72. Leiden: KITLV Press.

Robinson, K. 1986. *Stepchildren of Progress.* Albany, NY: Suny Press.

Turner, V. 1990. "Are there Universals in Performance in Myth, Ritual, and Drama?" In *By Means of Performance: Intercultural Studies of Theatre and Ritual*, ed. Richard Schechner and Willa Appel, 8–18. Cambridge: Cambridge University Press.

4

A Bugis *Imam Desa*

An Authoritative Voice in a Changing World

Kathryn M. Robinson

Introduction

The indigenous people of Sorowako, a community now at the centre of a modern mining town in the remote north of South Sulawesi province, were relatively late to embrace Islam, in spite of centuries of links to supra-local trade through the coastal Islamic sultanate of Luwu. This polity regards itself as the cradle of the Islamisation of Sulawesi from the early 17th century (Pelras 1995; Reid 1993).

According to the received history, the Islamisation of South Sulawesi occurred in the 17th century, relatively late in the archipelago,[1] when local rulers finally embraced this religion that had come to their shores in the context of international trade, especially focused on the port of Makassar (Reid 1993). The Sulawesi rulers had a common mode of Islamisation: it took the form of subsumption of religious authority under the power of the court. A pattern emerged in Bugis and Makassar polities that Islamic practices and principles, termed *sara'* (Bug.), became incorporated as an element of customary regulation under the authority of the court (Mukhlis and Robinson 1985: viii). The court appointed an official known as *kadi* who was responsible for the administration of Islam, and in the farthest reaches of court power, prayer leaders (imam) were appointed as part of the court bureaucracy

(Azra 2004: 88; see also Wahyuddin Halim; Adlin Sila, this volume). Hence, in these places far from centres of Islamic learning, village imams were bearers of Islamic doctrine and practice, holding official positions of status and authority (Mattulada 1974). These were hereditary positions of the realm, passed usually from father to son (Djamas 1985); and they conferred prestige and status honour (Mukhlis and Robinson 1985). Azyumardi Azra (2004) notes this formalisation of the position of village imam encouraged many itinerant preachers/ proselytisers to settle in Sulawesi. These officials have had a critical influence on the quotidian religious practice of communities, including the transformation (Islamisation) of life cycle rituals in addition to everyday religious practice.

This chapter examines the process of Islamisation in the region of Lake Matano in the mountains of the interior of Sulawesi, focusing on a particular lineage of village imams who have wielded significant influence in shaping local accommodations to waves of political and religious influence throughout the 20th century. It examines the impact of material changes in everyday life, as well as novel doctrinal influences, on religious and ritual practices of Sorowako Muslims.

Sorowako–Matano

Sorowako, located on the shores of Lake Matano, is now the centre of a nickel mining and processing industry, a quintessential outpost of modernity in an otherwise remote rural area (Robinson 1986). Historical records, in particular traveller's accounts[2] and oral histories, indicate that in the late 19th century Sorowako was under the authority of a polity named Matano, centred on Lake Matano. This was a vassal of the realm of Luwu at the time of colonial conquest. The area had been a site for smelting iron ore since the mid-15th century (Bulbeck and Caldwell 2000). Iron was the source of local power, and the form of tribute to the Datu of Luwu. Matano had long trade links to the coastal sultanates, in particular Luwu, connected through ports at the top of the gulf of Bone; and Bungku[3] located on the east coast, now part of Central Sulawesi. The relation between Matano (or Matana in Bugis) and Luwu had been cemented through marriage between a noble woman from Matano and a kinsman of the Datu of Luwu, and there were also genealogical connections to Bungku.

The political economy of the mountainous interior of Sulawesi was very different from that of the coastal states. Scattered populations practised shifting cultivation and exploited the jungle for food through hunting and collecting. With the expansion of the international dammar trade in the 19th century, trade goods followed the routes previously established for the trade in iron ore (Schrauwers 1977). The small local groups were engaged in endemic warfare and head hunting. In the early years of the 20th century, the people of Sorowako and Matano were "pagans and headhunters" but also under the despotic and "feudal" rule of Luwu (Robinson 1986: 71). The oral history of Sorowako indicates a cataclysmic defeat and destruction of villages in probably the late 19th century, and that a Luwu noble was central to the resettlement in the current village site (Robinson 1986: 60). Albert Grubauer (1913), who visited the area in 1911, mentions meeting a local Bugis Luwu noble.

Muslim traders (mostly Bugis) inhabited the coastal port of Malili and also established inland trading centres, such as Timampu on the shores of Lake Towuti, attracted by the rich resources of the interior (especially dammar resin in the later half of the 19th century) that were traded on global markets. However, their influence as propagators of Islam was apparently slight. Whereas elsewhere in the archipelago, trade (and intermarriage of traders with local populations) were significant vectors of Islam (van Leur 1955: 4), trade and marriage links to Luwu (and Bungku) did not result in widespread conversion to Islam in the area around Lake Matano—even though there is evidence of intermarriage between the Luwu and Matano nobles.[4]

Colonial Rule as a Vector of Islam

At the turn of the 20th century, there was a dramatic shift in Dutch colonial policy towards the coastal sultanates of Sulawesi. Military action ended the "hands off" policy and the sultans were forced to sign "short declarations" (*korte verklaring*) "[b]y which they empowered the colonial administration to give them directives for the exercise of their authority" (Vlekke 1959: 328), subsuming them under Dutch power. European influence had until this time been principally through Christian missionaries who were based in central Sulawesi from 1890 but who explored this interior region more widely. Linguist Nicolaus

Adriani and Albertus Christiaan Kruyt employed a novel "ethnographic method" in their missionary activities (Schrauwers 2000: 51). They report some Muslim influence for example in burials, but not the embrace of the faith.

Dutch administration was established through indirect rule (the model they had followed in Java). In the region around Lake Matano, they relied on the traditional political authority in the territory formerly claimed by the Makole Matano. They appointed Andi Cabo, a Luwu noble who also had genealogical connection to Matano, as the district head (*kepala distrik*) of Onderafdeling Malili in 1906 and gave her the title of local ruler, *makole*. However, the Dutch geographic appellation for the political domain was Nuha not Matano, and the "palace" was built in Sorowako, not Matano. The Dutch replaced her with her daughter Andi Halu in 1908. Indirect rule in the interior of Sulawesi through the Kerajaan Luwu had the Dutch supporting the power and legitimacy of the Islamic rulers of Luwu.

The German ethnologist Grubauer (1913) photographed Andi Halu in Malili in 1911 at a celebration of the birthday of the Dutch queen. He describes her "palace" in Sorowako as a "Luwu-style" house. The photographs show that it exhibits the symbolic accoutrements of a noble's house: as well as being larger than the surrounding houses, it has crossed buffalo horns on the gable, three gable flaps (*timpa laja*) and a *tamping* (an internal gallery below the level of the floor of the main room, where guests seeking audience would sit at a lower level to the noble inhabitants) (see Robinson 1993). Her children intermarried with members of the local "elite", descendants of the Makole Matano and the powerful families of Sorowako, such as the descendants of headman La Salima, also pictured in Grubauer's (1913) book.

Rice and Religion

This colonial reach into the interior after 1906 was an unlikely—and unwilling—agent of Islamisation: the principle vectors of Islam at this time were not religious scholars, but the Dutch-appointed indirect ruler (*makole*) and people she recruited to implement the colonial directive to encourage the people to adopt settled wet rice cultivation. This was linked to the ethical policy tenet of Volksverheffing (lifting the population from their situation). It went hand-in-hand with a policy of disarming the inhabitants of the interior and banning head-hunting, a practice that was central to the sustaining of customary religion and ritual.

To achieve these end goals, the Dutch administration moved shifting cultivators down from their scattered hillside hamlets and settled them in nucleated villages; and introduced them to intensive wet rice cultivation. To fulfil this latter directive, in a number of villages under her authority Andi Halu recruited Bugis who had migrated to the coastal port of Malili at the top of the Gulf of Bone. Many were from Sinjai, a maritime region on the east coast of the western Sulawesi peninsular. Its people are well known for their religiosity and their ability to read the Qur'an, as well as their skills as seafarers and warriors.[5] Aside from coastal fisheries and trade, there are extensive wet rice fields in its hinterland. Andi Halu also supported the building of mosques and appointed imam (prayer leaders) in several communities in the territory under her authority.

In Sorowako, she appointed both a *mantri sawah* (agricultural extension officer) and an imam. The mantri sawah, Daeng Masale, was charged with developing *sawah* (wet rice fields) on the wide plain on the shores of Lake Matano. He is remembered as the propagator of Islam. A trader from Sinjai whose family had moved to Malili, he arrived in Sorowako in 1911. According to the current imam (his son), at that time the people of Sorowako were "animists" and kept pigs.[6] He came from a line of imams in Sinjai and, as well as instructing them in cultivating sawah, he began to convert the people to Islam. According to his son, he was very busy with his agricultural work and trading, and did not at first become imam. In the late 1940s, when he was an old man, he was finally persuaded to take this role. His son described him as "illiterate" as he could not read Latin script, but he could read Bugis script (*aksara lontara*). He also was not literate in Arabic, although he could chant the Al Qur'an.

He and his wife (also from Sinjai) were the vectors not only of Islam but of Bugis custom, especially in relation to life cycle rituals. The imam's wife was the *dukun pesta* (ritual expert for festivals), advising on ritual and protocol aspects of weddings and other rites. Pre-Islamic practices in regard to birth, marriage, death, house construction and moving into houses were gradually replaced with Bugis-inflected Islamic practice ("traditional" Islam)—the "everyday" Islam the propagator knew from Sinjai. The teaching of the Qur'an and *salat* (ritual prayer) were the core activities of Islamisation as well as circumcision and the prohibition on eating pork. Like many communities in South Sulawesi that practise "traditional" Islam, they would recite a popular poem recounting the life of the Prophet (*barzanji*) at life cycle rituals and thanksgiving (*selamatan*)—replacing previous ritual chants on important occasions[7] (Pelras 1996: 203).

The children of the *mantri sawah*/imam intermarried with the village elite, including with the family of Andi Halu (whose members also intermarried with "locals"). This ensured that his offspring spoke the local language which they could use for religious instruction intensifying the possibilities for proselytising.

Once Islam had a presence in Sorowako, we see patterns similar to those we have found in other parts of eastern Indonesia, especially those under Bugis and Makassar influence. The position of imam passed from father to son and became one of great prestige, for example, expressed in the intermarriage between the imam lineage and the lineage of the Luwu nobles. The current incumbent is Imam H. Ahmad Djufri, whose wife is the daughter of a Luwu "noble", Opu Mappaware, who was the son of Andi Halu. When I first met the imam in 1977, it was clear that he was regarded as the authority on matters concerning ritual (life cycle rituals, Islamic calendric rituals) and his wife advised on practices around rituals of birth, marriage and death. Hence the form of Islam that was practised was the locally inflected form characteristic of Bugis communities in South Sulawesi (Pelras 1996; Djamas 1985). This brand of Islam is highly tolerant of local practices such as those supporting the celebration of marriage, a key ritual in Bugis communities (see Alimi, this volume).[8]

It is not clear how many of the local people had embraced Islam in the period before the Darul Islam rebellion in the 1950s (discussed below). It seems, however, that the village elite and their close families had embraced Islam and also made marriage alliances with descendants of Luwu nobility (the Andi Halu family). Indeed the family of village headman Magani claim he independently converted to Islam while on a trading mission to Malili (Robinson 1986: 75). The descendants of both Daeng Masale and Magani told me that each of them was detained in the colonial period for "allegedly forcing people to convert to Islam" (ibid.).

Colonialism and Conversion

Dutch colonial presence favoured an expansion of missionary activity, and a Minahasan missionary B. William Ruru, remembered as Guru Tua ("the old teacher") arrived in Sorowako in 1915. He lived in comfortable neighbourliness with the Sorowakan people. Many people in the region converted to Christianity. By the time of independence in the mid-20th century, the region around Lakes Matano and Towuti was a mosaic of Christian and Muslim communities as the influence of both religions spread. (This is unlike the situation in the highlands of Toraja, and Mori and Poso in what is now Central Sulawesi, where the embrace of world religion by these "animists and pagans" mostly favoured Christianity.) The indigenous population of Sorowako, who term themselves the Orang Asli Sorowako ("original" or indigenous people), are today universally Muslim. The indigenous people of Sorowako and Guru Tua's sons who grew up in Sorowako, say that the local people treated the missionary-teacher respectfully and cordially, and that he and Muslim headman Magani were very close. But most of his parishioners were from a related group who lived nearby, the Karongsi'e, a group that had been relocated to the shores of Lake Matano by the Dutch (Robinson 1986: 77). "We watched Guru Tua walk through the village to the church in the Karongsi'e village each Sunday", I was told. Post-independence, when the village was forcibly relocated by the Darul Islam rebels (see below), Guru Tua and his parishioners were forcibly converted, and accompanied the villagers to the relocation site.

The indigenous people of Sorowako speak of themselves as if always Muslim, but in recent years memories are surfacing (or are finally being articulated) of at least a few of them who were Christian converts, even some who were planning to attend a school to train pastors (*pendeta*) at the time of the outbreak of the Darul Islam rebellion.

The Impact of Darul Islam (1951–64)

In the turbulent years of the transition from colony to sovereign nation, the interior of Sulawesi was the heartland of an Islamic-inspired rebellion against the newly-formed government of Indonesia, led by the charismatic figure Kahar Muzakkar (Boland 1982; van Dijk 1981). His Darul Islam rebellion (Darul Islam/Tentara Islam Indonesia DI/TII, henceforth DI) joined with other similarly inspired rebel groups in West Java and Aceh, waging an armed struggle demanding that the new republic be constituted as an Islamic state (van Dijk 1981; Boland 1982; Feillard and Mardinier 2011).

During this interregnum (from the early 1950s to 1965) there was violent disruption of the religious face of the region, with many Christians fleeing rather than accept forced conversion to Islam (Robinson 2017). The strict regime DI imposed put its stamp on the practice of Islam and customary ways of expressing piety with its particular brand of reforming doctrine, a strict adherence to the religious practice of the Prophet Muhammad as revealed in the Qur'an.

Kahar had been a soldier in the republican army fighting for independence. Educated in a Muhammadiyah school in Java before joining the military, he developed a "modernist" approach to Islam and an intolerance of practices of the "enculturated" style of Islam that had developed in South Sulawesi, which encompassed what he saw as "impurities" within Islam. This included religious beliefs and practices linked to the body of La Galigo stories that had roots in pre-Islamic South Sulawesi societies (see Djamas 1985), especially when seen to be in conflict with strict application of textually-derived doctrine. He was intolerant of the hierarchies of the Bugis sultanates, the hereditary nobles who professed divine descent and associated beliefs and practices, which were rooted in the La Galigo textual/religious tradition (Pelras 1996: 203), and regarded the practices of the nobility and the courts as practices of *kafir* (non-believers); offensive to the pure practice of Islam. DI burned noble houses and ritual paraphernalia and many nobles fled to the cities, which were controlled by the government. In recent years I was told a story by a woman in Sorowako who was a young child at the time of DI, that she saw rebel troops enter a house and shoot someone; in her memory because they were nobility (*bangsawan*).

This interregnum had a dramatic impact on the religious practices and customary ways of expressing piety in the regions under DI control. The rebels introduced sharia law as the legal basis of everyday life and this was enacted through a body called the Dewan Fatwa (Council of Religious Pronouncement). In practice, this allowed for cruel and arbitrary justice, exercised by DI troops in the field. There was strict and immediate punishment for transgressions such as theft (cutting off the hand); or for sex outside marriage (*berzinah*), for which the punishment was 100 strokes. If the "culprit" was a girl or woman who was pregnant, the punishment was applied after she gave birth. Alternatively, they could be "*dirajam*", buried to the waist and stoned until dead. People in Sorowako recounted having seen these punishments administered. For example Imam Djufri says he once saw a woman *dirajam* in what is now Sulawesi Tenggara.

Elaborate death feasting that had been characteristic in the area around Lake Matano (described by Grubauer 1913) was banned, as were the circle dances (*dero*) performed at festivals and rituals, characteristic of peoples in the interior and southeast peninsular of Sulawesi. These dances involved males and females holding hands and exchanging *pantun* (couplets), which elderly people remember with smiles as occasions for flirting. Even Islamic practices such as recitation of barzanji (see above) at life cycle/life crisis rituals and the ritual of *tahlilan*—where collective prayers for the deceased were said 1, 7, 40 and 100 days after death—were banned. These practices were considered to be *bidah* or innovation.

Sorowako, located on the shore of Lake Matano and at the end of the road to Malili on the coast, was a strategic gateway to the remote interior of the island; the village was burned and the populace forced to relocate in rebel territory on the other side of the lake, to a site inaccessible by road. There they suffered privation. All goods, including medications and basic food items like salt, were in short supply (Robinson 1983). People still remember this as a time of suffering and trauma. Their forms of religious practice were transformed, and their religiosity intensified along the modernist model promoted by the rebels. Even the Minahasan missionary, who accompanied them in the *penyingkiran* (place of refuge), was forced to adopt Islamic worship.

Rebel rule lasted almost a decade and a half and had a dramatic impact on everyday religious practices and customary ways of expressing piety in regions under DI control. I remember an incident in the late 1970s when a beloved old man from Sorowako was killed in a vehicular accident. His son decided to take an unusual course of action, one dating back to the days prior to DI. He undertook to slaughter a buffalo for a feast after his father's burial, in part because the old man had been trying to catch the buffalo in the days prior to his unexpected and shocking death.[9] The older sister of the deceased arrived at the house where the meat was being cooked and she became very upset when she learned that specific customary ritual practices had not been conducted at the slaughter. His son was very upset: "We didn't know", he said, as he had never seen those practices carried out.

A brief ceasefire in 1962 allowed return to the village site, in particular, resumption of cultivating the sawah, but conflict was reignited and lasted until 1965 when the rebels were defeated by the Indonesian army. In the Sorowako imam's words: "*orang napas lagi*" (people could breathe again). The period of DI rule ensured that the people of Sorowako had a strong commitment to their Islamic identity and had become very pious in everyday practice. The highly culturally inflected form of Islam that had been introduced by the mantri sawah/imam from Sinjai included many practices that were not tolerated. Other cultural practices, such as circle dances (*dero*) that had been reproduced alongside Islamic observance, had dropped away. Following their return to the village, their everyday Islamic practice was heavily influenced by the experience of DI, in particular by the "modernist" approach of Kahar Muzakkar and his intolerance of the kind of traditional Islam that had been introduced by the Sinjai Bugis. They had become a pious community, diligent in daily practice. On a visit in June 2009, a woman, who had been a school-aged child at the time of DI, speculated to me: "I wonder if we would have been Muslim today, if it weren't for DI?"

Inco Arrives

Not long after the people had returned from Seluro, their place of refuge in rebel territory across the lake, the consequences of the regime change to Suharto's New Order (ushered in by the 1965 coup) began to hit. The new focus on foreign investment meant geological exploration teams came into the area, even before the rebels had been totally overcome in the region. The new regime was hoping to revive the nascent mining industry that had operated in the colonial period.

The subsequent minerals exploration and development of the mining project transformed this turbulent rural backwater into a modern urban centre. By 1968 a contract had been signed with International Nickel of Canada. Mineral exploration and construction of a process plant and townsite in Sorowako, a port at Malili, and roads connecting sites were soon underway (Robinson 1986). By 1972, the indigenous people had been forcibly dispossessed of their agricultural land and surrounding forests. They only just managed to fight for their village site, which became encompassed by the mining town. Further, their livelihoods now depended on finding employment as unskilled and often casual labourers in the modern enterprise, and living in a cosmopolitan mining town inhabited by people from all over Indonesia, all over the world. The village imam, as a respected leader and a man with charisma and calm who invites respect, has had an important (but ultimately disheartening) role as one of the mediators in the many ongoing conflicts between the community and the mining company. He has also negotiated with the government which has failed to protect their livelihoods and environment.

Many of the immigrants (including managers) were and are still Muslim, and the indigenous community now finds itself as part of a bigger Muslim population where members are subject to influences on their religious practice, and also to new kinds of religious authority (see below).

Imam H. Ahmad Djufri

During the period of initial development of the project, in the early 1970s, the old imam who had led his congregants during their time in exile elected to give up his post and the residents chose to appoint his son. The current imam says that his father was very strong in his desire for his children to be educated beyond the religious education that he was able to provide. But they were not able to pursue secular education because the rebel-controlled area was cut off. However, Imam Djufri's older sister had married a DI commandant and he was able to follow this influential brother-in-law to Kolaka Utara, in what is now Southeast Sulawesi, where he attended the DI *kader* school, which provided military and religious education.

This education has profoundly affected his approach to religious practice and, while he has no formal affiliation to any organisation, he has taken on the modernist interpretation in the Muhammadiyah mode that had influenced Kahar. Hence on many matters his position differs from that of his father. He has continued to reinforce the modernist approach to piety that had been applied in the DI period, but with compassion, tolerance and humanity, rejecting the application of arbitrary punishment that he had witnessed, for instance.

Figure 4.1 Imam H. Ahmad Djufri reading the Qur'an at the Majlis Taklim. Photo by Kathryn Robinson.

In keeping with the accommodation of religious and customary status that characterises Bugis communities, he married the granddaughter of Andi Halu, the former Makole Nuha whose son remained in the village as an influential figure. The imam is regarded by all as an important community leader, joining his father-in-law (the late Opu Mappaware) and his brother-in-law (Andi Baso) in negotiating between the mining company and the local community. For example, joining forces with a Muslim expatriate worker from Australia, the imam prosecuted the issue of the contamination of the community's water source, including the water for ritual ablutions in the mosque, resulting in the company piping in chlorinated water to stand pipes to provide clean drinking water in the village (Robinson 1985). The mining company and local government have frequently tried to harness the imam's authority, engaging him in consultation but, in his view, not respecting his counsel. On one of my visits in recent years, his wife said: "Bapak [lit. father, respectful term of reference for adult males] is really tired of the way they call on him and take his name all the way to Canada but don't act on any of the things they discuss."

While the influence of DI was strong in regard to religious practice, when I first went to Sorowako in 1977, there were still regular practices that reflected pre-Islamic traditions and the imam was regarded as authority in matters of everyday religious practice and religious understanding for the indigenous people of Sorowako. But he was also the authority for ritual matters (see also Alimi 2014 and this volume). He led prayers five times daily in the mosque; officiated at births, marriages and deaths, as well as rituals for building and moving into houses and for thanksgiving; and carried out halal slaughter of animals for ritual feasts. He formerly taught all village children to read the Qur'an in classes held after school hours. While he does not align himself with any organisation, his approach to religious questions is scripturalist, and in his interpretations of what is right and proper he always returns to the life and teachings of the Prophet.

Other ritual specialists had ritual authority as well, such as traditional midwives in regard to birth and ritual practices surrounding birth, or house builders in regard to technical and ritual aspects of house construction, or the *dukun pesta* (ritual specialist) who guided the correct conduct of wedding rituals, a position originally held by the wife of Daeng Masale. These ritual specialists worked in concert with the imam. For example, while he would conduct the *akad nikah* (marriage contract), the *dukun pesta* would be responsible for the conduct of the rituals relating to the social celebration and recognition of marriage, at stages such as the meeting of the bride and groom, and *duduk bersanding*, the social moment of marriage (Robinson 1986: 235; for Bugis weddings see Millar 1989). The authority of the imam and these other ritual specialists was generally unchallenged.

Life cycle events and rituals reflected the strong influence of the old imam and his wife, and also the intermarriage of the people of Sorowako with people from other Bugis Muslim communities most usually from Malili and other parts of Luwu. The Islamic practices that had been established in Sorowako followed the pattern set up by Daeng Masale, and were heavily inflected with practices common in Bugis communities. As noted above, the teaching of the Qur'an and salat (ritual prayers) were the core Islamic activities as well as the prohibition on eating pork. Like many communities in South Sulawesi that practise traditional Islam, they would recite barzanji on important occasions, a practice that Pelras (1996: 203) speculates replaced recitations from the La Galigo corpus. While the imam does not endorse this as a current practice, and it has not been revived in Sorowako post-DI, he noted that reciting barzanji in the past had the benefit of familiarising people with Qur'anic recitation. The DI rebels strictly outlawed barzanji as "innovation" (*bidah*), a practice that was not based on the activities undertaken by the Prophet. (It was written in the 18th century, long after the Prophet's death.) The rebels also outlawed the ritual of *tahlilan*. The imam does not support this practice but neither does he ban it. Some of the pre-DI practices emerge periodically but without controversy. In Sorowako today, as people become more affluent and can invite neighbours to commemorative funerary feasts, tahlilan continues as a popular practice. In contrast to the DI enforcement of religious orthodoxy in precise detail, the imam emphasises that if people know what is "right", practices that fall outside the codes of Islam will fall away.

Forty years on, many of the rituals around, for example, birth and house building that I regularly witnessed in the 1970s, have fallen away; and while some of these changes perhaps can be attributed to changing religious ideology, much of it can also be linked to changes in everyday life practices associated with the modernity that has been induced by the development of the mine. Material changes (positive and negative) in the wake of the project have had an impact on both cultural and religious practices.

Impact of the Secular Development of the Mine on Religious and Ritual Practice

House Building and Rituals

When I first arrived in Sorowako, the people lived in elevated wooden "platform houses" (*rumah panggung*) (Robinson 1993). The important first step, the erection of the prefabricated frame, involved collective labour. It was undertaken at an auspicious time determined often by the imam, utilising the Bugis calendric system for identifying favourable times and dates for endeavours (Robinson 1996). Most often, it occurred either before dawn prayers or after sunset prayers. On these occasions, the imam would also recite prayers and mantras (*baca baca*), and oversee the ritual paraphernalia that was placed under the pole, deemed the sacral central post of the house, to guarantee the auspicious life of its inhabitants. The neighbours who came to help were rewarded with a collective snack or meal provided by the house owner.

When the time came to inhabit the new dwelling, when it had a roof and (usually temporary) walls, the imam also officiated at a house-entering ritual, circumnavigating the house, reciting prayers and preceding the householders up the steps of their new dwelling. Ritual paraphernalia common in Bugis house rites, including a bunch of green bananas, was placed at the ritually significant centre post.

Sorowakan people now build brick and cement houses, often flush to the ground, following urban fashion. This now-common choice, even in rural communities in South Sulawesi, reflects the high cost of timber these days, compared to brick and cement. Changing house fashions also reflect the importance of houses as symbols of affluence and social status. Professional teams, no longer using collective labour, build these modern houses. I asked a friend who recently built a wooden second storey on her brick and cement house if she had conducted any rituals. "No", she replied "because construction was done at the timing of the building contractor (*tukang*) and anyway he is a Christian from central Sulawesi". Hence the imam does not have a role in house rituals. This seems to be as much a process of secularisation as it is a product of the piety movement (see chapter by Nisa, this volume).

Changing Wedding Practices

The *akad nikah* or marriage contract is the core of Islamic marriage. In Sorowako in the 1970s, this was a private affair conducted in the bride's home with only close family of the bride and groom—and of course the imam—present. The bride was not present. On one dramatic occasion, I sat in the bedroom with the bride dressed in a house dress (*duster*) while her prospective spouse and her *wali* (guardian) finalised the contract with the groom uttering his marriage vows in front of witnesses. The *akad nikah* was a family affair that involved no public feasting and took place in the days, or in some cases weeks, prior to the public event of the *pesta* or reception.

During the period of Islamisation (in the colonial period) the wife of the mantri sawah and first imam served as the *indo botting* (Bug. "wedding mother") or *dukun pesta*, with knowledge of the spells, rituals and practices necessary for a good wedding. Islamisation went hand-in-hand with the adoption of Bugis custom. Weddings came to follow Bugis adat practices, with a series of rituals including what Sorowako people referred to as *tamatkan al Qur'an*, meeting of the bride and groom, and *pesta* (reception) which featured *duduk bersanding* (bride and groom sitting side-by-side on a raised dais in front of the assembled guests), arranged at an auspicious time. Scheduling was determined according to a calendrical system derived from Bugis custom that has also come to be influenced by the Islamic calendar. Wedding custom, including the costumes, was an important marker of *suku* (sociocultural group) distinctiveness under the New Order. That the indigenous people of Sorowako have adopted Bugis custom for weddings was remarked on by an Inco mine manager from Java (in the 1970s) who reportedly asked one of the men under his authority, "If you don't have your own wedding adat maybe you can use mine?" That is, it was seen as a mark of inauthenticity that they did not wear a distinctive local dress, but chose a costume that underscored their identity as Muslim people of South Sulawesi.

There have been many changes in wedding practices over the years. Today, although there are seven mosques in Sorowako town (which now encloses the original village), Imam Djufri from the original village mosque is still the only officially recognised marriage celebrant in Sorowako; he is authorised by the government Religious Affairs Department, locally manifest in the KUA (Kantor Urusan

Agama). As I will show below, his authority in regard to marriage is still important in many ways. But the celebrations surrounding the marriage have been dramatically changed as the community becomes more affluent and subject to outside trends. In addition, the entry of migrants brings a wide range of ritual practices but also of assumptions in regard to monogamy, polygamy and divorce.

The *akad nikah* is nowadays an elaborate affair with a large invited audience and a feast. It sometimes occurs in the hours prior to the reception (which features the *duduk bersanding*). Weddings formerly took place in and around the house of the bride and, to a lesser extent, the groom. The elevated wooden house was extended (through collective volunteer labour) by opening one of the walls and adding a large temporary terrace-like space to accommodate guests. This practice of *sambung rumah* (extend the house) was one of the first celebratory events in a wedding cycle, accompanied by much jollity and feasting for the people who came to help. People now on the whole no longer live in *rumah panggung* (elevated wooden houses) and houses are crowded close together in the village, leaving no space to "*sambung rumah*". Parents of the bride hire tarpaulins (*tenda*) which they erect in the street as an approximation of hosting the ceremony in the bride's home. But increasingly they follow what is now the common urban practice in Sulawesi of hiring an auditorium.

Formerly those who followed Bugis-style wedding custom completed an elaborate sequence of rituals, including the *tamatkan al Qur'an* at the bride's house on the evening prior to the wedding where sometimes the bride, but more frequently her brother or even the imam, read from the Qur'an (see also Alimi 2014 and this volume). The reception (*pesta*) was held the following day in the extended house, or now the tent or the auditorium. The bride and groom sit together (*duduk bersanding*) dressed in elaborate costumes which, following conversion to Islam, are usually Bugis-style silk and brocade sarongs. The costumes are meant to be "courtly" as the bride and groom are the "king and queen for a day". After some speeches the guests come one by one to greet them and line up at tables to fill plates with the food that has been cooked by a merry volunteer crew over the previous day and night. The reception formerly happened in the day time and that evening the bride's close family escorted her to the groom's house for further feasting and gifting to the bride from her parents-in-law, after which the groom would be escorted back to the bride's house for their wedding night.

Over the years I have known Imam Djufri, the practice in regard to the *akad nikah* has changed. While the bride is still not present at the *akad*, it is now commonly conducted as a public ceremony with a large audience. It is followed by the cultural tradition *penjemptutan suami isteri* where the groom approaches the room of his (now) wife, and a group of women stage a mock battle in trying to prevent him entering. His escorts accompany him to greet the bride, nowadays sitting modestly but beautifully costumed on the bed. He reaches out to touch her and the place of the touch is regarded as symbolising the way the relationship will develop. The bride and groom then walk, usually holding hands, through the rowdy crowd of (mostly) women to return to the place on the floor where the *akad nikah* has taken place. The new bride sits next to her husband while he recites out loud the *taklik talak* (conditional divorce) which is printed on the back of the marriage certificate (*buku nikah*). It sets out the conditions under which women acquire rights to sue for divorce (Robinson 2006). In overseeing this public acknowledgment of rights and obligations, the imam says he is following instructions from the Department of Religious Affairs and he sees it as very important. I attended a wedding in a neighbouring village where the imam who officiated did not require the formal reading of the *taklik talak*. I asked imam Djufri why this was different from his own practice and he commented that the way of the other imam was "*belum sempurna*" (not yet perfect).

Wedding rituals are important events for claiming and validating social status in South Sulawesi and new fashions influence the conduct of wedding rituals, especially in the context of the new forms of affluence for many people in the community. In one notable instance, in 2012 a young woman university graduate returned home for her wedding to an engineer. Followers of the campus Tarbiyah (religious reform) movement, they elected to have a reception which followed a style that the locals called "*kawin* Islam" (see also Alimi, this volume). The bride wore a white dress and elaborate *jilbab* (tight veil covering hair and neck) rather than the usual colourful Bugis-style silk sarong and transparent *baju bodo* (Bug. short blouse). A curtain separated the male and female guests and the bride and groom stood on opposite ends of the dais each with a group of same sex relatives, and greeted only guests of their own sex. This innovation was regarded as a failure in the court of public opinion, as husbands and wives arriving as guests were directed to their same-sex section of the venue: the men were caught off guard, without the customary "*amplop*" (envelope) containing money that guests deposited in a jar after greeting the wedding party. The *amplop* were in the wives' handbags and hence many men were left feeling shamed. That is, innovations are not always readily accepted, or have positive impacts on social status. And there are checks on innovation, especially in elements of the cycle in which the imam has authority. In the case of the "*kawin Islam*" ritual, at the *akad nikah*, that had occurred earlier in the day, the bride and groom did sit side-by-side (*duduk bersanding*) for the reading of the *taklik talak* (see above) as the *nikah* was conducted in accord with the imam's procedures. Imam Djufri firmly believes in this state-regulated practice as, in his view, it ensures that women know their rights. Perhaps his strong commitment to this practice stems from dealing with many cases of so-called "*kawin kontrak*" (contract marriages) in which women were tricked into often polygamous marriages by migrant men who abandoned their wives once their employment contract ceased.[10] Imam Djufri's *khotbah* (sermon), delivered at the time of the *akad nikah*, emphasises marriage as a partnership, and the importance of respect and co-operation between husband and wife.

The significant presence of migrants impacts the cultural traditions of wedding rituals but has also had an impact on the conduct of spouses in marriages. As noted above, many women found themselves unwitting second wives of migrant workers. The imam's position amounts to an effective ban on polygamy: he advises against it on the grounds that the requirement of Islam to treat all wives absolutely equally is not humanly possible—except for the Prophet. In the more complex social relations of the mining town, it is much more difficult for his understanding of marriage contracts to be enforced.

Imam Djufri obtained his Bugis-style religious learning from his father, and from DI where he learned to reject many of the Bugis–Islamic practices. I asked him when it is acknowledged that the pair are married, and he replied it was at the time of the *ijab kabul* (*akad nikah*)—the vow that mattered—hence the groom's utterance must be clear, audible to the audience and perfect. (Grooms often have to repeat the vow several times.) Other elements like the *penjemputan* or the *duduk bersanding* are only culture (*budaya*). He has no objection to them, and indeed enthusiastically joins in these rituals, not finding them offensive as the DI rebels did.

His conduct of the *akad nikah* with insistence on the reading of the *taklik talak* and his views on polygamy spring from his interpretive stance that the Qur'an delivers rights for women in marriage, a common theme in the sermons that he delivers at the time of *akad nikah*. And marriage is an area where his religious authority is intact because it is protected by the state, as well as his own charismatic and religious authority.

Childbirth

There has been a "secularisation" in regard to childbirth. In the late 1970s, women gave birth at home with the assistance of a traditional birth attendant (*dukun bayi*) of whom there were around three in the village, but some company employees' wives were beginning to call midwives from the company clinic to assist in home births, or even to give birth in the company hospital.[11] Workers and their families were entitled to free treatment at the company clinic and the workers' wives would also have attended ante-natal care. In the case of the customary home births, the imam attended soon after births at home to whisper the *azan* in the child's ear and recite prayers (*doa*) for the child.

In addition, in customary births, the *dukun* provided post-partum care, and also conducted the post-birth ritual of descending from the house three to five days after birth. This involved the *dukun* bathing the woman in the lake, and bringing a small panier of lake water back to the house to also bathe the newborn child. At the same time the mother's breasts were "smoked" with coconut husks heated on the hearth. The bathing ritual was regarded as propitiating the "*ue uoi*" (Sor. lord of the water) while smoking the breasts was intended to improve milk flow. The *dukun* also massaged the new mother and baby, and gave advice, especially in the case of a novice mother. A celebratory ritual (*selamatan*) held at the time of the hair-cutting ritual (*akekah*) was termed *melepe-lepe* because the requisite food comprised rice and coconut milk dumplings wrapped in banana leaf (*lepe-lepe*) which were cooked overnight and served with chicken or occasionally a goat. Prayers (*doa*) recited by the imam were an important prelude to the collective feasts, attended mainly by men.

Now all women give birth with assistance from a midwife from either the company clinic or the government health centre built in the last decade. The baby is *diazani* (called to Islam) by its father and the *melepe-lepe* ritual has given way to a more clearly Islamic *akekah*, involving the slaughter of goats, but also preparing the *lepe-lepe*.[12]

This transformation in religious practice which seems to exclude the imam from a customary sphere of his activities (in particular to *azani* the infant) would seem to be initiated by a secularisation and modernisation of childbirth, in the shift of birth to the modern health care sector; but the shifting practice from *melepe-lepe* is also linked to the trend to increased piety in Indonesia. Parents are adopting the practices of aspirational middle classes by practising these more Islamised rituals. Affluence and status claims are important here, as well as religiosity.

In a similar vein, circumcision of young boys is no longer conducted in the village. Parents rely on medically-trained personnel at the company and government clinics to conduct this significant Islamic ritual.

Religious Education

A dilution of the imam's authority as the principle source of Islamic education is perhaps the most significant transformation in his role, since the village developed into a cosmopolitan town. In the 1970s, Imam Djufri gave all children religious instruction in praying and reading the Qur'an, using the traditional method of *halaqah* (Gade 2004). The mining town is a complex and growing urban agglomerate which now has around seven mosques. The Sorowako village mosque, now beautifully renovated by local business men, is acknowledged as the oldest mosque (Masjid Jami).

The *masjid karyawan* (workers' mosque) in the town site behind the village has now become the largest and principle mosque. Its congregation are the new middle class comprising company and contract employees, local business people, etc. This urban growth centre attracts young, highly-educated *ustadz* (preachers) who seek opportunities to work. The *masjid karyawan* advertises for its imam, who is appointed by a selection committee, and necessarily has a high level of formal Islamic education.

Figure 4.2 Teaching children Muslim religious practice in the Workers' Mosque (Masjid Karyawan). Photo by Kathryn Robinson.

Figure 4.3 Women watching their children graduate from the TPA (Taman Pendidikan Al-Qur'an). Photo by Kathryn Robinson.

The private school for the children of employees, run by a foundation on behalf of the mining company, has a strong emphasis on religious education, and employs highly-educated professional religious teachers (including a graduate from Al-Azhar in Egypt). All of the mosques have been brought under a foundation which, among other things, organises the schedule of Friday sermons, and invites guest preachers from outside the community on special occasions, sometimes sponsored by the mining company. There is usually a company-sponsored "star" preacher to address the mass congregational prayers on Idul Fitri, the end of the fasting month, regarded as the Islamic "new year" celebration.

Religious education has been formalised under the auspices of this foundation. Children now attend one of several TPA (Taman Pendidikan Al-Qur'an) where they are instructed by young professional *ustadz* in religious practice including salat, *azan* and reading the Qur'an. These schools use modern instructional methods, for example in teaching the children to read Arabic script. One of the TPA takes place in the beautifully renovated and enlarged village mosque (masjid Jami) but the imam is not directly involved. He does, however, provide instruction to a *majlis taklim* (religious study group) of older women, who meet twice a week in his mosque. Here his talents are on show: not only his skill in understanding Arabic but also his explication of Qur'anic verses and *hadis* in the local language (Bahasa Sorowako) as well as in Indonesian, as many of the older women have only a basic everyday grasp of Indonesian. The economic transformation of the village has meant many of these women no longer farm into their old age. For elderly people in Sorowako, they can reap the fruits of their effort to educate their children in the relatively leisured lives their children provide for them. The mosque is an important focus of the daily life of the "retirees".

Impact of the Piety Movement

Sorowako is a pious community and Islam dominates the rhythms of daily life. The Orang Asli Sorowako have taken up the responsibility to make the pilgrimage (haj) to Mecca in large numbers since the late 1970s as monetary wealth began to circulate and accumulate in the mining town. This is a remote urban enclave that has strong cultural links with changes happening in Indonesia's cities, through educated

Figure 4.4 Women at the Majlis Taklim in the old mosque. Photo by Kathryn Robinson.

migrants and the young education migrants who return home from universities in Makassar and Java. The grandchildren of the women I first met in 1979, when they were tentatively trying out Western-style skirts and blouses, with matching kerchiefs as a nod to the idea of head covering, now frequently choose to wear the modern Muslim fashion (*busana* Muslim) associated with the pious in the urban middle class. Driving up from the capital city of Makassar in late 2016 I was struck by the fact that once one left the capital city, where this kind of dress is ubiquitous, in the small towns I passed through, the main groups wearing the *jilbab* were civil servants and school children for whom it was part of their uniform under local government Islamic regulations (*perda syariah*)—that is until reaching Sorowako, where the urban fashion for *busana* Muslim was once again ubiquitous.

The current wave of hard-line Islamism in South Sulawesi is linked to the heritage of the Darul Islam Movement. Prominent members of the group promoting the political strategy of implementing local regulations based on sharia (*perda syariah*) are descendants of Kahar Muzakkar. This group, KPPSI (Komite Persiapan Penegakan Syariat Islam; Committee of preparation for the implementation of Islamic law), is associated with conservative religious views, including in regard to women's rights. Imam Djufri acknowledges Kahar's modernist religious heritage in some matters such as not recognising the recitation of barzanji as a legitimate Muslim practice (on the grounds that it is innovation since the time of the Prophet) or not endorsing the *tahlilan*. However, his reliance on textualism and his humanitarian approach informs his approach to gender equity which is at odds with the current Islamist agenda. I asked about his view on the application of sharia law as state law, the idea promoted by KPPSI, and he replied: "We already have the 1945 Constitution and Panca Sila [the state ideology] so it is not possible or appropriate. You cannot apply Islamic law [*hukum* al Qur'an] in Indonesia because there are already secular laws [*undang undang*]." He then recited a verse from the Qur'an, that God created humankind in men in many different cultural groups (*suku suku*) so they can know each other. This is the value of tolerance (*toleransi*). He keeps a "weather eye" for people who might preach intolerance, for example in his mosque.

He has a strong view that individual responsibility in religious observance is an Islamic value. In the DI period all women were required to wear a headcovering and could not leave the house without it—but, he said, once the *gerombolan* (rebellion) was over, it disappeared (*hilang*) and only old women continued to wear it. Now, he went on, many young women are wearing *jilbab* (tight veil) if they want to. If they have heard the correct message through *dakwah* (preaching) on this topic then they choose to wear it. It is the right thing to do but only if it is a consequence of their conscious choice.

One of his important principles of religious observance is defined in opposition to the coercion experienced under DI.

He commented that, with Kahar Muzakkar the signature term (*istillah*) was not "choose for yourself", but "you are obliged to" (*harus*). He concluded: "If something is forced and the force goes, so does the practice; it doesn't come from within."

Conclusion

This local history can help us unpack some of the dynamics of the spread of Islam, for example the significance of the power struggles under colonial rule, and the complexities of the impact of the decade and a half of the DI rebellion. The contemporary significance of DI is not only as a forerunner of current movements for the implementation of sharia, but that it had a dramatic impact in some places on the culturally inflected forms of Islam (traditional Islam) that have been characteristic of Muslim communities in South Sulawesi.

The Islamisation of the village of Sorowako happened through the influence of a family of village imam with limited formal religious education, and in the absence of *ulama / kiyai*, religious institutions such as *pesantren*. Initially, Islam was more of an oral than a textual tradition. The current village imam succeeded his father and for many years was solely responsible for the religious learning and spiritual guidance of his community, many of whom were his kin and affines. He now operates in a complex social and religious environment where he faces novel social and cultural dilemmas. As a charismatic leader and someone who has the trust of his community, his religious authority has translated into secular authority as he joins with other local leaders to press the claims of local people to the mining company. In terms of his religious authority, today he needs to co-ordinate and co-operate with scholars with higher levels of formal education. The adaptability of his exercise of religious authority in this complex social arena is illustrated by his embrace of the stewardship of the women's *majlis taklim*.

There have been many changes in regard to the ritual practices associated with life cycle events, such as birth and marriage; and house building and occupation. In these events where often the imam shared the exercise of ritual authority with other ritual experts, changes have arisen as a result of the changed material circumstances in which people live their lives, consequent on the development of the mining project. The magnitude of the impact of the mine development and the rapidity of social change render visible the kinds of changes that are proceeding, perhaps more slowly, in other Indonesian Muslim communities. The village imam has had significant stewardship of religious and social change, but he himself acknowledges that he will not be succeeded by a religious authority of the same ilk.

Notes

1. Ternate, at the centre of the spice trade and the polities in its orbit, including Buton, had embraced Islam in the mid-16th century.
2. Abendanon (1916–18), Grubauer (1913), Sarasin (1931).
3. In the Treaty of Bongaya it was ceded as under the influence of Bungku (Andaya 1993).
4. We can only speculate on why they remained linked to, even intermarried with Luwu, in the case of the rulers of Matano, but did not convert to Islam. Schrauwers (1997) notes the value of headhunters to the Luwu rulers in dealing with enemies. Presumably one cannot be a Muslim and a headhunter.
5. Visiting Sinjai in 1995, I was shown a beautiful illuminated Al Qur'an that had been given to the grandfather of the current owner by the Raja Buleleng of Bali. It was a token of appreciation to the Sinjai warriors who had fought with his troops against the Dutch.
6. By the 1970s, the memory of this distinctly un-Muslim practice was explained to me by one man as "we kept pigs for sacrifices but we didn't eat them".
7. Christian Pelras (1996: 203) notes that reading barzanji gradually replaced reading texts from the epic La Galigo, the principal body of texts for pre-Islamic Bugis religion. Imam Djufri described to me how barzanji similarly replaced pre-Islamic ritual chants in Sorowako.
8. A religious leader in Sinjai said to me: "The Dato' [the legendary religious scholars credited with bringing Islam to South Sulawesi] were very smart—they found things people were doing and said—'See, you are already following Islam'."
9. The buffalo was kept in fields in Seluro, the site of refuge during DI as pasturage was hard to come by close to the village on account of the forced land dispossession, and the mining company security strictly enforced a ban on animals straying into the company townsite.
10. In the practice referred to by this term in Sorowako, women unknowingly entered in good faith into marriages to which migrant male

workers were committed only for the duration of their employment. The KUA, then in the nearby town of Wasuponda, showed me a cupboard full of unclaimed *buku nikah* (marriage certificates)—sorry evidence of this practice.

11. The sphere of influence went beyond the employees as the indigenous Sorowakan people were granted rights to be treated at the company health facility.
12. In some cases it is arranged at the Hidayatullah *pesantren* (residential school) in nearby Wawandula where the remainder of the slaughtered goat (or goats) is donated to the orphans at the school.

References

Abendanon, Eduard Cornelius. 1916–18. *Expedition de la Celebes Centrale. Voyages Geologiques et Geographiques a travers la Celebes Centrale 1909–1910* [Expeditions in Central Celebes. Geological and Geographical Journeys Across Central Celebes 1909–1910]. Leiden: E.J. Brill.

Alimi, Moh Yasir. 2014. "Islam as Drama: Wedding Rituals and the Theatricality of Islam in South Sulawesi." *The Asia Pacific Journal of Anthropology* 15 (3): 265–85.

Andaya, Leonard. 1993. *The World of Maluku: Eastern Indonesia in the Early Modern Period.* Honolulu: University of Hawai'i Press.

Azra, Azyumardi. 2004. *The Origins of Islamic Reformism in Southeast Asia: Networks of Malay–Indonesian and Middle Eastern 'Ulama' in the Seventeenth and Eighteenth Centuries.* Crow's Nest, NSW: Allen and Unwin; Honolulu: University of Hawai'i Press.

Boland, B.J. 1982. *The Struggle of Islam in Modern Indonesia.* The Hague: Martinus Nijhoff.

Bulbeck, David and Ian Caldwell. 2000. *Land of Iron. The Historical Archaeology of Luwu and the Cenrana Valley. Results of the Origin of Complex Society in South Sulawesi Project (OXIS).* Centre for Southeast Asian Studies, University of Hull; School of Archaeology and Anthropology, Australian National University.

Djamas, Nurhayati. 1985. "Varian keagamaan orang Bugis-Makassar" [Varieties of Bugis–Makassar religion]. In *Agama dan Realitas Sosial,* ed. Mukhlis and Kathryn Robinson, 273–396. Ujung Pandang, Indonesia: Hasanuddin University Press for the Indonesian Social Science Foundation (YIIS).

Feillard, Andree and Remy Mardinier. 2011. *The End of Innocence: Indonesian Islam and the Temptations of Radicalism.* Trans. Wong Wee. Singapore: NUS Press.

Gade, Anna M. 2004. *Perfection Makes Practice: Learning, Emotion and the Recited Qur'an in Indonesia*. Honolulu: University of Hawai'i Press.

Grubauer, Albert. 1913. *Unter Kopfjägern in Central Celebes* [Among the Headhunters in Central Celebes]. Leipzig: R Voigtländers Verlag.

Mattulada. 1974. "Bugis–Makassar: Manusia dan Kebudayaanya" [Bugis–Makassar: People and Their Culture]. *Berita Antropologi* 15: 12–25.

Millar, Susan B. 1989. *Bugis Weddings: Ritual of Social Location in Modern Indonesia*. Monograph Series no. 29. Berkeley, California: Center for South and Southeast Asia Studies, University of California.

Paeni, Mukhlis and Kathryn Robinson, eds. 1985. *Agama dan Realitas Sosial.* Ujung Pandang, Indonesia: Hasanuddin University Press for the Indonesian Social Science Foundation (YIIS).

Pelras, Christian. 1985 "Religion, Tradition and the Dynamic of Islamization in South Sulawesi." *Archipel* 29 (1): 107–35.

______. 1996. *The Bugis.* Oxford: Blackwell.

Reid, Anthony. 1993. "Islamization and Christianization in Southeast Asia: The Critical phase (1550–1650)." In *Southeast Asia in the Early Modern Era: Trade, Power, and Belief*, ed. Anthony Reid, 151–79. Ithaca, NY: Cornell University Press.

Robinson, Kathryn. 1983. "Living in the Hutan: Jungle Village Life under the Darul Islam." *Review of Indonesian and Malay Affairs* 17 (1–2): 208–29.

______. 1985. "The Soroako Nickel Project: a Healthy Development?" *International Journal of Health Services* 15 (2): 301–19.

______. 1993. "The Elevation of Status: the '*Rumah Panggung*' in Contemporary South Sulawesi." In *Cultural Expression Under Indonesia's New Order*, ed. V. Hooker, 228–42. Kuala Lumpur: Oxford University Press.

______. 1996. "Traditions of House-Building in South Sulawesi." In *Living Through Histories: Culture History and Social Life in South Sulawesi*, ed. Kathryn Robinson and Mukhlis Paeni, 168–95. Canberra and Jakarta: Anthropology ANU in collaboration with the Indonesian National Archives.

______. 2006. "Muslim Women's Political Struggle for Marriage Law Reform in Contemporary Indonesia." In *Mixed Blessings: Laws, Religion and Women's Rights in the Asia-Pacific Region*, ed. Amanda Whiting and Carolyn Evans, 183–210. Leiden: Brill.

______. 2018. "Can Formalization of Adat Law Protect Community Rights? The Case of the Orang Asli Sorowako and the Dongi." Lecture, Indonesian Study Group, ANU Indonesia Project, Australian National University, 9 May 2018. http://asiapacific.anu.edu.au/blogs/indonesiaproject/isg-can-formalisation-of-adat-law-protect-community-rights/.

Robinson, Kathryn, M. 1986. *Stepchildren of Progress: The Political Economy of Development in an Indonesian Mining Town.* Albany, NY: SUNY Press.

Sarasin, Fritz. 1931. *Aus Den Tropen. Reiseerinnerungen aus Ceylon, Celebes und Neu-Caledonien* [From the Tropics: Journeys in Ceylon, Celebes and New Caledonia]. Basel: Verlag von Helbing & Liehtenahn.

Schrauwers, Albert. 1997. "Houses, Hierarchy, Headhunting and Exchange: Rethinking Political Relations in the Southeast Asian Realm of Luwu." *Bijdragen tot de Taal-, Land- en Volkenkunde* 153 (3): 356–80.

______. 2000. *Colonial 'Reformation' in the Highlands of Central Sulawesi, 1892–1985*. Toronto, Buffalo, London: University of Toronto Press.

van Dijk, Cornelius. 1981. *Rebellion Under the Banner of Islam: The Darul Islam in Indonesia*. The Hague: Martinus Nijhoff.

van Leur, Jacob Cornelius. 1955. *Indonesian Trade and Society: Essays in Asian Social and Economic History*. The Hague: W. Van Hoeve.

Vlekke, Bernard. 1959. *Nusantara: A History of Indonesia*. The Hague: W. Van Hoeve.

5

The Reproduction of Imams and Their Changing Roles within the Contemporary Muslim Community in Wajo, South Sulawesi, Indonesia

Wahyuddin Halim

Introduction

The Qur'an memorisation programmes (*tahfiz al-Qur'an*) of the religious organisation As'adiyah[1] in Sengkang, the district capital of Wajo, South Sulawesi, play an important role in the production and provision of leaders of congregational prayer (*imam salat*) to mosques all over Indonesia, particularly in the eastern part of the country. Generally, in Islamic literature, imam (from Arabic) designates the spiritual leader or religious scholar of a Muslim community or group. In most Muslim communities in Indonesia, the imam is one of the religious functionaries at village and subdistrict levels whose tasks include: to perform marriage rituals according to Islamic law; lead and teach the community in religious matters; lead the communal prayers; and organise funerals.[2] The network of students and alumni of this religious educational institution, particularly in eastern Indonesia, facilitates the placement of students and alumni from the memorisation programme Tahfiz Al-Qur'an Masjid Jami (henceforth TQMJ) as imam. This institution provides two types of congregational prayer leaders: firstly, *imam rawatib*,[3] a permanent or professional leader of congregational prayer (*imam tetap*); and secondly, *imam tarawih*, a seasonal leader of congregational prayer during the fasting month of Ramadan.

Imam rawatib refers to the male who leads the five-times daily obligatory prayers (*salat jamaah*) performed congregationally in the mosque. Since the person who holds this job is in charge of leading all congregational prayers in the mosque on a permanent basis and, in most cases, also resides in the building complex of the mosque, he is often referred to as "*imam tetap*" (permanent imam). In many other mosques without a permanent imam, the imam leading different congregational prayers may change from time to time, depending on who is considered competent enough among the mosque community present at the time of prayer. Islamic texts dictate that every adult male Muslim may become an imam. This privilege is given first to someone who is considered by the community of the mosque to be the oldest, the best in faith and the finest in Qur'anic recitation and memorisation.

As'adiyah is considered by many scholars (such as Mattulada 1983; Azra 2004; van Bruinessen 1998) as the most influential Islamic learning institution in South Sulawesi in the second half of the 20th century, particularly in terms of the role of its *pesantren* (Islamic boarding school) in the reproduction of *ulama*[4] as well as the number of *madrasah*[5] that it runs within the region and beyond. Since the 1970s, As'adiyah has operated hundreds of madrasah (at elementary level or *madrasah ibtida'iya*) in nine districts in South Sulawesi and in the provinces of Central Sulawesi, Southeast Sulawesi, East Kalimantan, and Jambi and Riau on the island of Sumatra (Mattulada 1983). In addition to its Islamic education programmes, As'adiyah has numerous programmes in the field of Islamic preaching or mission (*dakwah*).

As part of its *dakwah* programme, during the month of Ramadan, As'adiyah assigns hundreds of students from its *tahfiz* (memorisation) programme as *imam tarawih*, the male leader of *salat tarawih*. *Tarawih* is an optional prayer that can only be performed during the Muslim fasting month of Ramadan (the ninth month in the Islamic lunar calendar). In Indonesia the tarawih prayers are performed in a mosque by a mixture of men and women (who are physically segregated). The number of cycles or prescribed postures and recitations (*rakaat*) is either 8 or 20 (see also Sila, this volume).[6] Also during Ramadan, students and teachers are assigned to serve as religious preachers or speakers (*mubalig*, Bug. *pattabellek* or *padda'wa*) in different places (see Halim 2015). Outside the month of Ramadan, many of the graduates of the tahfiz programme (called *hafiz*, preserver of the Qur'an) are appointed as imam rawatib in mosques in eastern parts of Indonesia and other parts of the archipelago.

As'adiyah and the Development of Islamic Education and Mission in South Sulawesi and Beyond

Pesantren As'adiyah was established by AGH Muhammad As'ad al-Bugis in 1930 in Sengkang. The young ulama was born in Mecca in 1907 to a devout Bugis Muslim family who had migrated there from Wajo in the late 1880s due to internal political conflict and chaos in the Wajo polity.[7] As'ad first obtained his basic religious education from his father and learned to memorise the Qur'an before he went to Madrasah Al-Falah, a formal Islamic school established by Muslim migrants from India (Walinga 1981: 29–30). At 14, As'ad had memorised the whole Qur'an (30 chapters) and for three consecutive years (1922–24), he was assigned by the authority of al-Haram mosque to lead the tarawih prayer in the most important mosque in the Muslim world (Manguluang 1990: 1). The assignment signified recognition of his exceptional fluency and eloquence in Qur'anic recitation and memorisation among non-Arab ulama in Mecca. At the age of 17, he had mastered most, if not all, classical branches of Islamic knowledge such as the Qur'anic sciences ('Ulum al-Qur'an), the sciences of the prophetic tradition ('Ulum al-Hadith), principles of Islamic jurisprudence (Ushul al-Fiqh), and sciences of Arabic language (Walinga 1981; Ismail 1989; Manguluang 1990).

In addition to his formal education at Madrasah Al-Falah, As'ad also extended his study to different branches of Islamic knowledge from a number of prominent ulama who taught in al-Haram mosque (al-Masjid al-Haram) in Mecca using the non-classical system which was known in the Islamic history of learning as *halaqah*.[8] Among the prominent ulama whose halaqah As'ad attended were 'Umar b. Hamdan, Sa'id al-Yamani, Hashim Nazirin, Jamal al-Maliki, Hasan al-Yamani, 'Abbas 'Abd al-Jabbar and Ambo Wellang al-Bugisi (Ismail 1989).

In 1928, As'ad left Mecca for Sengkang and soon began teaching classical Islamic Arabic books to a small number of students at the house of his brother-in-law, Ambo Emme, using the halaqah system (Bug. *mappangaji kitta*). He also taught Qur'anic memorisation (tahfiz) to a small group of interested students at the mosque near his house, built in 1930 by the local ruler of Wajo. Also in 1930, AGH As'ad established al-Madrasah al-'Arabiyah al-Islamiyah (popularly known as MAI) to accommodate the fast-growing number of students coming to his halaqah. Students were organised in different classrooms based on their age and level of understanding of basic Islamic knowledge. In its early years, MAI operated only at primary and secondary school levels and study durations ranged from one to four years. The emphasis was on teaching classical branches of Islamic knowledge in the classroom system. The halaqah teaching system, however, was included as an important part of the programme (Pasanreseng 1992).

AGH As'ad passed away on 2 December 1952, aged 45. A year later the name of his madrasah, Al-Madrasah al-Arabiyah al-Islamiyah (MAI), was changed to Madrasah As'adiyah, honouring his name.[9] The madrasah and pesantren he established continued, led by his two most senior students: AGH[10] Daud Ismail (leadership period: 1952–61) and AGH Muhammad Yunus Martan (1961–86). After his death in 1986, AGH Hamzah Badawi (1986–88) continued as leader for another two years before leadership was handed over to AGH Abdul Malik Muhammad (1988–2000) and AGH Abd. Rahman Musa (2000–02). Between 2002 and 2014, the pesantren, the madrasah, and the foundation was led by AGH Dr Muhammad Rafi'i Yunus (the oldest son of the third director of As'adiyah, AGH Yunus Martan), a retired professor from the Alauddin State Islamic University of Makassar.

The institutions founded by AGH As'ad have played a fundamental role in producing new generations of ulama, religious teachers, religious speakers and religious officials.[11] It can be said that most, if not all, subsequent important ulama in South Sulawesi have developed their religious authority through their personal teacher-student relationship with AGH As'ad or by attending one of various religious learning institutions that he founded in Sengkang. These ulama, in turn, have established their own institutions in various parts of South Sulawesi and trained new generations of Muslim scholars, teachers and preachers, generating a broad intellectual network that continues into the present (Al-Bone 1987; Arief 2008).

AGH Abunawas Bintang, a senior ulama in As'adiyah, told me of a popular Bugis saying among ulama in South Sulawesi that, "*De'gaga tau ri Sulawesi missengngi agamae ko de' napole mangaji ki Anregurutta Aji Sade*'" (No one knows the [Islamic] religion unless he has learned it from AGH Muhammad As'ad). Another popular saying is, "*De'gagatu topanrita komeye, panrita-panrita marioloe, pole maneng mangaji ri Anregurutta aji Sade*'" (There are no ulama here, that is, older ulama, except those that have come to study with AGH Muhammad As'ad) (Interview in Sengkang, 2012). These aphorisms attest to AGH As'ad's high religious authority in the last century.

Since the leadership of AGH Muhammad Yunus Martan in the early 1960s, As'adiyah as a socio-religious organisation has expanded to become not only the most important place of Islamic learning in South Sulawesi but also the centre of a variety of outreach programmes. Its religious and educational programmes serve the Muslim communities not only in the home district of Wajo, but also other districts in South Sulawesi and indeed other Indonesian provinces.

During the leadership of AGH Muhammad Yunus As'adiyah opened school programmes for general education at different levels: from kindergarten to senior high school as well as a college for Islamic studies at its headquarters in Sengkang. The organisation operates a radio station called "Radio Suara As'adiyah" (the voice of As'adiyah) to expand the scope of its Islamic outreach programme (dakwah), as well as to facilitate other public and government information services. Print media was developed to contribute to the spread of Islamic ideas in South Sulawesi and beyond. In 1941, for example, AGH As'ad started a trilingual journal, in Buginese, Malay and Arabic, entitled *Al-Maw'iza al-ḥasana* (Ar. Good Advice).

During the Japanese Occupation (1943–45), however, the journal had to cease publication (Walinga 1981). In 1956, under the leadership of AGH Muhammad Yunus Martan, As'adiyah published a monthly magazine, *Risalah As'adiyah* (The Message of As'adiyah), also in Bugis, Indonesian and Arabic, which lasted for almost 30 years. Since the 1990s As'adiyah has established an Islamic micro finance initiative called Baitul Mal wat Tamwil (BMT) As'adiyah that works not only in the cooperative enterprise sector within the pesantren community but also operates a mini market and real estate business for the community at large (Halim 2015).

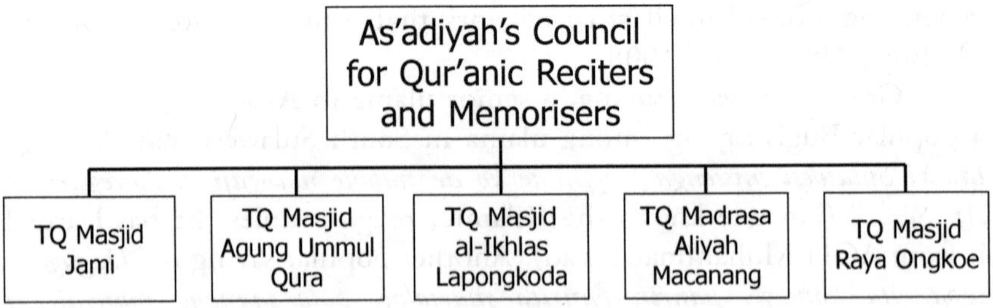

Figure 5.1 As'adiyah Tahfiz al-Qur'an (TQMJ) programmes

Currently As'adiyah manages tahfiz programmes in five different locations in Wajo, directed by a special council called Majlis al-Qurrā' wa al-Huffaẓ (Ar. Council for [the Qur'anic] Reciters and Memorisers) within the Central Executive Board of As'adiyah (Pengurus Besar As'adiyah) (see Figure 5.1).

A Brief History of Tahfiz al-Qur'an of Masjid Jami

Preserving Islam's most sacred text, the Qur'an, via memorisation, forms the fundamental basis of Muslim learning and has become an important foundation, if not the prerequisite, for further study in Islamic religious sciences (Eickelman 1978: 489). Those who memorise the 30 chapters of the Qur'an are recognised to be its "preservers" (hafiz), known for their specific talent, the ability to recite the Qur'an without the aid of a text. Special programmes or institutions of learning to memorise the Qur'an, called tahfiz al-Qur'an (from Arabic, meaning the "memorisation of the Qur'an"), are found in many parts of the Muslim world, including Indonesia.

The tahfiz al-Qur'an programme (*Menghafal Qur'an*, Bug. *makkapala korang*), established in 1930 by AGH Muhammad As'ad, has been one of the main religious programmes of Pesantren As'adiyah, indeed the oldest and now most prominent tahfiz programmes in South Sulawesi.[12] AGH As'ad planted the seed for the programme immediately after he arrived in the city in 1928 when he taught Qur'anic memorisation to a small number of students, mainly his own sons and the sons of his close relatives. As the number of interested students quickly grew, he invited his close Egyptian friend, Shaikh Ahmad 'Afify al-Misri, to assist him. The new teacher, known among his students and the Muslim people in Sengkang as Puang Masere ("the respected person from Egypt"), was a hafiz who had graduated from Al-Azhar University in Egypt. He dedicated his life to teach in the tahfiz programme and madrasah established by AGH As'ad in Masjid Jami before his death in 1951 (Surur 2011a: 505). As'ad continued the leadership of the tahfiz programme until he died a year later (Surur 2011b: 385). For AGH As'ad, becoming a hafiz had important religious value; he once said to his students that "Although you may not become *ulama* (Bug. *topanrita*), make the best of your opportunity to at least become a *hafiz*" (Natsir 2005: 75).

Among the most prominent graduates of this tahfiz learning programme were: H. Hasan Basri (As'ad's nephew) and H. Abd. Rasyid As'ad (As'ad's son); H. Muhammad Jafar Hamzah and H. Hasan (from Soppeng); H. Abd. Rahman (from Malaysia); H. Abd. Rasyid Hasanuddin (from Sengkang) and H. Abd. Karim Jafar (from Bulukumba); and Muhammad Amali, H. Muslimin, Abdullah Massarasa, Sunduseng, Dawisy and Sulaiman (from Bone); H. Muhammad Jafar Hamzah; and Abdul Hayyi, a blind hafiz who later also assisted AGH As'ad to teach Qur'anic memorisation in Masjid Jami (Surur 2011b: 384). These graduates were particularly important since most of them became ulama, established their own tahfiz learning centres in their place of origin or became teachers in existing tahfiz programmes that later produced the next generations of influential tahfiz teachers in the province.

After AGH As'ad's death, the tahfiz programme was directed respectively by H. Muhammad Ja'far Hamzah (1952–57), H. Hasan Basri (1958–60), H. Abdullah Massarasa (1961–70), H. Abd. Rasyid As'ad (1971–76) (Surur 2011b), and H. Muhammad Yahya from 1977 until 2017. They fulfilled two major leadership roles: firstly, to give daily direction to teachers (Ar. *mudarris*) who were themselves graduates of the programme and therefore qualified memorisers or hafiz; and secondly (and more importantly) to make sure that the ongoing care of memory of the Qur'an among their students could create what Anna Gade (2004: 60) noted as "a distinct and consistent subjectivity in terms of the ongoing nature of practice".

There is no extant record of the exact number of tahfiz students in Masjid Jami following its establishment until 1971, as in that year a massive fire resulted in the complete destruction of Masjid Jami, the library of the madrasah, teachers' personal book collections, and many important documents about As'adiyah. From 1971–76 there were 71 students and between 1980 and 2008, more than 475 students. Not all students enrolled in the tahfiz programme were able to fulfil the requirement of hafiz, to memorise all of the Qur'an within the average expected period. Usually only 30 per cent of any group of students attain the title of hafiz. For example, of 71 students enrolled in TQMJ between 1971 and 1976, only 11 achieved complete memorisation of the Qur'an. Between 2002 and 2007 there were 239 students enrolled in TQMJ, but only 46 of them succeeded in attaining hafiz. Most students were only able to memorise 5 to 15 chapters after spending 3 to 5 years—and finally gave up the programme. The data indicate that memorising the whole of the Qur'an is not easy and requires strong self-motivation, self-discipline and discipline of the body. Writing about the tahfiz programme in another institution in South Sulawesi in the 1990s, Gade (2004: 60) captures the complexity of this endeavour:

> The ongoing practice of committing and maintaining the Qur'an in memory requires that memorisers negotiate affectively the expectations for the social role and responsibilities of one who 'carries' the Qur'an in memory for the community. At the same time, they undertake the continual management of the technical challenges of safeguarding that memory on a daily basis. The confluence of social, cognitive, and emotional challenges facing Qur'an memorisers necessitates continual balancing of tasks, norms, and the self-understanding that comes with achievement. Memorising is thus a process of ongoing remaking of the self through a specifically Qur'anic involvement grounded in both the text and its social context.

The most important difference between TQMJ and four other places in Sengkang organised by As'adiyah is that in TQMJ students are required to devote their time exclusively to the memorisation of the Qur'an. They skip either junior or senior high school for two to four years to focus solely on Qur'anic memorisation, enabling them to finish the programme as quickly as possible. In other tahfiz programmes of As'adiyah, such as in Masjid Agung Ummul Qura of Sengkang, the students attend the tahfiz programme for occasional study only due to their full-time attendance at junior or senior high school. Based on the data from five tahfiz programmes organised by As'adiyah, more hafiz have been produced through TQMJ than in the four other places.

Figure 5.2 A *tahfiz* student doing his daily memorisation in the main hall of Masjid Jami. Photo by Wahyuddin Halim.

For example, in 2007 TQMJ conferred seven *huffaz* (plural for hafiz) and there were only two hafiz each from tahfiz in Masjid Agung Ummul Qura and Masjid Al-Ikhlas Lapongkoda in Sengkang (Dokumen TQMJ 2007).

Masjid Jami is one of the oldest mosques in the city of Sengkang, located on what is now KH Muhammad As'ad Street in the heart of the city. Since its establishment in 1930, both the wings and the front area of the mosque have been used as classrooms for students of the As'adiyah madrasah. The tahfiz programmes take place within the main hall of the mosque, which usually functions as a space for the performance of congregational prayers. The same hall has also been used for the halaqah programme since AGH As'ad's time until today.

Students of TQMJ live in houses located around the mosque that are either rented from local Sengkang residents or built by other district governments in South Sulawesi such as Bone, Pinrang and Soppeng, from where most tahfiz students of TQMJ originate. All daily activities of tahfiz students take place in and around Masjid Jami. The grand teacher, his students and many people in Wajo believe in the presence of "God's blessing" (Bug. *barekka'*, Ind. *berkat*, derived

Figure 5.3 Masjid Jami viewed from K.H.M. As'ad Street. Photo by Wahyuddin Halim.

from Arabic *barakah*) in the mosque. This blessing makes the effort of memorising the Qur'an in the mosque feel lighter than in any other place. "I keep telling my students", H. Muhammad Yahya, the director and grand teacher of TQMJ, told me in in 2012, "that it is in this mosque [Masjid Jami], not in any other place in Sengkang, that the *barekka'* resides and they should, therefore, spend most of their time in this mosque to memorise the Qur'an, not in their dormitories or any other places outside the mosque walls." Muhammad Yahya believes that the factor of *barekka'* for Masjid Jami is related to its long history as the place for learning the Qur'an and classical Islamic knowledge, started by AGH As'ad in 1928.[13]

Daily activities of tahfiz students are as follows: from after breakfast in the morning until late evening, students spend their time in the mosque in the daily process of memorising new verses, sections or chapters of the Qur'an and only pause to perform afternoon (*zuhur*), late afternoon (*'azr*), sunset (*magrib*) and evening (*isya*) prayers, as well as time taken for bathing and eating. After performing the communal evening prayer in Masjid Jami, around 7:15 pm, they submit or report their daily progress to their teachers.

Figure 5.4 Tahfiz students lining up after performing *magrib* prayer to submit their daily memorisation to their teachers (Ar. *mudarris*) in the main hall of Masjid Jami. Photo by Wahyuddin Halim.

The main role of teachers (Ar. *mudarris*) in the tahfiz programme is to routinely check that each student's memorisation conforms fully with the text. Every night after evening prayer (except Saturday night), each student sits face-to-face with a teacher and recites those parts of the Qur'an memorised within the last 24 hours. If he makes mistakes or misses parts of the verses being memorised, his teacher will correct him. If he makes too many mistakes, he may be required to resubmit, performing the same portion the following day, meaning that he failed to make progress that day. A student may also be advised and warned about the possible negative factors that are hindering his progress. Muhammad Yahya told me that the most difficult challenge and disruption for tahfiz students today is the use of the mobile phone. There is no strict regulation about what the tahfiz students should and should not do in their dormitories; they are free to do whatever they want as long as they appear in the mosque and submit their progress after evening prayer (*isya*).

In many cases, tahfiz students spend time in Internet cafes located near or around Masjid Jami, updating their Facebook status or surfing the Internet, which may include sites with pornographic content. The deputy director and some of the teachers of TQMJ complained to me that, exposure to malign images and videos would potentially affect the purity of their souls and minds, regarded as indispensable for Qur'anic memorisation. Although Internet-enabled mobile phones were formally prohibited by the programme, at the time of my research it was evident that some tahfiz students owned the latest smartphone with multimedia features to access the Internet and display pictures or play videos which may, as the director mentioned earlier, obstruct their progress.[14]

All teachers of the tahfiz programme are themselves hafiz. The most senior teacher and director, Al-Hafiz H. Muhammad Yahya (88 years old), serves as the grand master responsible for overseeing all tahfiz teachers and the progress of the students. He is assisted by a few junior teachers who have completed programme under his direction. Teachers at TQMJ are not paid in cash, but received services and gifts from students and their families when a student has completed the programme. However, H. Abdullah Mustafa, the deputy director of TQMJ, told me that in the last five years the director, his deputy and teachers of TQMJ have received a monthly incentive or honorarium from the Central Executive Board of As'adiyah, the umbrella institution that coordinates the programme. The amount, however, is very small and far from enough to be taken as the main source of monthly income.[15] But, given that teaching Qur'an memorisation is considered a noble task in Islamic tradition, teachers often receive services and gifts (money, meals, clothes) from the Muslim communities in and around Sengkang. For example, H. Muhammad Yahya told me that people from Sengkang and beyond frequently came to his house with groceries or cooked food.

H. Muhammad Yahya has worked as a teacher in this programme since 1972 and acted as director since 1975. Students coming to study under his guidance hope to acquire the blessing of being with him. Many teachers and students in South Sulawesi consider Muhammad Yahya as the most senior and charismatic tahfiz teacher in the region and other teachers often recommend that their students go to him in order to finish the last stage of their Qur'anic memorisation.

According to data for 1975 to 2005, students of TQMJ came from the provinces of Riau, Jambi, East Kalimantan, Central and Southeast Sulawesi, and the Moluccas. However, the largest number of students came from the South Sulawesi districts of Wajo, Bone, Soppeng, Pinrang, Luwu, Bantaeng, Gowa and Bulukumba. Most of these students were born into a Bugis family, either in South Sulawesi or in the diaspora. Other students came from Makassar-speaking districts such as Bantaeng and Gowa, but after a while came to speak Bugis fluently.

There are different motivations for these students to join the tahfiz programme. Some have been amazed and inspired by the performance of a student or graduate of this programme as imam tarawih, leading communal prayers in their home village during the month of Ramadan. When leading the prayer an imam recites lengthy verses of the Qur'an fluently and beautifully without the aid of a text. Some mentioned their dreams to become ulama in the future for which, according to them, the ability to memorise the whole Qur'an is an important, if not a required qualification. Other students mentioned the Prophetic tradition (*hadis*) pertaining to the great value of memorising the Qur'an and the great reward granted by God for those who achieve this.

From my interviews with many tahfiz students, I found another stimulus for these students to become memorisers of the Qur'an, that is, to win the Indonesian contest in reciting (*tilawah*), memorising (tahfiz) and interpreting the meaning (*tafsir*) of the Qur'an, popularly known as Musabaqah Tilawatil Qur'an or MTQ. The winners in the different skills sections in MTQ not only obtain popularity and appreciation from the Muslim community but also gain valuable material rewards (*hadiah*) from the organising committee. Many of the MTQ winners at national and international levels have been recruited as government employees (PNS) at national and local levels. It has become a tradition that the winners in different Qur'anic skills in MTQs at national level have been granted a pre-arranged pilgrimage to Mecca (haj) or, at least, a lesser haj pilgrimage (*umrah*) outside the 12th month Dhu al Hijjah.

A significant number of TQMJ students have won MTQs in district, provincial and national levels. Some national MTQ winners have gone on to succeed at the international level. Martomo Malaing, for example, was twice MTQ winner of the 20- and 30-chapter segments at district and provincial levels (2003 and 2005); winner and runner-up at the national level (2003 and 2005); third place in the international MTQ in Mecca in the 20-chapter segment (2003);

and second place in Libya in the 30-chapter segment (2005). Another graduate from TQMJ with an international reputation, Ihsan Ashari, won fourth place in an international MTQ in Mecca in 2003 in the segment of 20 chapters when he was only 15 years old and also in 30 chapters segment in the international MTQ convened in Dubai, UEA, in 2006. Humaidi Ali won fourth place in the 10 chapters segment of the international MTQ conducted in Egypt in 2006 (Surur 2011b: 394–5).

Training and Producing Permanently-assigned Imams

Many students and graduates of TQMJ are appointed as imam rawatib or permanently-assigned imam, especially in Sengkang but also other places beyond Sengkang and even South Sulawesi. By tahfiz "student" I mean one who is still participating in the memorisation programme in TQMJ on a daily basis which, as noted, can take between one to five years.[16] To be eligible for assignation as an imam tarawih a tahfiz student should have already memorised at least five chapters of the Qur'an. By tahfiz "graduate" I mean one who has memorised the whole Qur'an and been conferred with the title *al-hafiz* at a graduation ceremony. The main objective of these ceremonies is an open examination of Qur'anic memorisation by the tahfiz students being conferred the title hafiz. Two ceremonies usually take place: at TQMJ for all students from Sengkang; and a celebration with family in the home of a graduating student.[17]

The expectation to become an imam rawatib acted as an important motivation for children aged 12 to 15 to become hafiz. Although according to Islamic jurisprudence (*fikih*), the ability to memorise the whole Qur'an is not a formal requirement for a person to lead communal prayers, having such ability is preferred by mosque organisers and community members. It is still common that in South Sulawesi, many mosques appoint imam rawatib because he is the oldest member of the mosque or considered to be the most pious among others, and not because of his apparent beautiful Qur'anic recitation or extensive memorisation. The trend today, however, is that more mosques in Indonesia, particularly in urban areas, seek out hafiz to "hire" as imam rawatib for a period of time, for example, on a monthly or annual basis. Some hafiz eventually become permanent imams in such mosques.

I asked AGH Abunawas Bintang whether assigning young people, such as students of a tahfiz programme, as imam rawatib and imam tarawih had a normative textual foundation in Islam. He referred to the fact that even during the Prophet Muhammad's life time, teenagers like 'Abdullah ibn 'Umar (c. 614–93) had been given the opportunity to lead prayers. He also pointed to the fact that AGH Muhammad As'ad, at around the age of 17, had been appointed as imam tarawih at al-Haram mosque in Mecca for three consecutive years, on the basis of his fine memorisation and recitation of the Qur'an.

During research in Sengkang in 2012, I observed that almost all of the city mosques engaged imams who were either current students or graduates from tahfiz programmes of As'adiyah, except for the mosques aligned with the reformist Muhammadiyah organisation (with the notable exception of Masjid al-Ikhlas). Several of the mosques employed two to three such imams for different communal prayers. These imams received monthly salaries ranging from IDR 1,500,000 (approximately AU$150) to IDR 2,500,000 (AU$250). The *imam besar* (grand imam)[18] of Masjid Agung (the Grand Mosque) Ummul Qur'an in Sengkang, for example, was entitled to IDR 2.5 million (AU$250) as monthly wages plus IDR100,000 (AU$10) as a weekly honorarium for leading the Friday congregational prayer, and an additional IDR 7 million (AU$700 per month) for leading tarawih prayers during Ramadan. The mosque community often provides the imam with a place to stay, usually a small room attached to the mosque. In Sengkang, most imams rent houses near the mosque, but if their house is further away they commute to the mosque by motorcycle.

In Sengkang in particular, besides serving as imam rawatib many imams also attend school or university or teach in a Qur'anic learning centre for small children (*taman pendidikan al-Qur'an* or TPA). In such cases, the post of imam rawatib is temporary. Sudirman, for example, an imam rawatib in Nurul Muhajirin mosque in the north of Sengkang since 2010, told me that while serving as imam he also attended the As'adiyah Islamic College (Sekolah Tinggi Agama Islam As'adiyah). He had already graduated from As'adiyah Islamic Junior High School (Madrasah Aliyah) and attended tahfiz Qur'an in the grand mosque Ummul Qura for two years during his studies in madrasah, but could only memorise ten chapters. Coming from a low-income family in the district of Jeneponto on the south coast of South Sulawesi, about

270 kilometres from Sengkang, his college tuition fees came from his monthly honorarium as imam rawatib. When imam rawatib like Sudirman have finished their school or university studies, they usually look for a permanent job such as teacher, lecturer or civil servant. They can still, however, serve as imam rawatib if their permanent job is in the same location.

During fieldwork I visited a number of other district capitals in South Sulawesi. I observed that many mosques, especially the district mosques which are usually called *masjid raya* (great mosque), have graduates of tahfiz programmes of As'adiyah as their imam rawatib. I also observed that in the provincial capital of Makassar many mosques have imams who are alumni from tahfiz programmes of As'adiyah. This is even more evident during the fasting month of Ramadan.

Today, like other places in Indonesia, many district capitals in South Sulawesi also have a "grand mosque" (*masjid agung*).[19] Most have at least one imam from the tahfiz programme of As'adiyah. For example, Abd. Waris Ahmad, a graduate of As'adiyah tahfiz programme in Ongkoe, Belawa, is the current imam rawatib of Masjid Agung Ummul Qura in Sengkang, Wajo. Imam of Masjid Agung of the district of Bantaeng, Masjid Raya of the district of Bulukumba, and Masjid Raya of Makassar municipality are hafiz produced by tahfiz programmes of As'adiyah. Moreover, several alumni of TQMJ serve as imam rawatib outside South Sulawesi, even in Jakarta. For example, H. Martomo Malaing and H. Ihsan Ashari, the TQMJ alumni with international reputations mentioned above, have been serving as imam rawatib in Jakarta since 2010 and 2011 respectively. Martomo is one of the seven official imams in the state mosque of Istiqlal in Jakarta. Ihsan is the imam in the official mosque of Mahkamah Agung (the High Court) in Jakarta.

The story of Ihsan Ashari serves as an example of a "successful" hafiz from TQMJ. His success in winning a number of MTQs at district, provincial, national and international levels has inspired many young children, particularly from his home village in Langnga, in the district of Pinrang, South Sulawesi, to come to Sengkang and attend TQMJ. Ihsan won several national MTQ contests (held in Palangkaraya, Central Kalimantan in 2003 and in Gorontalo in 2005), and won fourth place at an international-level competition held in Mecca in 2003. Ihsan completed his tahfiz programme in Masjid Jami within two years, eight months and ten days and graduated in 2002.

After he graduated from TQMJ in April 2002 he left Sengkang for Jakarta to become imam rawatib in the Indonesian High Court (Mahkamah Agung) mosque. Ihsan was 23 when he accepted this position. Shortly after he completed his memorisation at TQMJ, aged 22, Ihsan married a young woman from Sengkang whose parents were among the well-off in that city.

In Bugis cultural practice, where a young man of modest origins marries a woman from a wealthy or aristocratic family, the groom is required to pay a large sum of money to the bride's family as bridewealth (Bug. *dui' menre*) and wedding party expenses (Bug. *dui' balanca*) (see Millar 1989). In the case of Ihsan, the marriage payment was not considered an issue as his "in-laws" had high respect for his status as hafiz.[20] In other words, Ihsan's Qur'anic memorisation became the priceless gift of the groom to the bride, acting as compensation for the large cash sum usually submitted by the groom's family as bridewealth. In order to maintain the respect of the bride's family and relatives, however, Ihsan gave them $3,000 (IDR30 million) from his own savings derived from MTQ prizes. Ihsan and his bride's wedding, while simpler than usually practised, was well attended by many guests.

I learned in interviews with tahfiz students from Pinrang district and their teachers, that the aspiration to follow Ihsan Ashari's career acts as one of the most important stimuli for becoming hafiz, and choosing TQMJ. Some students admitted that their parents had strongly encouraged them to take this course as Ihsan's achievement in respect to his astonishing talent in Qur'anic memorisation and recitation was renown among village residents in Langnga, Pinrang. Ihsan's career has been taken by many parents as an exemplary model that their teenage children should emulate.

Hence parents' hope for their children to become memorisers of the Qur'an may not be motivated solely by religious meaning, that is, to receive great reward in the hereafter, or to gain the respect of the Muslim community as the parents of Qur'anic memorisers. As a hafiz can generate a significant amount of income (at least as a part-time job) by his participation in MTQ, as well as by becoming imam rawatib or imam tarawih (as explained next), memorising the Qur'an and the appointment of "professional imams" may be considered as constituting, what Greg Fealy (2008: 16–17) has called, "Islamic commodification" in contemporary Indonesia.

There are many interesting stories concerning the appointment of graduates from As'adiyah tahfiz programmes as imam rawatib. Darto Gunadi, a graduate of TQMJ from sub-district Belawa, Wajo, was sent in 2011 to become imam tarawih in the grand mosque (Masjid Besar) Manuntung, Margasari, subdistrict, Balikpapan Barat, East Kalimantan. At the end of Ramadan, the mosque community wanted him to stay and become imam rawatib. They sent a formal request to the director of As'adiyah, who replied that Darto should first return to Sengkang and get permission from his parents. And because he was also doing his undergraduate study in a university in Pare-Pare, South Sulawesi, the director also suggested that Darto should first finish his undergraduate study before accepting the offer. A month later Darto moved to Balikpapan with a promise from the mosque community that they would fully support him to continue his undergraduate programme in an Islamic college in Balikpapan. The mosque community provided him with a place to stay near the mosque and a motorcycle. For his service as imam rawatib, Darto received around IDR 2.5 million (AU$250) as monthly salary and IDR 100,000 (AU$10) weekly incentive for leading the Friday congregational prayer. The director of As'adiyah and the deputy director of TQMJ recounted similar stories from communities in South Sulawesi and beyond.

Providing Imam Tarawih

According to the deputy director of TQMJ, H. Abdullah Mustafa, the annual programme to send tahfiz teachers and students to serve as imam tarawih began during the leadership of AGH Yunus Martan (1961–86). During Ramadan he would take one or two of his students who were hafiz and who had the most fluent and beautiful Qur'anic recitation to join him in his frequent visits to give religious sermons in mosques in Wajo and beyond. This student would lead tarawih prayer after the religious sermon given by AGH Yunus Martan.

As far as H. Abdullah Mustafa could remember, this programme became formalised from around 2000. Before that, selection and appointment of imam tarawih was done via direct personal communication between tahfiz programme students with mosque officials or through the personal network of alumni of tahfiz programmes. Since then, responding to many requests from the mosque officials in Wajo and beyond, one or two days before the first day of the month of

Ramadan, the director of TQMJ annually dispatches hundreds of tahfiz students, graduates and teachers to become imam tarawih. For mosques located within Sulawesi, tahfiz use land transport (bus) to get to their placement, and those from Southeast Sulawesi take the ferry from the port of Bajoe in Bone or Siwa in Wajo. For places such as East Kalimantan and Papua or West Papua, students travel by plane or ship. In most cases, they will travel alone or with one or two fellow tahfiz students who are placed in mosques located in the same district. Travel expenses are paid by the mosque officials who have invited them, usually transferred to their bank account in advance.

This placement of tahfiz students is regulated by the director, H. Muhammad Yahya. They usually stay in the house of one of the mosque officials. For several years, it has been the policy of the director of TQMJ to avoid sending a tahfiz student to become imam tarawih in the same place for two consecutive years. This policy is strictly implemented especially when the host community requests the same tahfiz student to become imam tarawih at the same mosque for two

Figure 5.5 *Imam tarawih* and *mubalig* (preachers) ready to be dispatched from the As'adiyah complex in Lapongkoda, Sengkang, to their places of duty in 2012. Photo by Wahyuddin Halim.

consecutive years. This policy is intended to avoid the recurrence of cases where a tahfiz student is requested to marry a local girl by her parents or/and the mosque community as a means for retaining him permanently to serve as imam rawatib in their mosque.

For their service as imam tarawih, these students normally receive an honorarium from the mosque community (*jemaah masjid*). The exact amount is never predetermined nor based on a mutual contract between the two parties. The director and deputy director of TQMJ told me that when they receive a request for imam tarawih from a mosque official (usually by mail or phone call), they ensure that the official will pay at least the current standard minimum honorarium to their students, which in 2012 was IDR 3.5 million (AU$350). However, a few tahfiz students revealed to me the amount received for acting as imam tarawih during Ramadan in 2012. I have estimated that on average they received IDR 5–10 million (AU$500 to AU$1,000). In addition to the honorarium, the mosque community often gives gifts, such as clothes, cakes, rice, fruit and other local specialties.

Another interesting tradition has emerged whereby tahfiz students are accompanied back to their home villages after their Ramadan placement in Wajo and surrounding districts such as Bone, Soppeng, Sidrap and Luwu. I could not get a clear answer as to when this became a ritualised practice, however. After the imam tarawih have finished their task, the mosque officials and community members will escort them back to their parents' homes, instead of to their school dormitory in Sengkang. Usually their final task as imam tarawih is to lead the Idul Fitri prayer in the early morning of the first day of Syawal (the Hijri month following Ramadan). The mosque community will rent one or two cars, usually 12-seat mini buses, to accommodate members of the mosque community who want to participate in the journey. The convoy may travel up to several hundred kilometres to meet the parents and close families of the imam in order to express their gratitude and appreciation for the excellent service the young imam has given to them. The cars are often loaded with rice, fruit, vegetables, eggs and other seasonal foods to bring to the home of the imam's parents.

H. Abdullah Mustafa reported that for Ramadan 2012 (coinciding with July–August), while 200 requests were made for imam tarawih, only 100 could be provided. The requests came from the provinces of Papua, West Papua, Southeast Sulawesi, Central Sulawesi, West Sulawesi, East Kalimantan and Riau (Sumatra). In most cases, the requests came from Bugis migrant communities who knew about TQMJ or had maintained a good relationship with As'adiyah by, for example, sending their children to study in As'adiyah religious education programmes in Sengkang. If their requests for imam tarawih cannot be met by the director of TQMJ, the mosque organisers usually turn to other institutions in South Sulawesi with smaller tahfiz programmes.

During Ramadan, the five daily prayer times are heightened and intensified because far more members of the Muslim community attend mosques than in other months, in particular, during the tarawih prayer. I observed in several mosques in South Sulawesi that, in the performance of tarawih, the entire Qur'an is read through over the course of Ramadan. It is not clear to me, however, whether this practice is found elsewhere in Indonesia, when a hafiz is taken as imam tarawih. What is clear is that in such mosques, the need to hire a hafiz as an imam, with a fluent and beautiful recitation is an imperative. There is a practical reason for this too. An important factor that attracts people to a particular mosque for tarawih prayer is the beautiful recitation (*tilawah*) of the imam tarawih. Good imam tarawih or imam rawatib usually come from a tahfiz programme such as those organised by As'adiyah because, students also learn to read according to the *tajwid* (Bug. *mattajawi'*) system. This is the rigorous system of vocalisation for correct Qur'anic recitation. Although not taught formally in TQMJ, students are encouraged to learn *tilawah* or technical aspects of proper recitation of the Qur'an independently or from other teachers of the Qur'an. Most tahfiz students of TQMJ utilise digitised Qur'anic recitation available on electronic devices such as mobile phones and mp3 players.

To some extent, mosque officials compete with each other; the greater the attendance for tarawih prayers, as well as the five communal daily prayers, the deeper the sense of communal blessing in the month of Ramadan. Also the more people attending tarawih prayer, the more numerous the donations for mosque maintenance as Muslims are especially motivated to give charity during Ramadan. Several verses of the Qur'an and the Prophetic traditions (*hadis*) mention the multiplicity of God's rewards for those who have performed good deeds and actions during Ramadan, including giving charity. Usually money is placed in the donation boxes (*kotak amal*) provided by the mosque at each entrance or circulated by the mosque officials to people coming to perform tarawih prayer. In several mosques, during Ramadan the donation box is also circulated after every one of the five daily congregational prayers.

A mosque official in Sengkang told me that, in the past, due to the limited number of mosques there were fewer options for tarawih prayer, or congregational prayers in general. For example, in the subdistrict (*kecamatan*) of Tempe, which includes the city area of Sengkang, the capital of Wajo district, there were only three mosques in the 1930s, including the one renovated and expanded by the local ruler for AGH Muhammad As'ad to use as a place for his halaqah learning sessions (discussed above). According to data from the Central Statistics Centre Bureau in 2011, there were 62 mosques and 10 prayer houses (*musholla,* not used for Friday congregational prayer). Today in Wajo, in a small village (*desa* or *kelurahan*) of 1,000 persons, for example, we can typically find at least four mosques.

How have the tahfiz programmes of As'adiyah become the most popular source for imam tarawih and imam rawatib in eastern Indonesia? The reason is related to the wide network of As'adiyah alumni. Requests to TQMJ for imam tarawih come mainly from mosques located in places where there are a significant number of alumni of Pesantren As'adiyah or parents whose children have spent some time studying in madrasah managed by As'adiyah, in Sengkang and elsewhere. The people of Wajo are well-known for their mobility and outward migration into widely scattered regions of the Malay world since the 16th century, particularly for the reasons of escaping political unrests and uplifting their economic and social status (see Lineton 1975). Large numbers of migrants—and their descendants—from Wajo can be found today in places such as Jambi and Riau in the island of Sumatra and many places in East Kalimantan, Central and Southeast Sulawesi, Papua and West Papua (see Bakti 2010).

The As'adiyah alumni network has played a significant role in maintaining the relationship between the people in the Wajo heartland and those in the diaspora. This relationship is maintained in many ways but mainly through the sending back of children from the diaspora to study in Pesantren As'adiyah and the recruitment of As'adiyah alumni into the roles of *mubalig* and imam in distant migrant places as far as Merauke in West Papua to the east, to Poso and Luwuk Banggai in Central Sulawesi to the north, and to Riau and Jambi in

Figure 5.6 A group picture of students of TQMJ with their director and teachers (Oct. 2012). Photo by Wahyuddin Halim.

Sumatra to the west. As'adiyah alumni often become pioneers in the establishment of mosques in a newly-opened village area and then become its first and permanent imam and *khatib* (that is, the male person who preaches the sermon in the Friday congregational prayers) due to their well-known competence in religious knowledge from years of studying in Sengkang. The assignment of As'adiyah students and alumni as *mubalig* and imam tarawih to many (including remote) places in different parts of Indonesia has become one of the most effective ways to encourage prospective students in those places to enrol in pesantren and madrasah of As'adiyah in Sengkang.

Concluding Remarks

Since its establishment in the early decades of the 20th century, As'adiyah has played an important role in the dissemination and spread of Islamic reform in Wajo in South Sulawesi and among Bugis across the archipelago. There are two particular fields in which this role can be observed.

Firstly, in the field of Islamic education, As'adiyah pesantren and madrasah—in which the teaching of different branches of classical Islamic knowledge has been given great emphasis—have been influential in producing new generations of Muslims scholars (ulama) in

South Sulawesi. Most of the influential ulama in South Sulawesi in the 20th century were students of AGH Muhammad As'ad, the founder of As'adiyah, or graduates of the madrasah (al-Madrasah al-Arabiyah al-Islamiyah or MAI) he established, which later became Pesantren As'adiyah.

Secondly, As'adiyah has played a fundamental role in Islamic proselytisation (*dakwah*). From the early days of his arrival in Sengkang from Mecca, AGH Muhammad As'ad was primarily concerned with the Muslim community in Wajo whom he perceived as still believing and practising elements of pre- and non-Islamic belief. His efforts were mainly directed at transforming the life of the Muslim community in Wajo to be in conformity with the Islamic orthodoxy as prescribed in Islamic scriptures and its classical interpretations by ulama. Beside his direct involvement as a religious preacher and teacher, As'ad started his halaqah (religious learning circle) as well as *tahfiz al-Qur'an* (Qur'anic memorisation) programme to transform the traditional practice of Islam in the Wajo community.

Through his religious learning institutions, MAI and later Pesantren As'adiyah, AGH Muhammad As'ad introduced a new tradition: that those assuming the role of imam rawatib and imam tarawih should be qualified as hafiz (the memoriser or preserver of the Qur'an). In effect this prerequisite sidelined the custom of the past that an imam should be the eldest and most pious (*takwa*) among the mosque community, or someone descended from a line of imams (initially appointed by the Bugis ruler), regardless of his competence in Qur'anic recitation and memorisation. Today, if someone has memorised most, if not all, parts of the Qur'an and has reached maturity (*balig*), he would be considered the most competent to become an imam.

The role of imam in Bugis mosque communities has long been a voluntary or unpaid job; the spiritual value and social reputation that an imam obtains from serving the community in the mosque are believed to be incalculable. In the era of independent states (sultanates) in South Sulawesi such as Gowa, Bone and Wajo, elements of sharia were incorporated into their political systems, and mosque functionaries such as imams were appointed by the rulers. The local Muslim community, however, managed to partially support the livelihoods of these mosque functionaries in various ways, for example by giving direct donations (mainly in the form of livestock) or through religious charity (*sedekah*) and annual alms-giving (*zakat*).

It can be seen in the case of the imam how As'adiyah, through its religious education, has challenged the forms of religious authority associated with the customary courts (see Kathryn Robinson, this volume and Adlin Sila, this volume). Now, religious authority, such as required by mosque functionaries for practical religious tasks, can be attained by any person from all social classes within the community provided that they hold a recognised qualification in Islamic knowledge. In addition to forging new bases of religious authority, in contemporary Indonesia, leading congregational prayers both as imam rawatib and imam tarawih has become an income-generating activity and part of the Islamic religious economy.

Notes

1. In this chapter, As'adiyah refers to the broad context of this religious institution as a social and religious institution which includes, most importantly, the *pesantren* and *madrasah* (see footnote below). "Pesantren" literally means "place of the *santri*"; an Islamic boarding school. Pesantren is derived from the word *santri* meaning "student" (Dhofier 1999). In many parts of Indonesia, however, the pesantren system of education assumes different names.
2. The term "imam" is used this chapter in its limited sense as the male who leads congregational prayer (*salat Jumat*) in the mosque or other places used for the same purpose. An imam in the broader sense can also perform the tasks of the *imam salat.* However, a person appointed as *imam salat* is not permitted to perform the broader functions of imam (although this occasionally occurs) due to it being a formal religious position in the Muslim community.
3. The job is sometime called "professional" since it is actually a "paid" job although the payment is not normally considered "salary" but "honorarium" or "incentive" since, as far as Islamic doctrine is concerned, the task is considered as part of the religious ritual which should be exercised with sincerity and spiritual purpose.
4. From Arabic, "'*ulamaa*'" meaning "learned"; the term used for Islamic religious leaders or learned scholars. In this study, ulama (its Indonesian form) is used to indicate both singular and plural. In Javanese society, these scholars are commonly called *kiai* or *kyai* (see Geertz 1960; Dhofier 1999).
5. *Madrasah* is an Indonesian term originating from the Arabic which means "schools". The *madrasah* system is common in many Muslim countries since the beginning of the 12th century (Dhofier 1999). The

first *madrasah* in Indonesia was established in 1906 (Yunus 1979). Today it refers to Islamic religious schools of a modern type which teach mainly religious and some secular subjects.

6. For a detailed description of how fasting and other special rituals during the holy month of Ramadan become highly esteemed by Javanese Muslims in particular, or by Indonesian Muslims in general, see Möller (2005).
7. Before its integration into the Republic of Indonesia in 1946, Wajo was one of the seven major traditional polities in present-day South Sulawesi province, which existed from around the end of the 14th to the early 20th century, when it was vanquished by the Dutch (see Pelras 1996).
8. Found in many parts of the Islamic world, this old model of learning requires students to sit around a teacher, listening and making notes while the teacher is reading, translating and explaining the meanings of a book on Islamic knowledge written in Arabic. In Indonesia this book is usually referred to as *kitab kuning* (yellow book) due to the yellow colour of the paper used in this type of book. For a comprehensive discussion of the importance of *kitab kuning* in the Indonesian pesantren milieu, see van Bruinessen 1990.
9. As'adiyah derives from the Arabic world *As'ad* (also the last name of Muhammad As'ad) which literally means happiness, fortune, or luck, plus *iyah* (*ya' al-nisbah* in Arabic) now meaning the follower or the people of As'ad.
10. "AG" is an abbreviation of the Bugis term "*anregurutta*" (literally "our great teacher") used to refer to senior ulama. The letter H (for haji) indicates that the person has performed the haj pilgrimage to Mecca (see Bosra 2008). AGH preceeding the name of respected Bugis ulama stands for Anregurutta Haji.
11. Religious officials (Bug. *parewa sara'*) in the era of the Bugis sultanates were in charge of conducting Islamic rituals and festivals: mosque officials (in the mosques); *qadi* (the highest religious authority and official within the kingdom); imam (prayer leader); *khatib* (preacher in Friday prayer); *bilal* (the person who calls the congregants) and *modin* (responsible for mosque wellbeing) (see Pelras 1996; also Bosra 2008). Since Independence, religious affairs are managed by the Ministry of Religious Affairs (Kementerian Agama) through its provincial, district and sub-district office levels.
12. Several small centres for learning the basic teachings of Islam, including how to read and memorise the Qur'an, had existed since the second part of the 19th century (see Hamid 1983: 380). Most of them were conducted in the house of an ulama and only a few in the mosque or transformed into learning centres similar to what is called pesantren today such as the one in Pulau Salemo of Pangkep (As'ad 1989).

13. The term "*barekka*'" is frequently mentioned in ordinary conversations, classroom instructions, religious speeches and the religious works of ulama from As'adiyah. For ulama, teachers and students in Pesantren As'adiyah, the meaning of *barekka*' is much more complex than the popular English translation "blessing". In general, *barekka*' is used primarily to refer to blessing from God which can attach itself either to people like Muslim saints such as As'ad himself or to places such as the Jami mosque. People in Sengkang, like Muhammad Yahya, the director of TQMJ, believes that as a Muslim saint, As'ad possessed *barekka*' in extraordinary quantity, even after death, which can be transferred to others through the act of learning in his *madrasah* and in his mosque. Other words associated with the term *barekka*' are abundant good effect, long-lasting effect (such as in Qur'anic memorisation), less effort but more result (such as pursuing worldly affair), less in quantity but having much more benefit (as in the case of wealth) (for a detailed discussion on the importance of *barekka* in Pesantren As'adiyah, see Wahyuddin Halim 2015: 154–8).
14. The tahfiz students were not excluded from a growing trend among most Indonesian youth to own a smartphone and spend much time playing with it. Some of these students sent me Facebook (FB) friend requests after I finished my fieldwork in 2012, and invited me to join their special FB group for TQMJ students. Students used their smart-phones to go online and update their FB status. Among the topics of discussions or postings on their FB groups were the plan for reunion, fund raising for their programme and teachers, sharing information about new imam placement and recruitment, information about upcoming tahfiz contests and sharing information and photos about activities in and around the Jami mosques related to tahfiz programme. For a more detailed exploration of the engagement of As'adiyah's pesantren community (including TMQJ students) with social media, see Halim (2018).
15. According to Abdullah Mustafa the monthly incentives are: director (IDR160,000 or AU$16), deputy (IDR147,000 or AU$15), and teachers (IDR112,000 or AU$11). As a comparison, these amounts were far below the minimum monthly salary usually received by a madrasah teacher in Pesantren As'adiyah (around IDR700,000–1,000,000 [AU$70–100]).
16. When the research for this paper was conducted in 2012, nine months was the record for memorising 30 chapters of the Qur'an in the history of TQMJ programme, accomplished by Muhammad Iqbal Natsir.
17. Examiners usually comprise the director of TQMJ and his deputy, and often the director of As'adiyah when he is also present. The three examiners first read some verses (*juz*) from the Qur'an selected randomly and then instruct the candidate to continue reciting the verse and some

following verses without the aid of the opened text. Next, the candidate is asked to identify the name of the particular chapter being read and its location within the standard Qur'anic text (*mushaf*), specifically, the page number, left or right page, top or bottom of the page, and so on.

18. "*Imam besar*" is the official title for an imam who is in charge of leading all communal prayers and other religious rituals conducted in a grand mosque (*masjid raya* or *masjid agung*) in the district capital.
19. Naming a mosque "grand mosque" (*masjid agung*) is a new phenomenon in Indonesia. In the past, people only recognised a great mosque (*masjid raya*) as an "official" or state mosque located in the district or sub-district capital. "Grand mosque" nowadays indicates either a newly-built, bigger and better architecturally-designed mosque in the district capital or a newly-renovated longstanding great mosque (*masjid raya*).
20. Qur'anic memorisation by the groom, valued in the bride price, has a precedence in the life of the Prophet Muhammad. In a *hadis* narrated by Sahl bin Sa'd As-Sa'idi, one of the Prophet's companions, a poor man, believes he has nothing to offer as a bridal gift to the woman he wants to marry. The Prophet asked the man if he knew some chapters of the Qur'an. The man replied, "I know such *sura* [Qur'anic chapter] and such *sura*", proceeding to count them. The Prophet asked further, "Do you know them by heart?" To which the poor man replied, "Yes". The Prophet said, "Go, I marry her to you for that much of the Qur'an which you have" (*Sahih Bukhari* 7:62:24). Muslihin, a graduate of the As'adiyah tahfiz programme in Ummul Qura mosque told me a story of the wedding ceremony of his close friend in the district of Bone, South Sulawesi. On the day of the marriage ceremony, the groom started reciting the Qur'an from memory (or without the aid of a text) beginning after the dawn prayer (*subuh*) almost until the time of the evening prayer (*magrib*). This recitation was attended and checked by the extended relatives of the bride. Only after the bride's parents had witnessed the groom's perfect and comprehensive memorisation of the Qur'an could the marriage ceremony be performed.

References

Ahmad, Abd. Kadir. 2008. *Ulama Bugis.* Makassar: Indobis Publishing.

Al-Bone, Abd. Azis. 1987. *Peranan Kyai di Sulawesi Selatan (Studi Kasus KHM As'ad di Sengkang Wajo).* Jakarta: Pusat Penelitian dan Pengkajian, Pengembangan Pesantren dan Masyarakat (UnitE-P3M) Pesantren Ciganjur.

Arief, Syamsuddin. 2008. *Lokalitas Islam: Dinamika Islam dan Jaringan Pesantren di Sulawesi Selatan.* Yogyakarta: LKiS.

As'ad, Muhammad. 1989. "Sejarah Sosial Pulau Salemo." In *Persepsi Sejarah Kawasan Pantai*, ed. Mukhlis, 128–37. Ujung Pandang: P3MP Universitas Hasanuddin.

Azra, Azyumardi. 2004. *The Origins of Islamic Reformism in Southeast Asia: Networks of Malay-Indonesian and Middle Eastern 'Ulama' in the Seventeenth and Eighteenth Centuries*. Crows Nest, NSW: Asian Studies Association of Australia in association with Allen & Unwin; Honolulu, HI: University of Hawai'i Press.

Bakti, Andi Faisal, ed. 2010. *Bugis Diaspora di Alam Melayu Nusantara*. Makassar: Ininnawa.

Biro Pusat Statistik Kabupaten Wajo. 2011. *Kabupaten Wajo dalam Angka 2011*. Sengkang: BPS-Wajo.

Bosra, Mustari. 2008. *Tuang Guru, Anrong Guru dan Daeng Guru: Gerakan Islam di Sulawesi Selatan 1914–1942*. Makassar: La Galigo Press.

Dhofier, Zamakhsyari. 1999. *The Pesantren Tradition: The Role of the Kyai in the Maintenance of Traditional Islam in Java*. Tempe, AZ: Monograph Series Press, Program for Southeast Asian Studies, Arizona State University.

Eickelman, Dale F. 1978. "The Art of Memory: Islamic Education and its Social Reproduction." *Comparative Studies in Society and History* 20 (4): 485–516.

Fealy, Greg. 2008. "Consuming Islam: Commodified Religion and Aspirational Pietism in Contemporary Indonesia." In *Expressing Islam Religious Life and Politics in Indonesia*, ed. Greg Fealy and Sally White, 15–39. Singapore: Institute of Southeast Asian Studies.

Gade, Anna M. 2004. *Perfection Makes Practice: Learning, Emotion, and the Recited Qur'an in Indonesia*. Honolulu: University of Hawai'i Press.

Geertz, Clifford. 1960. "The Javanese Kijaji: The Changing Role of a Cultural Broker." *Comparative Studies in Society and History* 2 (2): 228–49.

Halim, Wahyuddin. 2015. "As'adiyah Traditions: The Transformation and Reproduction of Religious Authority in Contemporary South Sulawesi." PhD diss., The Australian National University.

———. 2018. "Young Islamic Preachers on Facebook: Pesantren As'adiyah and its Engagement with Social Media." *Indonesia and the Malay World* 46 (134): 44–60.

Hamid, Abu. 1983. "Sistem Pendidikan Madrasah dan Pesantren di Sulawesi Selatan." In *Agama dan Perubahan Sosial*, ed. Taufik Abdullah, 323–457. Jakarta: Rajawali Press.

Ismail, Daud. 1989. *Al-Ta'rifu bi al-'Alimi al-'Allamah al-Haji Muhammad As'ad al-Bugisy*. Ujung Pandang: Bintang Selatan.

Lineton, Jacqueline Andrew. 1975. "An Indonesian Society and its Universe: A Study of the Bugis of South Sulawesi (Celebes) and their Roles within a Wider Social and Economic System." PhD diss., School of Oriental and African Studies, University of London.

Manguluang, H. Hamzah. 1990. *Ana wa Syaekhi (Riwayatku dan Mahaguruku).* Sengkang: n.p.

Mattulada. 1983. "Islam di Sulawesi Selatan." In *Agama dan Perubahan Sosial*, ed. Taufik Abdullah. Jakarta: Rajawali Press.

Millar, Susan B. 1989. *Bugis Weddings: Rituals of Social Location in Modern Indonesia.* Berkeley: Center for South and Southeast Asia Studies, University of California at Berkeley.

Möller, André. 2005. *Ramadan in Java: the Joy and Jihad of Ritual Fasting.* Lund, Sweden: Department of History and Anthropology of Religions, Lund University.

Nasir, M.H. 2005. "Efektifitas Metode Pembelajaran Tahfiz Al-Qur'an As'adiyah di Masjid Jami' Sengkang Kabupaten Wajo." Master's diss., Universitas Muslim Indonesia, Makassar.

Pasanreseng, Muh. Yunus. 1992. *Sejarah Lahir dan Pertumbuhan Pondok Pesantren As'adiyah Sengkang.* Sengkang: Pengurus Besar As'adiyah.

Pelras, Christian. 1996. *The Bugis.* Oxford: Blackwell.

Surur, M. Bunyamin Yusuf. 2011a. "KH. As'ad bin KH. Abd. Rasyid Al-Buqisy: Perintis Ulama Huffaz di Sulawesi Selatan (1907–1952)." In *Para Penjaga Al-Qur'an: Biografi Huffaz Al-Qur'an di Nusantara*, ed. Muhammad Shohib and M. Bunyamin Yusuf Surur, 483–513. Jakarta: Lajnah Pentashihan Mushaf Al-Qur'an Badan Litbang dan Diklat, Kementerian Agama RI.

______. 2011b. "Pondok Pesantren Tahfiz Al-Qur'an As'adiyah, Sengkang, Wajo, Sulawesi Selatan." In *Memelihara Kemurnian Al-Qur'an: Profil Lembaga Tahfiz Al-Qur'an di Nusantara*, ed. Muhammad Shohib and M. Bunyamin Yusuf Surur, 377–407. Jakarta: Lajnah Pentashihan Mushaf Al-Qur'an Badan Litbang dan Diklat, Kementerian Agama RI.

van Bruinessen, Martin. 1990. "Kitab Kuning: Books in Arabic Script Used in the Pesantren Milieu". *Bijdragen tot de Taal-, Land- en Volkenkunde* 146 (2–3): 226–69.

______. 1998. "Muhammad As'ad Bugis [Wajo, South Sulawesi, Indonesia, 1907–1953]." In *Dictionnaire Biographique des Savants et Grandes Figures du Monde Musulman Périphérique, du XIXe Siècle à Nos Jours, Fasc. no. 2*, 22–23. Paris: CNRS-EHESS.

Walinga, Muh. Hatta. 1981. "Kiyai Haji Muhammad As'ad hidup dan perjuangannya" [KH Muhammad As'ad's life and struggle]. Honours thesis, IAIN Alauddin (State Institute of Islamic Studies), Makassar.

Yunus, H. Mahmud. 1979. *Sejarah Pendidikan Islam di Indonesia.* Jakarta: Mutiara.

6

Negotiating a Space in the Mosque

Women Claiming Religious Authority

Eva F. Nisa

Introduction

In Indonesia the main significance of the mosque has been as a locus for praying; however, there has been a continuous effort to revitalise its function, including on campuses, to mirror the role of the mosque in the time of the Prophet Muhammad in which it served as a community centre. During that period, the religious, social and political lives of Muslims were centred in mosques which functioned as a public space for education, *dakwah* (proselytisation), politics and social interaction (see also Wahyuddin Halim, this volume; Nakosteen 1964; Zaimeche 2002).

This chapter focuses on female university students in Makassar, who are followers of contemporary Islamist and Salafi movements that acquire spaces in university mosques. There are a growing number of such movements, attracting followers in Indonesia, especially among young university students; and this has led to contestation over space in campus mosques. In this chapter, I explore the role of university mosques in accommodating diverse versions of Islamic understandings and practices. University mosques can be seen as a representation in miniature of the multiple voices of Islam in Indonesia and how Muslims accommodate these voices.[1]

Almost all local and transnational Islamist and Salafi movements in Indonesia have established university campus mosques as sanctuaries to spread their influence.[2] An important moment was the emergence of campus Islam in the 1980s.[3] During this time many university students became interested in Islamic movements, with either Sunni or Shi'i based ideology. One of the best-known and largest university-based movements using campus mosques was the Tarbiyah Movement or Gerakan Tarbiyah (Education Movement) (see Fealy and Hooker 2006: 48) which used the Salman Mosque at Bandung Institute of Technology as its main locus of activities. Young students attracted to this movement were inspired by the ideas of Islamic revival initiated in Egypt by Hasan al-Banna (1906–49) and Sayyid Qutb (1906–66) of Ikhwan al-Muslimin/Ikhwan al-Muslimun (The Muslim Brotherhood) and, to a lesser extent, by Abu al-A'la Mawdudi (1903–79) of the Jama'at-i-Islami in Pakistan (Fox 2004: 10). The young, urban, educated youth in this study associate themselves with the Islamic study groups of Islamist and Salafi movements (Tarbiyah[4], Hizbut Tahrir Indonesia or HTI[5], and Salafi factions[6]). Islamism refers to "ideologies and movements that strive to establish some kind of an 'Islamic order'—a religious state, sharia law, and moral codes in Muslim societies and communities" (Bayat 2013: 4). The term "Islamist movement" refers to a diverse spectrum (see Mandaville 2007; Ayoob 2008; Bayat 2013), ranging from legal political parties (for example, Partai Keadilan Sejahtera [Prosperous Justice Party, or PKS] in Indonesia and Partai Islam Se-Malaysia [the Malaysian Islamic Party, or PAS] in Malaysia)[7] and oppositional movements (for example, HTI), to a political strategy not only to redefine Islam and what being a true Muslim entails, but also to implement sharia.

In addition to their attendance at lectures, the lives of some university students have been centred on and shaped around their activities in religious study circles (*halaqah* or *halqah*[8] also known as *usroh* or *usrah*[9], *liqo*, *keputrian*, *mentoring*[10], *taklim*, *tarbiyah*[11], *kajian*[12] and *pengajian kelompok*[13]). Female students are more visible than male students in informal campus mosque religious circles. Much of the writing on "campus Islam"[14] has neglected the role of women, however. Many scholars have argued that women are victims within these kinds of movements (see Othman 2006: 339) in which patriarchal powers are apparent. However, nowadays a number of scholars have begun to argue that religious revival movements have empowered women in numerous ways (for example, Mahmood 2005; Deeb 2006; see also Nisa 2012a, 2012b; Rinaldo 2013). Women's inclusion in prayer spaces and leadership is regarded as detestable by some male Muslim clerics, hence, the presence of female Muslim activists in university mosques is the result of a progressive effort by women to have a public abode there. In this chapter I address this trend in which young Muslim women at universities have felt empowered by their activities in the mosques and their attachment to their religious movement.

I draw on one year of ethnographic fieldwork that I conducted among student activists belonging to Islamist and Salafi movements in Makassar. The city of Makassar was not chosen randomly. While I have observed female university students in other campus mosques in different cities, particularly Jakarta, West Java and Yogyakarta, I found that the dynamism of women's activities in Makassar differs from activities in other cities, particularly due to the presence of the Makassar-based Salafi movement, Wahdah Islamiyah, which is very active in recruiting young followers (see Nisa 2012a). Their goal was to spread their influence among university students who are committed cadres and achieve their goal of forming branches in all large cities in Indonesia by 2015. Wahdah's zeal in gaining new recruits and cadres in universities has caused other Islamist movements, including other Salafi groups, to become more competitive. Hence, the dynamism of activities in campus mosques is more robust than in other cities. Many university mosques, in Jakarta, West Java and Yogyakarta, for example, are divided along lines of ideological affiliation. When a university mosque aligns with a certain group other groups will usually try to build their "nests" elsewhere, in mosques close to the universities, or *musholla* (prayer halls) on university campuses. (Similar dynamics are to be found in mosques in Western countries, usually divided along ethnic, racial and sectarian lines [see, for example, Shannahan 2014: 131].) This chapter focuses on how university mosques in Makassar accommodate diverse Islamic understandings and practices. I argue that, rather while in competition for followers they also manifest "imagined solidarity" (Bayat 2005) that binds different Islamist movements based on their "imagined commonality" (2005: 901).

Figure 6.1 Students at the campus mosque in Makassar. Photo by Eva F. Nisa.

Campus Mosque Activism and the Emergence of Women Activists

The birth of informal Islamic study clubs and religious circles at Indonesian campus mosques and prayer halls occurred as a direct response by university students to a policy issued by the Suharto regime in 1979; Normalisasi Kehidupan Kampus (NKK, the Normalisation of Campus Life), which aimed to control student political activity. From the late 1960s to the mid-1980s, the Suharto regime took a harsher attitude than previously towards Islamic groups (Liddle 1996: 614; see also Crouch 1981). This suppression led to students choosing to become active in small Islamic study clubs and study circles rather than attending public gatherings and activities, such as demonstrations and orations (see also Machmudi 2008: 116).

The activity of female students in university mosques became more visible during the 1980s and onwards, coinciding with the emergence of campus Islam and the broader phenomenon of the post-1970s resurgence of piety across the Muslim world. This could be seen through young Muslim women adopting *jilbab* (or "tight veil"), a new version of head covering in Indonesia.[15] Female students active in campus religious study circles popularised the adoption of Muslim dress (see Brenner 1996: 673; Robinson 2009: 172; Amrullah 2008: 22). These young female students became known as *aktivis dakwah kampus* (campus proselytisation activists) in their group Jemaah Tarbiyah (the Education Movement) inspired by the Middle Eastern Muslim Brotherhood. In 1998, it formed the Islamist political party Partai Keadilan or the Justice Party, which, from April 2002, has been known as Partai Keadilan Sejahtera (PKS, the Prosperous Justice Party).

Women's Inclusion in Mosques

The presence of female Muslims in mosques is regarded by ultra conservative Muslims as a violation of a legal consensus made by Muslim jurists—Sunni and Shi'ite—during the formative period of Islamic law (see Sayeed 2001: 10). Women, especially those who are young and/or attractive should keep a distance from mosques to avoid *fitnah* (sexual temptation which can lead men to sin) caused by their presence (see also Sayeed 2001: 10).[16] As a result, females are less visible than males in many mosques, not only in Indonesia (see Shannahan 2014: 126; Woodlock 2010: 51). Women are more likely to be present in rituals related to major religious festivals, such as Idul Fitri and Idul Adha prayers (see also Shannahan 2014: 127), the celebration of the Prophet's birthday, and His Isra Mi'raj (Miraculous Night Journey).

Recent scholars have studied women's access to mosques (Sayeed 2001; Reda 2004; Melchert 2006; Holmes-Katz 2014) and their mosque-based activities (Jaschok and Jingjun 2000; Aryanti 2013), including the debate on how mosques have enabled the production of a certain pious self (Mahmood 2005; Frisk 2009) and discussion of women's leadership and gender justice (Hammer 2012; Aryanti 2012; Hoel 2013). Some studies have also focused on the architecture of women's space (*maqsuurah*) in the mosques (Dişli 2015). I take up these discussions in this chapter and address how young Muslim women in diverse campus movements in Makassar negotiate and shape the public sphere to adjust to their Islamist and Salafi agendas.

An important finding of this study is the role of campus mosques in producing "imams" from female university students, and how these future female "imams" have monopolised campus mosques in Makassar.

In this context I employ "imam" not to mean the leader of a mosque or the leader of prayers but turn to other definitions of imam. The Qur'an uses the term seven times in its singular form "imam" and five times in plural form "*a'immah*", referring to diverse meanings such as leader (the Qur'an 2:124, 21:73, 28:5, 32:24) and revelation as religious guidance (the Qur'an 46:12, 11:17). The term "imam" in this chapter also refers to religious and socio-religious leaders. The female students whose activities centre in the mosque can be regarded as future leaders of their Muslim communities. Like the women in Saba Mahmood's (2005) study of women's pietist movements in Egypt, the young female students in this study engage in the project of ethical formation or moral cultivation to become better Muslims. They do this by being active in campus mosques, including in religious lessons. Mahmood describes the women who participate in pietist movements as docile agents, criticising the Western feminist tradition that frames agency as resistance to patriarchal domination. This notion of human agency, according to Mahmood, is not suitable to understand "the lives of women whose desire, affect, and will have been shaped by non-liberal traditions" (Mahmood 2001: 203). She uses the term "docile agency" to refer to ways the women intentionally "seek to cultivate virtues that are associated with feminine passivity and submissiveness…" (Mahmood 2001: 203). Following Michel Foucault and Judith Butler, in her explanation of resistance, Mahmood contends that "[k]ey to this formulation is what Foucault calls the paradox of *subjectivation:* the very process and conditions that secure a subject's subordination are the means by which she becomes a self-conscious identity and agent" (Mahmood 2001: 17). Mahmood's emphasis on the two paradoxes: the *paradox of subjectivation* and the *paradox of piety*, however, has been challenged by Pnina Werbner who suggests the third paradox: the *paradox of (ascetic) self-denial* (2018: 81). Werbner argues "[i]n my view, … her analysis misses the fact that like other proselytizing fundamentalist movements, in this one, too, self-fashioned virtue is ultimately activist, claiming new spaces for women" (2015: 230–1). Further, Werbner contends:

> Mahmood … denies that women in the mosque movement are motivated in any simplistic sense by a 'desire for autonomy or gendered equality in the feminist liberal sense'. While accepting her argument that binaries of submission or resistance gloss over the complexity of

> the women's project, we need also to recognise, following Foucault, that embodied, ascetic self-denial and self-mastery may lead, paradoxically, to a capacity for power and authority over others (2018: 86).

Echoing Werbner, I argue that young Muslim women's activities around campus mosques, especially those activities of religious study circles can be regarded as a way to claim religious authority and challenge the status quo of male Islamic authority.

Mosques and Women's Mobility

Many scholars (Milani 1992; Göle 1997; and Deeb 2006, 2009) have argued that the discussions about women's visibility, mobility and voices are the main issues relating to the public sphere in Muslim countries. Conservative Muslims tend to control women's participation in the public sphere, for example, through the prohibition of *ikhtilat* (the social mixing between men and women). There is also a tendency for commentators to regard Islamist movements as social movements that control the public visibility of Muslim women. For example, Nilüfer Göle contends that, "[g]ender issues, such as communitarian morality, women's modesty, and the social mixing between men and women, are central to Islamist politics' desire to differentiate itself from modernist liberal projects and Islamists' endeavors to control the public sphere" (1997: 63). Her work demonstrates how Islamist politics in Turkey have endeavoured to control women's public visibilities (Göle 1997: 63).

Attempts to restrict women's mobility is problematic if implemented in Indonesia. Kathryn Robinson (2009: 175) asserts that women in Indonesia have enjoyed great freedom to be active in the Indonesian public sphere and Islam has not historically been used to limit women's mobility in public (Robinson 2004: 195). Therefore, it is not uncommon to see many women members of groups active in Indonesian public spaces.[17] The presence of female students in campus mosques is also part of Muslim women's visibility in the Indonesian public sphere. Many Muslim communities regard mosques as male-dominated places (see also Hammer 2010). Mosque attendance by women has been an important point of discussion for Islamic jurists: hotly debated because the Qur'an does not address this issue. Since the second century AH (Anno Hegirae, the base year for the Islamic calendar, which is 622 CE) to the modern period, Sunni and Shi'ite jurists have emphasised that it is preferable that women's prayers are conducted in the mosque (Sayeed 2001: 10). However, later developments show that the most prominent jurists of Sunni *mazhab* (schools of law)—Hanafi, Maliki, Shafi'i[18] and Hanbali—oppose the presence of women in mosques for fear of *fitnah*. This is especially emphasised for young female Muslims because they are attractive. Therefore for some jurists, the presence of young female students in campus mosques can be considered a significant violation of *fikih* (Islamic jurisprudence). However, in Makassar it is young female students who tend to "monopolise" the campus mosques.

It is worth noting that there are alternative opinions among Muslim jurists on this issue. The most famous originates from Ibn Hazm of Zahiri mazhab who based his opinion on one of the Prophet's sayings (*hadis*) that congregational prayers are preferable by 27 degrees; meaning the reward is 27 times greater than solitary prayers, in God's eyes (Sayeed 2001: 10). According to Ibn Hazm, this *hadis* is not specific to men. He also mentioned that during the Prophet's lifetime, women prayed in the mosques. Indeed the Qur'an does not specify that access to the mosque is for men only. QS. 7:31, mentions: "O children of Adam! Take your adornment to every mosque". This verse demonstrates that attending a mosque is not solely men's activity.

Proponents of women's attendance in mosques also argue that historical accounts of mosque architecture demonstrate that women may be seen in that space. Nevin Reda (2004) mentions that between the years 610–32, during the prophetic ideal period or the beginning of the Prophet Muhammad's career, there was no evidence of segregation or limitations on women's access (2004: 77). Reda argued, "In the Makkan and Madīnan periods, houses surrounded the courtyard [where people prayed] and no barriers separated the men from the women. Even the sacred space was not enclosed by a wall" (2004: 81). Further evidence of women's inclusion in the mosque is the presence even today, of female and male pilgrims without segregation in the most crowded mosque in Mecca (Reda 2004: 81). Segregation emerged during the reign of the second Caliph (634–44), Umar b. Khattab (Reda 2004: 77; Melchert 2006: 59). It can first be seen in the presence of a separate compartment in Jerusalem's al-Aqsa mosque, which was regarded as the most important mosque built during its time (7th century). During this period some scholars began to prevent women from accessing mosques (Reda 2004).

What about nowadays? Although the Prophet Muhammad provided women and men equal access to mosques, gender constraints often exist nowadays. Akel Ismail Kahera argues that "[i]n many traditional Muslim societies, a set of rigorous, male-formulated rules restricts the use of the mosque by women" (2002: 15). Mahmood (2005) also mentioned that in Egypt mosques are by and large male-dominated places. In the 1950s, however, Zaynab Al-Ghazali (1917–2005), a prominent female figure within the Muslim Brotherhood circle, began giving lessons in mosques. According to Mahmood (2005) such activities did not continue after her death until the emergence of the mosque movement.

The presence of women in mosques has been the main struggle articulated by many Muslims, including Muslim feminists and activists. For example, Juliane Hammer argued that Muslim women's inclusion in American mosques means the embodiment of "gender-just interpretation of the Qur'an" (2010: 26). The effort of Amina Wadud to oppose male-dominated mosque leadership by becoming the imam (prayer leader) and *khatib* (preacher) in a mixed-gendered congregation is, therefore, considered a response to the exclusion of women from the main space of mosques as well as from leadership positions in mosques and Muslim communities (Hammer 2010: 27).[19]

In Indonesia, some religious leaders and scholars advocate limiting the presence of women in mosques. According to one of the heads of Forum Komunikasi Majelis Ta'lim (Communication Forum of Islamic Study Gatherings), Ustazah Uun Maimunah, the majority of female religious gatherings in Jakarta are not located in mosques. Rather they are held in either *musholla* (prayer halls) or in the houses of *ustazah* (female preachers) or congregants where women can serve as leaders of other women and exercise religious authority. Therefore, across Indonesia, there are some *musholla* constructed specifically to accommodate Muslim women's gatherings and congregations. An example of this is the establishment of a women's mosque for Aisyiyah (the women's wing of Muhammadiyah) in 1922, which aimed to provide a separated women's space for public worship to avoid *ikhtilat* (Aryanti 2012: 378). Thus, the way female students use campus mosques in comparison to male counterparts can be regarded as a

Figure 6.2 Female students at their weekly religious programme held in the campus mosque. Photo by Eva F. Nisa.

new current in the development of the mosque in Indonesia, and of women's rights.

Mosque Crisis: Young Muslim Women as the "Imam"

In Indonesia the mosque is often seen as in crisis as some of them struggle to attract congregants. Some mosques are increasingly used only for prayer. There is a tendency for people to only attend mosques at certain times, in particular for Friday congregational prayers and, sometimes, the daily Magrib prayer, as well as during the first weeks of Ramadan. Therefore, one of the Indonesian government's campaigns regarding the development of mosques is "*meramaikan masjid*" (enliven the mosque) and "*memakmurkan masjid*" (make the mosque prosperous). This kind of mosque crisis does not hold true, however, when we consider campus mosques, especially their female sections in Makassar.

In her critique of Mahmood's ideas of docile agency, Werbner draws on Foucault's concept of the ethical subject, arguing that these women's ascetic self-discipline and discursive knowledge will enable

Figure 6.3 Male students of HTI in a special (not regular) public discussion on the caliphate. Photo by Eva F. Nisa.

them to gain power in the religious sphere (2010: 253). "Much of the pedagogical effort women invest in regular mosque lessons and courses is devoted to the acquisition of literacy in classical Islamic texts and hermeneutical traditions which, over time, qualifies them to act as instructors of other women" (Werbner 2010: 253). The experience of the zealous female activists of university campuses resonates with Werbner's view. The small religious circles that they have formed have produced leadership positions amongst them.

The women maximise their share of mosque space to conduct their religious activities. Their dedication to using the mosque as religious sanctuary far exceeds that of their male counterparts. Ima, a 25-year-old student at UIN (Universitas Islam Negeri or State Islamic University) Alauddin Makassar, said: "It is very rare to find male informal religious circles during the day, Kak (sister). The mosque is always packed with us [female students]." During one of the focus group discussions that I conducted with students, many young men admitted that female religious circles outnumbered those of men. This phenomenon aligns with studies mentioning that women are more active in religious attendance than men (Miller and Stark 2002;

Hackett et al. 2016). Mumtaz, an 18-year-old male student of UNM (Universitas Negeri Makassar or Makassar State University), shared his thoughts: "Male students also have informal religious circles [in the mosque]. Usually, we hold them very late in the afternoon or sometimes there are also some circles at night. However, it is true the number of our religious circles is far less than those of females."

Women attaching themselves to Islamist and Salafi movements can be regarded as manifestating their "public piety", to borrow Lara Deeb's (2009) concept. Their activities are located in the public sphere and can be regarded as part of their contribution to the common good or to the development of dakwah for their own groups (see Deeb 2009: 249), due to their eagerness to ask others to be closer to Islam. The activities of these young students also express "active piety" which for Bayat characterises "those who not only practice their religion, but also preach it, wanting others to think and practice like them" (Bayat 2005: 894).

The trend found in five big universities in this study: UNISMUH (Universitas Muhammadiyah Makassar), UMI (Universitas Muslim Indonesia), UNM, UIN Alauddin Makassar and UNHAS in Makassar, demonstrates three primary religious affiliations popular among students: Wahdah Islamiyah; HTI;[20] and KAMMI[21] (Kesatuan Aksi Mahasiswa Muslim Indonesia, the Indonesian Muslim Student Action Union) which was founded by activists of Jemaah Tarbiyah in 1998.[22] Unlike in the early years, nowadays informal religious circles of these Islamist and Salafi movements exist not only at state universities but also at Islamic universities (see, for example, Arifin 2005: 123).

Why Join Such Movements?

There were plenty of answers to this question. Students most often mentioned, first and foremost, peer pressure. Qia, a 21-year-old student, shared her experience: "I know the HTI religious circle because many of my friends in my rented house are HTI followers. They often asked me to join, so eventually I followed their advice." The second most common reason was the methodology of learning Islam in a particular group. These informal religious circles commonly offer learning step-by-step based on the knowledge of the disciples. Most of the followers argue that the study circles in the campus mosques have a simpler and easier curriculum compared with the well-established

Muslim mass organisations, such as Nahdlatul Ulama and Muhammadiyah. Maziya, a 19-year-old student, recounted: "If I want, I could also join an Islamic study circle around my neighborhood, like *majlis taklim* [Islamic gathering for learning Islam]. Unfortunately, the themes discussed in *majlis taklim* are usually too advanced for me." Many of the students who joined this kind of religious circle had been exposed to such circles in their high schools. Their low levels of Islamic learning differ from those students graduated from *pesantren* (Islamic boarding school) or *madrasah* (Islamic school) traditions who have stronger and more thorough understandings of Islam.

The eagerness of students attending Islamic study circles to become better Muslims is facilitated through meticulous self-monitoring of their weekly religious achievements. This form of supervision aims at controlling the participants' individual piety, such as whether they perform the recommended prayers, read the Qur'an, and perform recommended fasting. This kind of control might seem too demanding for some Muslims. Alika and Jannah, however, stated: "We need this kind of controlling, Kak.[23] It encourages us to stick to our religious routine. In addition to this, the evaluation of our attendance has made us aware that we have to be consistent and serious in learning Islam to be better Muslim women." Some study circles have a scheduled test, such as that of Wahdah Islamiyah (see Nisa 2012a). Some demand that under-performing students repeat their level of study, to maintain quality assurance.

Thirdly, the method of organising the disciples or groupings is also an important factor for the participants. They are grouped according to their level of understanding. Newcomers usually feel insecure if they attend the conventional *majlis taklim* where there is no such structure. Usually, the maximum number of participants in one religious circle is limited to 5–10 disciples in order to ensure meticulous supervision by one mentor, a senior activist who has a higher level of Islamic knowledge.

The majority of students who choose to be active in dakwah of Islamist and Salafi movements are new students, in their first to fourth semesters of study. Their activities in the mosques provide them succour and relief from the anxiety of being newcomers on campus, and from their sense of alienation and dislocation. The university mosque plays a significant role in "protecting" them from the campus lifestyle, often strange to them. It has enabled them to find new friends, new sisters in Islam, and new mentors who are able to act as their confidants and provide spiritual comfort from the anguishes of life.

When these students feel that their hearts are committed to the study circles, their condition is like that of the pious women in Mahmood's study (2005). They will voluntarily adopt the norms introduced by their religious circles as part of their self-fashioning, including adopting a strict Islamic bodily regime for the sake of inculcating Islamic virtues, especially modesty and being better Muslim women (see also Mahmood 2005: 129–30). This is evidenced in the way these young women adopt their religious circles' distinguishable "uniform" or standard of modesty. Women of Wahdah Islamiyah, for example, wear a thick, somber, long *abaya* (a long sleeved, full-length garment) or *jubbah* (a head-to-toe wrap, like an open coat) and veil. Many also wear the *cadar* (face-veils) (see Nisa 2012a). The majority of female activists of another Salafi group in Makassar, known as MANIS, wear a thick, somber, long *jubbah* or *abaya* and *cadar* in black. Female followers of HTI wear long *gamis* (a head-to-toe wrap) and long colourful veils, while followers of Jemaah Tarbiyah wear a long skirt and top, sometimes *gamis* and long colourful veils. All of these different styles of attire express the movements' understandings of proper Muslim dress.

Passing and Competition among Diverse Voices

Many of the students whom I met had experienced moving (*hijrah*) from one movement to another before they committed to a particular group. Ni'ma, for example, initially joined Pengkaderan Muhammadiyah (Muhammadiyah Caderisation) called DAD (Darul Arqam Dasar). Her university (UNISMUH) had a policy that required all students to join this *pengkaderan* (caderisation programme) which encompassed training based on Muhammadiyah ideology. After joining DAD, she tried Wahdah Islamiyah. Her "journey" ended up at HTI. She said of her current affiliation: "*Insya* Allah (If Allah wills) I will be *istiqaamah* (committed) with HTI, but not sure [smiling]." Maziya has had a different experience from Ni'ma. She is now a committed supporter of HTI. However she also occasionally joins activities of Wahdah Islamiyah. She said that she has to try out diverse groups as part of her journey to find one where she feels accepted. Maziya, therefore, can be regarded as a "nomadic follower" or seeker of the

Figure 6.4 A flyer typically found in campus mosques. Photo by Eva F. Nisa.

most appropriate religious sanctuary, eager to try diverse religious movements. I discovered many "nomadic followers" in Makassar, such as Khadijah, a 21-year-old student who I met in the KAMMI study circle. She recounted her journey: "I am now in between Wahdah and KAMMI, Kak. But I think I am a lot closer to KAMMI." I found the phenomenon in Makassar differed from what I had found in previous research on young female students in Jakarta and Yogyakarta (Nisa 2012b). Not only are there diverse study circles of different religious groups occupying one mosque, but associated with this there are many "nomadic followers", neither of which I found in Jakarta or Yogyakarta.

For these "nomads" a campus mosque is akin to a "buffet" where they can try diverse meals before finally deciding on their favourite. The temptation to move from one circle to another is facilitated by the presence of numerous flyers (see Figure 6.4) inviting those who want to experience and learn something new or more Islamic about Islam. Wahdah Islamiyah, as a Makassar-based Salafi organisation, is particularly important. It is a well-organised Muslim mass organisation that strives hard to win the hearts of Muslims. It has its own Forum

Muslimah Dakwah Kampus (Muslimah Forum for Campus Dakwah). At the time of my field research, Forum Muslimah Dakwah Kampus envisioned the establishment of campus dakwah throughout Indonesia by 2015, through Muslimah student associations that follow the ideology of Ahli Sunnah Wal-Jamaah.[24]

Wahdah Islamiyah is popular due to its ability to offer thorough teachings of Islam. Although it has a literalist and strict understanding of Islam, in the Makassar map of dakwah it can be regarded in the middle of two major poles of dakwah organisations: the political and apolitical Islamist groups. It is known among the students that the two groups that represent political Islam are Jemaah Tarbiyah (PKS) and HTI. Two groups that do not have a political agenda, according to many of them, are Wahdah and MANIS,[25] another famous Salafi group in Makassar. Although they are both known as Salafi groups that focus more on individual piety, Wahdah is perceived by many as being the more moderate group, and as having a clearer direction for developing the Muslim community (Nisa 2012a).[26]

It is widely believed among activists in informal religious circles that the mentors in MANIS and Wahdah Islamiyah have more thorough understandings of Islam than those of other groups, so some activists of HTI and Jemaah Tarbiyah also join their study circles to "charge" their Islamic knowledge. Those who decide in the end not to be part of MANIS or Wahdah do so mainly because they oppose some of their literalist interpretations of Islam, their strict code of conduct and the nature of their indoctrination. This resonates with Bayat's argument that this kind of disagreement is born from two sources: "divergence of interests and/or in interpretations" (2005: 901).

There is intense competition among the Islamist and Salafi movements to gain influence at campus mosques in Makassar and all have the same target: new university students. The cadres feel the competition strongly, and it is exacerbated by the many nomads. Maryam, a 19-year-old student, was typical in her experience:

> I have tried all the different religious study circles on campus, but I ended up with the Salafi group (MANIS) because it suits my conscience. I can find my new life and new me through the guidance of my current mentors. I feel that this is the real Islam. For me, other groups are too busy with worldly matters, especially power and politics, such as Wahdah,[27] PKS or KAMMI and HTI.

Nomadic followers will usually experience social punishment from their previous group. It is common nowadays, however, to see certain participants move from one circle to another. Hamidah said: "I often *hijrah* [move] from one circle to another. My mentor knows. She tried to approach me. But I think she should not limit my effort to find a more correct Islam".

Negotiating Your "Spot"

What can be seen from these future female "imam" and their activities is that they try to negotiate their own spaces and influence in the mosques. Everyday campus mosques are busy with religious study groups with different affiliations, and many study groups are also held during weekends and long holidays. Some universities are known as the hub of certain groups.[28] Wahdah Islamiyah, for example, is known to have a strong foothold at the UNHAS campus mosque. At UMI, HTI has more female followers than other religious groups. It is understood that this is because UMI has been very important in the history of the advent of HTI in Makassar. Activists of LDK (Lembaga Dakwah Kampus or Islamic Campus Predication) at UMI played a significant role in the dissemination of HTI ideology in Makassar (see also Rijal 2011: 256).[29] Followers of KAMMI, on the other hand, are spread throughout these five universities. These Islamic study circles have all found convenient places to conduct their Islamic studies, and in every mosque there are de facto spots in corners or verandahs for specific groups. At UMI, for example, HTI uses the ground and second floors of the mosque, while KAMMI uses the opposite side of the second floor, and Wahdah uses the third floor of the mosque.

Wahdah Islamiyah is the motor that has shaped the dynamics of campus mosques in Makassar, due to its systematic and intensive mode of Islamic learning. Members of Wahdah Islamic study circles are classified based on their competency and need to pass examinations to move from one level to another. Many young Makassarese have responded positively to this strict method. This has resulted in Islamist groups becoming concerned about the possibility of losing recruits. Therefore, the competition for space in mosques has intensified in Makassar.

Despite the fact that each of these groups cannot reach consensus regarding certain points, in particular religious issues, members and

Figure 6.5 Female students greeting and talking to each other before their *halaqah*. Photo by Eva F. Nisa.

supporters strive to respect each other's choices. Inside campus mosques, students can be seen greeting congregants of other religious circles and shaking each other's hands prior to leaving. Therefore, although they are different in certain ways, they believe that they have a shared goal—namely to develop dakwah and strengthen Islam on campus. The place is important in this context: they understand that the mosque is a symbol of Islamic unity and this is a key factor that enables the encounters of different groups to be peaceful.

They are certainly not a monolithic bloc: some groups are political and others are apolitical. Those that engage in politics, such as PKS and HTI for example, have different agendas. PKS strives to change the Indonesian nation to become more Islamic by being inside the system; while HTI chooses to struggle for its Islamist political agenda outside the system of formal politics. However, despite their conflicting positions on many issues, the groups can accept each other's presence in the mosque due to their shared "imagined solidarity": each of the movements aim for the betterment of Islam and the life of Muslims, and the implementation of sharia Islam. They also believe that Islam is the solution (*al-Islaam huwa al-ḥall*) to a range of contemporary problems, and that Muslims need to learn their religion to have better understandings of the importance of Islam in all aspects of their lives. Thus, they have "*partially* shared" interests, to borrow Bayat's concept (2005: 902). Bayat argues that this concept of imagined solidarities in some Muslim countries has brought the agents to work and act together, such as in the case of Iran's Reform Movement (2005: 902). The partially shared interests among these campus-based Islamist and Salafi study circles have brought active agents in these study circles to act together, for example in organising events or dialogue.[30] In contrast, in spite of their partially shared interests, there are also "harsh" rumours and gossip concerning the shortcomings of differing study circles. These kinds of disputes are understood to be a consequence of the practice of "active piety" (after Bayat [2005]). "Active piety" leads to the members of these Islamic study circles seeking recruits and competing with other groups to find followers.

Conclusion

Muslim youth, especially female students, are active participants in maintaining the dynamic functions of campus mosques. Students in Makassar are known to be active in voicing their aspirations, including religious aspirations. The inter-group competition among diverse Islamist movements and the presence of Makassar-based Salafi groups that have gradually won traction from Makassarese Muslims, have resulted in intensifying competition between Islamist and Salafi groups. Female cadres play a key role in strengthening the influence of each group.

Women are the most visible agents in the public settings of university mosques in Makassar. In many campuses, mosques cannot be regarded as exclusive male spaces. This can be seen as a progressive development. The presence of women in the mosques can be the point of departure to see how, in recent times, campus mosques are being used in the same way as at the time of the Prophet, namely, not only as the locus for worship. A campus mosque is especially important for newcomers who do not have any affiliations or feel "lost" in the campus lifestyle and need to increase their self-esteem. These campus mosques often adopt the role of "schools" or "homes" where these women not only learn about their religion but also self-fashion themselves by learning to inculcate Islamic virtues. Their mastery of religious knowledge can lead to public religious leadership positions, at least among women within the movements. These women's mastery of religious knowledge has placed them as the source of authority, not only within their mosque study circles, but also outside the study circles, albeit still within their own movement. In Indonesia, Muslim youth have become the backbone of various Islamist and Salafi groups, especially the groups which took shape in the late 1970s and 1980s. Therefore, all Islamist and Salafi movements in this study view the campus mosque as an important and strategic public space in the dissemination of their ideologies. The campus mosque is akin to a free, open pulpit that is able to accommodate diverse ideologies. However, it is noteworthy that religious activities in campus mosques in Makassar are more dynamic than those of campuses in other parts of Indonesia, mainly because of the presence and significant growth of the Makassar-based Salafi movement, Wahdah Islamiyah. The contestation over orthodoxy and the question of what are true Islamic teachings propagated by diverse Islamic groups in Makassar is more robust. This can be seen in the topography of every campus mosque space in Makassar. The everyday presence of Islamic study circles in campus mosques indicates that each group needs to maintain a strong influence within the universities of Makassar.

The seeds of Islamist and Salafi movement ideologies in Indonesia have developed from university campuses. Further, for some groups in Makassar, women are not the epiphenomenon of their movements. Their movements have appealed to many interests *grâce à* women's active piety.

By virtue of their religious authority enabled by the university mosques these women are positioned to become the future "imam" of other female Muslims. The establishment of Muslimah (female Muslim) institutions within the campus environment affiliated with HTI, Tarbiyah Movement, and diverse Salafi movements, including Wahdah Islamiyah, illustrates an overarching phenomenon of the growth and dynamics of such movements in Indonesia. In comparison, the informal religious circles of mainstream Muslim mass organisations, such as Muhammadiyah and Nahdlatul Ulama, are far less popular among the young female activists of campus mosques.

Through the mastery of the knowledge gained via the lessons they attend, these women have initiated an important change through which they can gain the power and privilege of influencing their sisters in Makassar. Their activities in religious study circles in mosques have enabled them to become qualified to transfer religious knowledge to others. Through their dakwah calling, hundreds of cadres and future cadres are trained in and subsequently start similar activities in their campus mosques around Makassar. There is the potential that the presence of these informal religious circles and the birth of these new female imams could change the map of Islamist and Salafi movements in Makassar in the future. Such changes may happen very quietly within the campus mosque. Signs include the presence of zealous female cadres, including alumni of universities around Makassar, who attend their alma mater mosques to help "produce" female imams. Hence, the campus mosques have become active sites for the development of future female imams.

Notes

1. Wiktorowicz (2002: 196) argued that the mosque, for diverse Islamist groups, has played a significant role as the "religio-spatial mobilizing structure".
2. This includes the nation's radical movement, Darul Islam/DI (Domain of Islam), that successfully recruited students to be part of the *usrah* (lit. family) or discussion groups (see Fealy 2004: 111).
3. During this period, Indonesia also witnessed the spread of Shi'ism among university students, especially those at Indonesia's state universities, who were influenced by the success of the Iranian revolution in 1979 (see Zulkifli 2013: 38).
4. The movement emerged in the mid-1980s (see Machmudi 2008).
5. HTI is the Indonesian chapter of Hizbut Tahrir/HT (Party of Liberation) which first appeared in Indonesia in the early 1980s (Ward 2009: 150) and was banned by the Indonesian government in July 2017. The aim of the establishment of HT is to revive a global Islamic Caliphate on the basis of sharia (see Fealy 2004; Ward 2009; Muhtadi 2009; Osman 2010).
6. The Salafi movement was founded in the 18th century. The root of classical Salafism, however, can be traced back to the thoughts of Taqi al-Din Ahmad Ibn Taymiyya in the 14th century and Ahmad Ibn Hanbal in the 9th century. The Salafi movement started to become perceptible in Indonesian campuses in the 1990s (see van Bruinessen 2002: 134; Fox

2004: 11 f.26). It is a movement that calls for a return to the foundational text of Islam and purifying Islam as was practised by the Prophet Muhammad and his companions (see DeLong-Bas 2004; Meijer 2009). The Salafi movement consists of diverse factions. The current three major factions are: purist, political and jihadi. For more discussion on diverse Salafi factions, see Wiktorowicz (2006), Mandaville (2007) and Meijer (2009).

7. In 1996, Asef Bayat introduced the term "post-Islamism" to describe an emerging trend within political Islam (2013: 7), elaborating the main differences between Islamism and post-Islamism as follows: "[w]hereas Islamism is defined by the fusion of religion and responsibility, post-Islamism emphasizes religiosity and rights. Yet, while it favors a civil and nonreligious state, it accords an active role for religion in the public sphere" (2013: 8). PKS is also categorised as a post-Islamist party that has shifted its attention "from establishing an Islamic state to focusing on *maqāsid al-Sharīʿa* ([Ar.] the purposes of the divine law) as the real objective of Islam, which it defined in terms of justice, good governance, and human rights" (2013: 15; see also Hasan 2013).
8. The term *halaqah* is often used by HTI's small study group. The activity within this *halaqah* is called *kajian/ngaji* (learning Islam).
9. This is a small secretive religious circle or discussion group inspired by a model of the Muslim Brotherhood style cell.
10. The terms *liqo*, *keputrian* and *mentoring* are mostly used interchangeably by followers of Jemaah Tarbiyah at Indonesian schools and campuses. The terms refer to their weekly religious circles (see Damanik 2002). However, it is also known by some of the followers that *mentoring* is generally used for beginners, while *liqo* is used for more advanced levels of this circle.
11. In Makassar, this term is often used by followers of a Salafi movement, Wahdah Islamiyah. It refers to a small study group held once a week.
12. *Kajian* or *pengkaderan* is a term often used by followers of Ikatan Mahasiswa Muhammadiyah (IMM, Muhammadiyah University Student Association).
13. The popularity of all these informal religious study circles can be seen not only on campuses, but also in schools, community houses and offices. However, the activities within campus mosques have been particularly notable.
14. Campus Islam refers to diverse university-based movements, particularly Jemaah Tarbiyah, HTI and Jama'ah Tabligh or Tablighi Jama'at (Preaching Community) (Fealy and Hooker 2006: 48).
15. The term *jilbab* is used to distinguish it from *kerudung* (loose veil), which was more common before the growing popularity of *jilbab*, since the 1980s (see Brenner 1996: 673; Robinson 2009: 122).

16. It is not only mosques that are considered by many jurists as "taboo" places for Muslim women. Attending university itself can also be regarded as "taboo" for some ultra conservative scholars, who consider university attendance as public visibility, which can also lead to *fitnah*.
17. However, it is noteworthy that some women belonging to Islamist and Salafi groups may find public mobility more difficult than other Muslim women. This is because they uphold a strict understanding of women's mobility. These women can mostly be seen in public when they attend *taklim* (religious lessons) (Nisa 2012b).
18. The majority of Muslims in Indonesia are of the Shafi'i *mazhab* (school of legal thought). Shafi'i himself (d. 204) emphasised that it is neither part of obligation nor part of recommendation for women to attend congregational prayers in the mosques (Sayeed 2001: 10).
19. For a substantial account of debates regarding women's leadership in Indonesia, for example, in the role of president, and the interpretations of Muslims, see Robinson 2004.
20. Members and followers of HTI on campuses have their own HTI campus organisation, called Chapter. Each university that has members and followers of HTI mostly has its own Chapter, such as MHTI (Muslimah Hizbut Tahrir) Chapter Kampus (Campus) UMI (Universitas Muslim Indonesia), and MHTI Chapter Kampus UIN Alauddin. Being active and having commitment to their study circles is one of the requirements for all HTI followers to be recognised as HTI members.
21. The term "KAMMI follower" is popular among students at Makassar universities to define the followers of Jemaah Tarbiyah study circles. Many of the students are reluctant to be defined as PKS supporters. They said, "Kita mau ikutan KAMMInya saja bukan PKSnya" (We just want to join the KAMMI not its PKS).
22. Besides these three affiliations, there are also other group affiliations. However, they are not part of this study, because they do not use mosques extensively as the main centre of their activities. These affiliations include HMI, PMII and IMM (Ikatan Mahasiswa Muhammadiyah/the University Students' association of Muhammadiyah). Generally those who are active in these three organisations are students whose attachment is to the two biggest Muslim mass organisations in Indonesia, Nahdlatul Ulama and Muhammadiyah. Although IMM sometimes have an informal study circle in the mosque of UNISMUH, its circle is not popular among students who are active in the campus mosques.
23. "Kak" is a term that my informants used when addressing me.
24. The ideology of Ahli Sunnah Wal-Jamaah (people of the tradition of the Prophet and Community) refers to an ideal ideology that has to be upheld by true Muslims. Throughout history, Sunni Muslims in general,

ranging from the more conservative to the more radical, have used this term to refer to themselves. Therefore, the majority of Sunni Muslims in Indonesia, including the followers of the biggest Indonesian Muslim mass organisation Nahdlatul Ulama, refer to themselves as Ahlus Sunnah Wal-Jamaah. In recent times, however, Salafi movements have become particularly eager to monopolise the claim that they are the bastions of this ideology.

25. MANIS stands for Ma'had As-Sunnah Makassar (Makassar As-Sunnah Islamic Boarding School). This Salafi group is known as the main rival of Wahdah Islamiyah in Makassar.
26. It is noteworthy that during its early establishment Jemaah Tarbiyah focused more on personal morality and piety (van Bruinessen 2002: 133). William R. Liddle also argued that initially the 1970s they focused on "[u]nderstanding and practicing the Qur'anic do's and don'ts of personal behaviour" (1996: 624).
27. Although Wahdah often claims an apolitical position, the presence of some elites or former elites of Wahdah Islamiyah and its close connection with one of the political parties has left an impression of a political agenda for some Muslims.
28. Almost all Islamist and Salafi movements in Makassar have their own study group (*kelompok studi*) affiliation with their main organisation. For example, at UMI, HTI has FOSIDI (Forum Studi Islam Ideologis or Ideological Islamic Study Forum) (see also Rijal 2011: 258), Wahdah Islamiyah has LDK Ashabul Kahfi, and KAMMI has LDK Fitrah.
29. The first HTI Islamic study circle in Makassar was founded in 1995 by activists of LDK at UMI (see Rijal 2011: 256).
30. During this research, for example, I attended a public discussion held by HTI that invited elites from PKS and Muhammadiyah to discuss the position of Muslim women in Indonesia.

References

Amrullah, Eva F. "Indonesian Muslim Fashion: Styles & Designs." *ISIM Review* 22 (2008): 22–3.

Arifin, Syamsul. 2005. *Ideologi dan Praksis Gerakan Sosial Kaum Fundamentalis: Pengalaman Hizb al-Tahrir Indonesia*. Malang: UMM Press.

Aryanti, Tutin. 2012. "Women's Prayer Space: Body and Boundary." *The International Journal of the Constructed Environment* 2/3: 177–90.

______. 2013. "A Claim to Space: Debating Female Religious Leadership in a Muhammadiyah Mosque in Indonesia." *The Muslim World* 103: 375–88.

Ayoob, Mohammed. 2008. *The Many Faces of Political Islam: Religion and Politics in the Muslim World*. Ann Arbor: University of Michigan Press.

Bayat, Asef. 2005. "Islamism and Social Movement Theory." *Third World Quarterly* 26 (6): 891–908.

———. 2013. "Post-Islamism at Large." In *Post-Islamism: The Changing Faces of Political Islam*, ed. A. Bayat, 1–32. Oxford, New York: Oxford University Press.

Brenner, Suzanne. 1996. "Reconstructing Self and Society: Javanese Muslim Women and 'The Veil'." *American Ethnologist* 23 (4): 673–97.

Crouch, Harold. 1981. "Indonesia." In *The Politics of Islamic Reassertion*, ed. M. Ayoob, 190–207. London: Croom Helm.

Damanik, Ali Said. 2002. *Fenomena Partai Keadilan: Transformasi 20 Tahun Gerakan Tarbiyah di Indonesia*. Jakarta, Bandung: Teraju.

Deeb, Lara. 2006. *An Enchanted Modern: Gender and Public Piety in Shi'i Lebanon*. Princeton, NJ: Princeton University Press.

———. 2009. "Emulating and/or Embodying the Ideal: The Gendering of Temporal Frameworks and Islamic Role Models in Shi'i Lebanon." *American Ethnologist* 36 (2): 242–57.

DeLong-Bas, Natana J. 2004. *Wahhabi Islam: From Revival and Reform to Global Jihad*. Oxford, New York: Oxford University Press.

Dişli, Gülşen. 2015. "Women's Prayer Space in the Case Studies of the Historic Mosques in Three Balkan Countries." *Postor* 23 (2): 197–207.

Fealy, Greg. 2004. "Islamic Radicalism in Indonesia: The Faltering Revival?" *Southeast Asian Affairs*: 104–21.

Fealy, Greg and Virginia Hooker. 2006. *Voices of Islam in Southeast Asia: A Contemporary Sourcebook*. Singapore: Institute of Southeast Asian Studies.

Fox, James J. 2004. "Currents in Contemporary Islam in Indonesia." *Harvard Asia Vision* 21: 1–24.

Frisk, Sylvia. 2009. *Submitting to God: Women and Islam in Urban Malaysia*. Seattle: University of Washington Press.

Göle, Nilüfer. 1997. "The Gendered Nature of the Public Sphere." *Public Culture* 10 (1): 61–81.

Hackett, Conrad, Caryle Murphy, David McClendon, and Anne Shi. 2016. *The Gender Gap in Religion Around the World*. Washington, DC: Pew Research Center.

Hammer, Juliane. 2010. "Gender Justice in a Prayer: American Muslim Women's Exegesis, Authority, and Leadership." *Hawwa: Journal of Women of the Middle East and the Islamic World* 8 (1): 26–54.

———. 2012. *American Muslim Women, Religious Authority, and Activism: More than a Prayer*. Austin: University of Texas Press.

Hasan, Noorhaidi. 2013. "Post-Islamist Politics in Indonesia." In *Post-Islamism: The Changing Faces of Political Islam*, ed. A. Bayat, 157–82. Oxford, New York: Oxford University Press.

Hoel, Nina. 2013. "Sexualising the Sacred, Sacralising Sexuality: An Analysis of Public Responses to Muslim Women's Religious Leadership in the Context of a Cape Town Mosque." *Journal for the Study of Religion* 26 (2): 25–41.

Holmes-Katz, Marion. 2014. *Women in the Mosque: A History of Legal Thought and Social Practice*. New York: Columbia University Press.

Jaschok, Maria and Shui Jingjun. 2000. *The History of Women's Mosques in Chinese Islam: A Mosque of Their Own*. Richmond, Surrey: Curzon.

Kahera, Akel Ismail. 2002. *Deconstructing the American Mosque: Space, Gender, and Aesthetic*. Austin: University of Texas Press.

Liddle, R. William. 1996. "The Islamic Turn in Indonesia: A Political Explanation." *The Journal of Asian Studies* 55 (3): 613–34.

Mahmood, Saba. 2001. "Feminist Theory, Embodiment, and the Docile Agent: Some Reflections on the Egyptian Islamic Revival." *Cultural Anthropology* 16 (2): 202–36.

______. 2005. *Politics of Piety: The Islamic Revival and the Feminist Subject*. Princeton, NJ: Princeton University Press.

Machmudi, Yon. 2008. *Islamising Indonesia: The Rise of Jemaah Tarbiyah and The Prosperous Justice Party (PKS)*. Canberra: ANU E Press.

Mandaville, Peter. 2007. *Global Political Islam*. London and New York: Routledge.

Meijer, Roel. 2009. *Global Salafism: Islam's New Religious Movement*. New York: Columbia University Press.

Melchert, Christopher. 2006. "Whether to Keep Women out of the Mosque: A Survey of Medieval Islamic Law." In *Authority, Privacy and Public Order in Islam*, ed. B. Michalak-Pikulska and A. Pikulski, 59–69. Leuven: Peeters.

Milani, Farzaneh. 1992. *Veils and Words: The Emerging Voices of Iranian Women Writers*. Syracuse: Syracuse University Press.

Miller, Alan and Rodney Stark. 2002. "Gender and Religiousness: Can Socialization Explanations Be Saved?" *American Journal of Sociology* 107 (6): 1399–423.

Muhtadi, Burhanuddin. 2009. "The Quest for Hizbut Tahrir in Indonesia." *Asian Journal of Social Science* 37 (4): 623–45.

Nakosteen, Mehdi. 1964. *History of Islamic Origins of Western Education, A.D. 800–1350*. Colorado: University of Colorado Press.

Nisa, Eva F. 2012a. "*Cadari* of Wahdah Islamiyah: Women as Dedicated Actors of Ultra-conservatism." *Intersections: Gender and Sexuality in Asia and the Pacific*, Issue 30. http://intersections.anu.edu.au/issue30/nisa.htm.

______. 2012b. "Embodied Faith: Agency and Obedience among Face-Veiled University Students in Indonesia." *The Asia Pacific Journal of Anthropology* 13 (4): 366–81.

Osman, Mohamed Nawab Mohamed. 2010. "Reviving the Caliphate in the *Nusantara:* Hizbut Tahrir Indonesia's Mobilization Strategy and Its Impact in Indonesia." *Terrorism and Political Violence* 22 (4): 601–22.

Othman, Norani. 2006. "Muslim Women and the Challenge of Islamic Fundamentalism/Extremism: An Overview of Southeast Asian Muslim Women's Struggle for Human Rights and Gender Equality." *Women's Studies International Forum* 29: 339–53.

Reda, Nevin. 2004. "Women in the Mosque: Historical Perspectives on Segregation." *American Journal of Islamic Social Sciences* 21 (2): 78–97.

Rijal, Syamsul. 2011. "Indoctrinating Muslim Youths: Seeking Certainty through An-Nabhanism." *Al-Jami'ah* 49 (2): 253–80.

Rinaldo, Rachel. 2013. *Mobilizing Piety: Islam and Feminism in Indonesia.* Oxford, New York: Oxford University Press.

Robinson, Kathryn and Sharon Bessell. 2002. "Introduction to the Issues." In *Women in Indonesia: Gender, Equity and Development*, ed. K. Robinson and S. Bessell, 1–12. Singapore: Institute of Southeast Asian Studies.

Robinson, Kathryn. 2004. "Islam, Gender and Politics in Indonesia." In *Islamic Perspectives on the New Millennium*, ed. V. Hooker and A. Saikal, 183–96. Singapore: Institute of Southeast Asian Studies.

———. 2009. *Gender, Islam and Democracy in Indonesia.* London, New York: Routledge.

Sayeed, A. 2001. "Early Sunni Discourse on Women's Mosque Attendance." *ISIM Newsletter* 7 (1): 10.

Shannahan, Dervla. 2014. "Gender, Sexuality and Inclusivity in UK Mosques." In *Studying Islam in Practice*, ed. G. Marranci, 124–34. London, New York: Routledge.

van Bruinessen. 2002. "Genealogies of Islamic Radicalism in Post-Suharto Indonesia." *South East Asia Research* 10 (2): 117–54.

Ward, Ken. 2009. "Non-Violent Extremists? Hizbut Tahrir Indonesia." *Australian Journal of International Affairs* 63 (2): 149–64.

Werbner, Pnina. 2010. "Religious Identity." In *The Sage Handbook of Identities*, ed. M. Wetherell and C.T. Mohanty, 233–58. Los Angeles, London: SAGE.

———. 2015. "Religion and Identity: Ritual, Pilgrimage and Frontier Encounters." In *Religious Diversity Today: Experiencing Religion in the Contemporary World*, ed. A. Panagakos, 215–37. Santa Barbara, California: ABC-CLIO.

———. 2018. "Between Islamic Piety, Agency and Ethical Leadership: Paradoxes of Self-Transformation." *Contemporary Levant* 3 (1): 79–90.

Wiktorowicz, Quintan. 2002. "Islamic Activism and Social Movement Theory: A New Direction for Research." *Mediterranean Politics* 7 (3): 187–211.

———. 2006. "Anatomy of the Salafi Movement." *Studies in Conflict & Terrorism* 29 (3): 207–39.

Woodlock, Rachel. 2010. "The *Masjid* is for Men: Competing Voices in the Debate about Australian Muslim Women's Access to Mosque." *Islam and Christian–Muslim Relations* 21 (1): 51–60.

Zaimeche, Salah. 2002. "Education in Islam: The Role of the Mosque." Foundation for Science Technology and Civilisation. http://www.muslimheritage.com/uploads/ACF2C23.pdf

Zulkifli. 2013. *The Struggle of the Shi'i in Indonesia*. Canberra: ANU E Press.

7

Mosques and their Communities in Northern Ambon, Maluku

Exploring Local Traditions as Islamic Practice in Indonesia[1]

Phillip Winn

Introduction

This chapter considers some key physical and social features shared by community mosques on the northern coastline of Ambon Island in Maluku province, Indonesia. This area comprises the district of Leihitu on a peninsula of the same name, which Ambonese Muslims associate with the earliest presence of Islam. I give particular attention to the roofs of local mosques and highlight one aspect that may represent a distinguishing feature of indigenous mosques in Maluku and a distinct tradition among the diverse expressions of Muslim religiosity existing in Indonesia: the *tiang alif* or *alif* pole, a structural element at the highest point of the mosque roof.[2] The tiang alif is redolent with profound symbolic significance among Ambonese Muslims in Leihitu, attracting significant ritual and ceremonial activity in its placement, removal and renewal. I suggest that the tiang alif can also be regarded as a quintessential expression of the historical openness of Islam to local cultural traditions, a characteristic that undoubtedly formed an integral part in its successful early propagation in Maluku as elsewhere in the archipelago.

The appearance of contemporary mosques has developed over many centuries, and while certain features are widely found, differences also exist between regions and populations. Three features are often considered universal or at least, invariably present: a large open space free of furniture for performing prayer; a niche in the centre of one wall which denotes the direction of the ka'bah in Mecca known as a *mihrab* (in Indonesia often taking the shape of a decorated doorway); and lastly is an elevated structure somewhat akin to an elaborate pulpit with several steps or a small staircase from which an address is delivered each Friday as part of a weekly gathering for communal prayer. *Mimbar*—as these structures tend to be called in Indonesia—are often heavily ornamented, usually with an awning, and are located at the front area of the mosque typically to the right of the *mihrab* (when facing this feature). General descriptions of mosques throughout the world also may highlight exterior courtyards and minarets as common elements, along with a domed roof, the interior of which may well feature Arabic calligraphy (religious phrases, names of prophets etc.) and/or geometric patterns or other non-figurative decoration.

Of all these elements, the shape of a mosque's roof regularly plays a conspicuous part in descriptions of variations in design. While no typological schema is universally accepted, references to regional mosque styles inevitably tend to emphasise this aspect, with references, for example, to a central, flattened dome ("Anatolian" or "Ottoman") or more bulbous triple domes ("Mughal" or "subcontinent"), while structural techniques to support domes and their effect on the internal space of the mosque is a recurring focus of discussion (see for example, Hassan and Omer 2013). Traditional forms of mosques in Southeast Asia, in their turn, are regularly characterised by the presence of a "central pyramidal or hipped" roof *instead* of a dome (Frisman 2002: 13). However, despite being widely acknowledged as a central even defining historical element in mosque design, relatively little attention has been given to the implications of mosque roofs within Muslim religiosity, whether in Indonesia or elsewhere. When mentioned, a diversity of perspectives are found. There are those who dismiss mosque roofs as lacking any significant spiritual or symbolic significance (for example, Al-Jasmi and Mitias 2004: 209). More common is the suggestion that domed roofs in particular express some degree of political and religious symbolism, though not liturgical focus, in attesting publicly and visually to the presence of Muslims and to a space they consider important (see Hillenbrand 1992: 53). Still others assert that an interior domed roof space is an essential part of Islamic ideology and prayer as a "cosmic symbol representing the vault of heaven" (Sliwoski 2007: 30).

Muslim communities on the north coast of Ambon Island agree that an open space for prayer, a *mihrab* and a *mimbar* are all important general features of community mosques. But in terms of their *own* mosques, other components are also emphasised, in particular, a feature of the mosque roof: the tiang alif pole that sits at the highest point of the roof. The other important aspect of this design are four pillars which support the roof. For Muslims on the north coast of Ambon, the tiang alif is an essential element of an authentically local mosque; its absence does not negate a structure's status as a mosque, particularly outside their home communities, but its presence substantially deepens the numinous potency a mosque possesses as a localised space of activity concerning the sacred. And it serves as material testament to claims of age-old Muslim community identity.[3] As an object imbued with considerable meaning and importance, the removal of a tiang alif whether for restoration or replacement is a significant act surrounded by ceremony, as is its re-erection. Accidental loss (for example, being blown down in a storm) is a highly portentous event for the community linked to the mosque concerned. To make sense of this, it is necessary to appreciate several aspects of social life among Ambonese in coastal Leihitu, beginning with local understandings concerning the status of specific settlements as socio-political entities known as *negeri*.

Mosques in Northern Ambon

National backing for decentralisation and the direct election of district (*kabupaten*) heads in the post-New Order period saw the emergence of new district regulations (*peraturan daerah*) in Central Maluku which sought to incorporate and reflect visions of traditional governance in the administrative structures of local communities (see Bräuchler 2015). The sub-district (*kecamatan*) of Leihitu, which takes in most of the northern coast of Ambon Island, is one of many where the former settlements categorised as *desa* under the 1979 Law on Village Administration (Law 5/1979) have been gradually renamed negeri, a change allowed by the 2004 and 2014 Village Laws (Vel and Bedner 2017; see also Bräuchler 2011). Each has status either as *negeri adat*—a settlement envisaged as having longstanding, usually pre-colonial social and territorial roots—or as a *negeri administratif*, denoting settlements which are unable to assert such a claim (especially those established during the New Order period or as part of the central government's transmigration programme).[4] The 11 negeri that constitute Leihitu district are all recognised as *negeri adat*. Their population is wholly Muslim and predominantly ethnic Ambonese, though with minority populations of in-migrants largely from Southeast Sulawesi's Buton region, which tend to be concentrated into hamlets at the edges of negeri.[5]

In the pre-colonial period Ambonese settlements were generally located in mountain areas adjacent to the coast. It is here that Ambonese in Leihitu suggest their ancestors first encountered and began to embrace Islam. The mountain-based negeri are considered to have been largely autonomous political entities, and each of the contemporary negeri in Leihitu has its own specific traditions concerning the process by which Islam became established in their community. In general terms, local narratives suggest no single source was involved and that Islam arrived independently of regional Sultanates—viewed as exerting little authority in this locale—but instead through the direct influence of Muslim proselytisers (*mubalig*) from the Middle East who began visiting numerous trading venues that emerged along the north coast. Local relationships with political centres are acknowledged, however, as later contributing to religious knowledge among Leihitu's Muslims and to the character of local religious practice. While broad-brush historical depictions of the "spread of Islam" in the Indonesian archipelago frequently cite the historically prominent northern Maluku sultanate of Ternate as the key source of Islam for the Maluku region as a whole (for example, Azra 2006), Leihitu accounts instead emphasise the importance of the northern port-cities of Java, and also sometimes the less well-known northern Maluku sultanate of Jailolo. Ternate is viewed as having exerted far more influence in the Hoamoal peninsula of nearby western Seram than on the Leihitu coast.

Ambonese Muslims in the Leihitu negeri, in common with Ambonese elsewhere, are members of local clans known as *mata rumah* or *fam*. And many clans also have their own traditions concerning the process by which individual ancestors first encountered and embraced Islam. Some provide the names of Arab or Javanese visitors to Leihitu as key historical actors in the process, often linked to particular objects among the clan heirlooms (*pusaka*) preserved in the source or origin house of the clan (*rumah tua* or *rumah tau*). Early handwritten copies of the Qur'an and special Arabic language prayer-forms are among such heirlooms, and may be used by senior members of a clan on specific occasions. There are also clans that claim descent from Arab traders who settled in the area permanently, some of which trace their origins to Iran ("Persia") and to Yemen.

In addition to the presence of clans, a second dimension of local social organisation needs to be noted: that of the *soa*. This term has a complex history in the Maluku region (see Pannell 1999). In a general sense soa are best conceived as a social grouping with greater scope than an individual clan, encapsulating a range of political and/or territorial boundaries. The specific character and functions ascribed to this grouping differ from place to place throughout Maluku and on Ambon Island. In the contemporary negeri of Leihitu, soa generally signify a village subdivision made up of several, usually unrelated, exogamous clans. Soa are often seen as having emerged originally among clans living in close proximity at particular locations in the pre-colonial period, forming an early expression of political collectivity. Some of the ancient mountain settlements in Leihitu are said to have consisted of a single soa, while others are viewed as having comprised several. Importantly, the presence of a mosque during that period is understood as an additional critical marker of a socially and politically bounded community. Mosques in the original mountain settlements are variously considered to have been associated with individual soa—and therefore reinforcing a sense of soa-based political identity—or shared among soa, a situation in which the political significance of the soa themselves was diluted.

A period of determined armed resistance to the Dutch presence occurred in the Leihitu region in the mid-17th century and is still known as the Wawané and Kapahaha wars.[6] Following defeat, mountain populations of northern Leihitu were gradually relocated to the coast by colonial authorities, creating discrete settlements more or less proximate to the positions of current negeri. In some instances, according to local accounts, this created dilemmas for soa who had formally been relatively autonomous but now found themselves residing alongside other soa in a single bounded settlement. This was reportedly the case, for example, with the contemporary blended negeri of Negeri Lima and Seit. In the case of Negeri Lima, local narratives suggest that five soa—each of which had possessed their own mosque in the mountains—made a conscious decision to erect just one mosque on the coast as a sign of new geographic and political unity. The historically separate status of the five soa nevertheless continued to be reflected in the name of the negeri. Informants suggest Seit also was originally composed of five independent soa, each with their own mosque. In this case following their relocation to the coast four of the soa maintained this pattern, constructing individual mosques. As a result negeri Seit today possesses four separate mosques in close proximity to one another, despite having a significantly smaller population than nearby Negeri Lima. Three of the mosques are each associated with the members of a single soa, the fourth with the members of two soa (who are said to have combined historically for this purpose given depleted numbers). The Seit mosques and their associated soa comprise:

	Mosque	*Soa*
1.	Mesjid Tua	Seith
2.	Kuha al Bayan	Hatuna
3.	Nur Yakin	"Lewas" (soa Lehulehu and soa Wasila)
4.	Ulu Paha	Lain

The same set of main mosque-based officials are found throughout Leihitu negeri: an imam (who leads daily prayers); a *khatib* (who presents an address at communal Friday prayers); and a *modin* (who has a range of duties explained below).

Each of the four mosques in negeri Seit have their khatib and modin appointed by *adat* (customary) leaders of the associated soa ("*tua-tua adat dalam soa*"). However, the community as a whole has just a single imam who is appointed at a joint gathering of the adat elders of all soa. In Seit as elsewhere the most regular distinctive function of the imam is to co-ordinate or synchronise those gathered to pray in the mosque (in local terms *bawah salat*—"carry" or "bear" the prayer) particularly in Friday communal prayers (*salat Jumat*). As a consequence, each Friday in negeri Seit the communal prayer occurs at only one of the mosques, a role rotated between the four on a weekly basis. A number of Seit informants emphasised that this practice, along with their single imam, attests to residents of Seit as a single united Muslim community despite the unusual number of mosques in such a small area. They also note that attendance at each of these mosques is not limited to members of the associated soa; residents who perform ordinary daily prayers at a mosque rather than at home generally attend whichever is nearest, with the associated modin acting as prayer leader. However, arrangements for hosting special annual calendrical events (such as commemoration of the Prophet's birthday, Maulid) are more complicated with festivities occurring at each of the mosques. This can involve some hurried movement by the imam (as well as the negeri head) in order to make an appearance at each gathering.

In neighbouring Negeri Lima, the imam, khatib and modin of the community's single mosque are each associated with particular soa, and here too it is the adat elders in the particular soa who appoint the individuals to these positions ("*orang tua-tua adat yang angkat*")—the imam with soa Soumena, the khatib with Soa Paihali and the modin with the remaining three soa, who share this responsibility. The latter is seen as an advantageous arrangement since modin are generally considered as having the most onerous duties among the various mosque officials. These include organising the call to prayer (*azan*) five times each day, as well as attending deaths to supervise arrangements (notably, preparation of the corpse for burial). Indeed, throughout the Leihitu negeri more than one modin (up to four) is viewed as ideal, though seldom attained, along with multiple khatib (often, two). No formal ranking applies to these mosque officials. The imam and modin are together seen as performing the most important duties, but neither could be said to manage or govern a mosque. The khatib is also viewed as a significant role. If the imam is absent, the modin will lead Friday prayer. If the modin is unavailable, the khatib substitutes. These officials are frequently referred to collectively in

Leihitu as *penghulu* and also as *lebeh*.[7] Appointment to the positions in all Leihitu negeri involves a prescribed process overseen by senior adat figures.

While soa retain a level of everyday local salience in Seit and Negeri Lima (where for example, soa names are used to denote neighbourhoods), in other Leihitu negeri their contemporary importance has narrowed considerably. In these communities soa are often regarded as having coalesced to a greater degree prior to the population moving to the coast, and as a result clans (*mata rumah*) are much more prominent. Here too, the positions associated with mosques are linked with one or more specific clans rather than soa. In Negeri Wakal, for example, the imam comes from the Lewaru clan; modin from clan Soulete; and khatib from clan Soupele. All such practices are believed to be reproducing historical arrangements carried from original mountain settlements to the coast, an interpretation that finds dramatic illustration in the case of Negeri Kaitetu.

Kaitetu residents maintain that a mountain-based mosque constructed by their ancestors appeared mysteriously in its current location under its own power. This mosque, known as the Masjid Tua Wapauwe was locally regarded to have been constructed in 1414 during contact with a second wave of Muslim proselytisers (*mubalig*) from Jailolo and Tuban and as a direct result of their instruction. In the Kaitetu language "*wapa*" refers to a wild forest mango ("*mangga hutan*"), while "*uwe*" means "below"—so the name signifies the "Old Mosque [from] below the forest mango", referring to its original site on Wawane Mountain.[8] The population associated with the mosque relocated to the coast under Dutch direction in 1664, leaving the structure behind. Soon after, the community is said to have awoken to find their mosque had transported itself to join them, occupying the location where it stands today. It appeared complete with all necessary items including a handwritten Qur'an; a carved wooden mosque drum (beaten immediately before the call to prayer); a set of scales linked to *zakat* payments; oil lamps; and an ornamented staff signifying the khatib role, held when delivering the Friday address (*tongkat khotbah*). The mosque is well-known among Muslims in the Ambon region as the oldest mosque in Maluku, though to the annoyance of Kaitetu people it is regularly linked in tourism materials to the larger negeri immediately adjoining Kaitetu in which the Leihitu sub-district office is located, that of Hila (as "the old Hila mosque").[9]

A second more spacious and centrally located mosque was erected in Negeri Kaitetu during the 18th century as the community grew and Mesjid Wapauwe was too small to host community gatherings at major festivals. A common pattern in Leihitu is that women do not join men in the main negeri mosque for Friday prayer or ordinary daily salat, but make use instead of smaller structures (*musholla*) built for the purpose, usually at some remove from the main mosque. In Kaitetu women may choose to make use of the older mosque for ordinary daily prayer, with men using the main mosque. The two groups also gather at separate mosques for Friday prayer, with women once again generally using the old mosque. A separate (male) imam is attached to each mosque, creating an unusual situation in Leihitu: the presence of two imams in a single negeri. However, the imams of the main mosque is viewed as the imam negeri and officiates at major festivals at that mosque such as Idul Fitri and Idul Adha. On such occasions women also join men at the main mosque, though seated in the yard surrounding the structure and separated by a large white cloth.[10] A second, smaller prayer event on these occasions also takes place later at the old mosque, led by its imam but involving all other mosque, adat and administrative officials of the negeri.

Sociality and Interior Space

In negeri mosques throughout Leihitu, specific places exist in the front line of the open prayer space that are nominally reserved for use by negeri officials—those associated with the mosque, but also a range of other individuals. These places are conceived in terms of their spatial relation to the *mimbar*. When facing forward (that is, looking towards the *mihrab*) certain officials sit to the right of the *mimbar*, and others to the left. In the case of negeri Kaitetu, those seated on the left are the penghulu (one or more khatib and modin along with the *marbut*) alongside a group of 12 adat elders (‘*orang tua-tua adat*’) known as the *tukang duabelas*. On the right are seven places reserved for the *bapak raja* (the administrative head of the negeri) along with his “staff” (*staf*), consisting of three *kewang* including a *kepala kewang* (officials with responsibility for controlling access to and use of resources in community-held forest areas), in addition to three soa heads (*kepala soa*). Those on the right side of the *mimbar* are often referred to as the “government” of the negeri (*pemerintah negeri*). However, in discussion with individuals occupying allocated places on both sides a view emerged that in contemporary democratic parlance, the right side of the *mimbar* might more accurately be considered members of an executive branch of political leadership (*eksekutif*), while the adat elders on the left are somewhat functionally equivalent to a legislature (*legislatif*). At the same time, all three distinct groups—the *raja* and his staff, the penghulu and the tukang duabelas—are regularly labelled altogether as the "three [groups of] traditional leaders" (*tiga tokoh adat*).

Throughout Leihitu, special salat occurs at the mosque on auspicious dates (*hari-hari baik yang tertentu*) that are not linked to the major Islamic festivals—these include the 15th and 27th days of the fasting month, and the 1st day of the month of Muharam. On such occasions in negeri Kaitietu individuals from all three leadership groups arrive earlier and enter the mosque before others in the negeri, forming a line in their specified places. According to some informants, a similar practice should ideally occur at each *salat Jumat* also.[11] The three groups are required to attend the mosque in this fashion because they are viewed as sharing special responsibility for their community in terms of interceding with God and the ancestors (*leluhur*) on its behalf in order to ensure the collective wellbeing of the negeri (such as avoiding disasters). Similar arrangements were said to occur in other negeri. When particular positions are not filled, or individuals are absent, the associated positions for salat at the front of the mosque floor stand vacant until immediately before prayer begins; at that point others present move forwards to fill the empty positions as it is seen as important to form complete lines in front of the *mihrab*. At *salat Jumat* this movement occurs immediately after the address (*khotbah*).

Existing officials say of the empty positions: "there is no-one yet who wishes to 'sit'" (*belum ada yang mau duduk*), that is, who are willing or able to occupy the associated role within mosque and negeri. Indeed, informants suggest it has become increasingly difficult in all Leihitu communities to entirely fill the positions involved, largely due to the gravity and/or demands of associated duties. In some cases, a clan may no longer have descendants to fill the role. But more important has been a growing level of reluctance to face the risk of making some kind of mistake. Informants noted that on taking up such a position one is required to be regular in religious observance with considerable potential for community scrutiny and censure as the positions bring one into closer relation with the *leluhur*—the ancestors. As such, errors of conduct are understood to carry potential community-wide consequences. Informants suggest that in the past, not only were individuals appointed to penghulu positions (particularly imam and modin) expected to behave in an exemplary manner, a similar expectation applied to their families. Any penghulu whose son engaged in drinking or gambling would face mounting pressure to withdraw (*mundur*) from their duties in advance of being asked to do so. Public opinion might manifest in an anonymous letter to the penghulu concerned, advising them of community concerns. Ultimately, when an imam or modin is slow to act under these circumstances, they could arrive at the mosque only to find their mat (*tikar*) removed from its reserved position and placed outside—a direct and very public form of community condemnation.

While the interior of a mosque may be free of major accoutrements such as furniture, spatial arrangements in the religious practices occurring there may vividly communicate a range of important aspects of social organisation and religio-political understandings. In Leihitu, these include community visions of the importance of local traditions and institutions. The presence of "reserved seating" in the negeri mosques of Leihitu provides some elucidation of a somewhat cryptic observation made by an Ambonese Muslim to previous researchers in this locale (von Benda-Beckmann 1988: 195) to the effect that "adat is done at the mosque" (*adat dibikin di mesjid*).[12] This idea of mosque and adat as mutually implicated can be illustrated further by considering the character of the tukang duabelas in more detail.

The Mosque Roof

Tukang duabelas refers literally to "12 workers", and consists of 12 individually-named positions linked to particular clans, which also form titles associated with the person occupying the position. These vary among negeri, and not all of the names are able to be translated or associated clearly with particular duties. But the tukang duabelas as a whole nevertheless have a close association with the physical structure of the community's mosque, with key responsibilities in relation to its maintenance and managing any needed repairs. In performing this role, they are viewed as "enacting directions passed from earlier generations" (*yang mengajarkan mesjid sesuai dengan diprentah oleh nenek moyang*). In Negeri Kaitetu, an established practice immediately before community prayers associated with the annual marking of Idul Adha (Hari Korban) involves members of the tukang duabelas collecting donations for the mosque from those assembled. This commences with a *pasawale*—a ritualistic exchange of formalised greetings and respectful acknowledgement carried out in local language between the penghulu and the tukang duabelas. In this performance the tukang duabelas bear a close association not just with ancestral knowledge but more specifically with those who constructed the original negeri mosque. Indeed, a widespread popular interpretation of the tukang duabelas is that they are contemporary representatives of these individual ancestors. A distinctive ceremony illustrating this point occurs also at Idul Adha at the main mosque at negeri Wakal, immediately prior to the main public events of the day. It involves a clan associated with community leadership (*raja*) marking the debt owed by the community as a whole to the tukang duabelas for their responsibility in building the original mosque (*membayar imbalan jazab/jazah kepada mereka tukang duabelas tadi yang membangun mesjid tua*). Negeri Wakal's tukang duabelas gather at the mosque in the early hours of the morning where they are presented with several chickens from the *raja* clan and others that have chosen to participate. The chickens are prayed over by the mosque modin, then killed, after which communal prayer (*doa tahlil*) takes place, without reference to writing, over a shared meal involving the penghulu and tukang duabelas along with other senior clan members. Informants note that these are the first animals ceremonially killed on a holy day on which the ritualised slaughter of larger animals (generally, goats) is at the centre of activity, underscoring community reverence for the historical role of the mosque-builders.

The dual character of the tukang duabelas as both responsible for organising ongoing maintenance and renovation of the negeri mosque as well as being contemporary representatives of the ancestral mosque-builders of the negeri, is enacted most dramatically in complex ceremonial activity surrounding components of the mosque roof: the periodic "replacing the roofing" (*ganti atap*) and less frequent, replacement of an object at the apex of the uppermost hipped roof-section (*kepala mesjid*) or dome (*kubah*) of a negeri mosque, widely known as the *alif* pole (tiang alif) or simply *tiang mesjid*. Both activities are widely cited among Leihitu Ambonese Muslims as the largest and most spiritually hazardous of the adat activities undertaken by negeri communities. In public scale they match or exceed activity surrounding the inauguration of a new negeri leader or raja (*pelantikan raja*), while their importance is viewed locally as far surpassing the renewal, or "warming up" of inter-village alliances (*bikin pela panas*)—a ceremony with considerable prominence in scholarly depictions of "Ambonese culture" in general terms.

Replacing the tiang alif consists properly of two separate large-scale public ceremonies which may be held several months apart: initially lowering the alif pole (*kasih turun tiang alif*) and later raising the pillar (*kasih naik tiang alif*). A number of associated activities take place which are not as public, but are nevertheless viewed as critical components by the communities involved and in which members of the tukang duabelas play a central part, including choosing and felling a tree to be fashioned into the new tiang alif and the process of disposing of the older tiang. For the purpose of establishing the symbolic importance of the mosque roof among Leihitu negeri it is sufficient to highlight just a few elements of both ceremonies and briefly consider local meanings attributed to the tiang alif itself.

Formerly, replacing mosque roofing—*ganti atap*—involved a type of thatching made from sections of sewn sago leaf. But with the exception of Kaitetu's Mesjid Wapauwe, corrugated roofing metal is ubiquitous among contemporary mosques in Leihitu. As a result, this occasion is far less frequent than in the past. When it does occur, it involves the clans or soa of a negeri making individual contributions of sections of mosque roofing, nowadays generally in the form of cash payments. Other communities that trace historical relationships to the negeri concerned also provide sections of roofing as an affirmation of that relationship. In the case of Kaitetu, for example, both Seit and Negeri Lima contribute towards the costs of its mosque roofing. These three negeri are understood as being in a *gandong* relationship, that is, as uterine siblings (*adik-kakak*) linked to a putative relationship between actual ancestors in the distant past. As sibling communities, they are each regarded as having an obligation to meet a share of the costs (*dong punya pembagian itu*). More unusually, a small hamlet of Christians residing formerly on disputed lands between the negeri of Kaitetu and Hila also routinely participated in the proceedings, contributing their own share of the replacement roof. From the perspective of the Kaitetu community, this formed a strong demonstration of the

Christian population's affiliation with their negeri as part of Kaitetu territory. Members of this community would sit quietly alongside other formal guests during the related collective prayer (*doa tahlil*).

It is evident then how mosque roofing manifests in a very tangible sense a range of social relationships, both within and between negeri, in addition to testifying to shared interpretations of the past. The mosque roof constitutes a substantial, material demonstration of history, which imbues it with a particular and substantive potency. The key responsibility of members of the tukang duabelas is to act in a manner that confirms this significance by conducting the physical replacement of roofing materials in a way that satisfies onlookers that established historical practices are being faithfully followed. Given the diverse interpretations and memories surrounding aspects of the event, errors (or perceptions of a mistake) inevitably occur. An action that may differ only marginally from narratives held by particular families or persons (for example, beginning to attach a specific section of roofline before another is completed) can result in spectators falling to the ground in a faint, convulsing, or running erratically about the crowded proceedings, shrieking or sobbing uncontrollably. Afterwards, popular analysis of the events proliferate—which possessions were feigned; which simply expressed overwhelming emotion or tension; which were real; the specific errors in action that provoked the ancestors and what if any events or consequences are foreshadowed for the community as a whole. In turn, individual tukang duabelas are critically assessed in the performance of their duties, and the event as a whole judged as a success or found wanting.

Replacing the tiang alif carries the same kinds of challenges for the actors involved (and risks for onlookers), if not more so in the sense that the object is especially charged. The tiang pole is not just at the pinnacle of the mosque roof, but it can be said to embody the mosque itself and the community to which it is linked. It could reasonably be described as the "ritual attractor" of this type of building in Leihitu, an object with "pre-eminence among the other parts of the [structure] and as such, represents, in concentrated form, the [structure] as a whole" (Fox 2006: 1). To appreciate this it is necessary to comprehend the symbolic dimensions of the tiang alif and how these are locally envisaged in terms of an encompassing religious and cosmological order.

Firstly, as noted earlier, mosques in Leihitu negeri generally feature four internal poles which support the building's raised ceiling (whether a central hipped roof section or dome). Popular interpretations of these pillars see them as emblematic of four of the five "pillars" or foundational principles of Islam (*rukun Islam*). The remaining, absent pillar is considered the first of the five, that is: the key profession of Muslim belief (*syahadat*) that there is only one God—Allah, and that Muhammad is Allah's prophet. And this *rukun Islam* is understood to be represented by the tiang alif. Physically absent from within the mosque, where the community gathers as Muslims engaging in activity relating to each of the remaining four *rukun* (prayer, fasting, alms-giving and pilgrimage), it sits atop and outside the mosque, rising above the imperfections of human practice. The term *alif* refers to the first letter of the Arabic alphabet, written as a single vertical stroke. The physical correspondence between the letter alif and a pole is one obvious dimension of their relation. However, as the first letter of the Arabic alphabet, alif is also described as the origin or source of the Arabic alphabet. In the lives of Leihitu Muslims, Arabic writing is closely associated with the Qur'an; the reason for learning the Arabic alphabet is for Qur'anic recitation. (This is a process all children engage in with village-based teachers.) Alif is in this respect also considered the source of the Qur'an, that is, the first letter of the language through which the Qur'an was received from Allah. It should be noted that alif is also the first letter of the word Allah and in esoteric understandings can stand for this word.

Leihitu informants suggest Islam *itself* can be described as emerging from alif, in all these senses; that is, that alif can be seen as the symbolic source of Islam, the vehicle through which Islam is manifest in the world. Some informants drew a parallel between this interpretation and that of viewing the alif pillar as a point from which the mosque can be seen as emerging downwards (much as an umbrella). Just as Islam descended from Allah to bound the Muslim community as a whole, the mosque, it was said, can be conceived as descending from the alif pillar to encompass the negeri as a Muslim community who gather beneath it to pray. In this perspective the alif pole becomes the symbolic anchor from which the rest of the mosque hangs; it is the source and anchor of the mosque and its associated community. But there is another, more esoteric significance explained to me by individual penghulu, tukang duabelas and others. It involves drawing metaphoric parallels between the tiang alif as the symbolic source of the Muslim community and the tiang alif as representing also the ultimate physical source of human community: sexual reproduction. So the alif pillar becomes the penis, with its placement into the mosque expressive of the original act that gave rise to all the clans of the negeri community associated with the mosque. This also provides a rationale behind the common practice of modestly wrapping the tiang alif in white cloth, at least until it is finally put in place. Clearly then, the replacement of this object constitutes a profound act on a range of levels as well as one necessarily generating the most intense interest from the ancestors as progenitors of the negeri.

The ceremonial removal and replacement of the tiang alif is more widespread in Maluku than the north coast of Leihitu. Ambonese informants from other localities affirm that it occurs at older community mosques throughout Ambon and the Lease Islands. The practice can reputedly also be found elsewhere in the central region of Maluku, including Seram and the islands off eastern Seram, while I have attended an event of this kind in the Banda Islands. Regional media has reported on the event in Seram and similar activity in Jailolo (Halmahera Island) in North Maluku.[13] Further research is needed, but it may be the case that a common constellation of ideas associated with what might be termed a "tiang alif ritual complex" could well represent a distinctive Malukan tradition (or perhaps, a unique variation of more widely shared significance attached to this element of mosque architecture) within the diverse expressions of Muslim religiosity currently existing in eastern Indonesia, and indeed, in the archipelago as a whole.

Discussion and Conclusion

Whenever it first occurred, the initial encounter with Islamic religious ideas by local populations in Leihitu represents the beginning of long engagement with an extended cosmopolitan Muslim world stretching across the Indian Ocean to the Middle East and North Africa. That extant cultural institutions and social values in Leihitu had a role to play in shaping local articulation of this engagement is hardly surprising, as are gradual transformations in character of institutions and values as new ideas (and those who carried them) became an established presence. Indeed, such dynamics continue to the present (see Winn 2012). At the same time it is critical to recognise that in historical terms Islam readily acknowledged and accommodated such processes. Perspectives that seek to emphasise a conceptual, even oppositional contrast between concepts of local custom (adat) and Islam—often via a rubric of "syncretism"—overlook the fact that custom has been recognised as a legitimate basis for regional variation in expressions of Islamic religiosity since the inception of Islamic schools of law (Shabana 2010: 5; Lisbon 2003: 69). In the classical Sunni period, the Arabic concept of *'ada*, from which the Indonesian term adat derives, was regularly invoked as a positive principle by Muslim judicial authorities.[14] This was particularly the case where core texts such as the Qur'an and *hadis* provided no definitive answer to a particular set of problems, but also in regard to ambiguity within Islamic jurisprudence and in broader terms, the oblique relationship that inevitably exists between law as an intellectual structure and law as realised through social practice. In the case of mosques, Qur'anic provisions relating to their built form are notably absent, while established *hadis* emphasise the blessings associated with their construction rather than their physical shape. Hence considerable scope has always existed to imbue these structures with local and regional traditions of design, including locally established imperatives to incorporate representations and/or embodiments of social as well as cosmological orders as a means to reinforce the position of the mosque as a centre and source of community ceremonial and ritual life.

There are numerous examples from between the 11th and 14th centuries of Muslim judges and legal authorities declaring the rejection of sound local custom and usage as counterproductive, bringing excessive difficulty and unwarranted harm to Muslim communities (see Calder 2010: 146–51). A widespread classical view held that local norms should be altered or obstructed only when absolutely necessary, notably where a custom directly conflicted with explicit provisions of the Qur'an; in other situations the wiser course involved broad accommodation to local custom (Faruq 2006: 363–5). This was an approach that became especially well-established in the Maliki school and demonstrably relevant also within Hanafi legal traditions, though is generally less researched in relation to the Shafi'i and Hanbali schools (Hannemann 2006: 187). It is entirely likely established judicial and legal principles of this sort helped to guide the earliest processes of disseminating Islamic religious understandings within the Indonesian archipelago, whether in Maluku or indeed, Java. Certainly early Qur'anic exegetes in the Malay language attest to a vibrant interest in variant interpretations (Riddell 2006: 317). Systematic study of early Malay or Javanese language commentaries and glosses of classic Arabic-language religious works (including interlinear and marginal notes) would be invaluable in shedding light on such processes. Unfortunately such work remains embryonic, hindered in part by a longstanding hierarchisation of Islamic discourse and languages that implicitly devalues the contribution and scholarship of Southeast Asian Muslims (Bruckmayr 2017: 27–30; see also Azra 2004: 2).

It remains the case that among Ambonese Muslims in northern Leihitu—as for many Indonesian Muslims—adat remains indelibly linked in an ontological sense to the domain of Islam from which the term emerges conceptually. And this situation exists despite considerable efforts by authorities in the colonial era to sharpen ideas of adat as a form of codified local customary law that can readily be distinguished from religion and in particular, the application of Islamic law (Kersten 2015: 185). It is entirely conceivable that an awareness of distinctive aspects of local customary practice as adat arose *within* and drew its key significances from an overarching Islamic worldview, rather than necessarily being at variance with locally emerging Islamic thought and identity, or requiring efforts at integration. That informants throughout Leihitu negeri inevitably characterise adat and Islam as "mutually interrelated" (*saling berkaitan*) and "mutually necessary" (*saling membutuhkan*) may well attest to just such a process. That is not to suggest Leihitu Muslims are unaware of contrary perspectives or tensions around this very issue in contemporary currents of reform in their religion; adherents of Wahhabism/Salafism and of Jemaah Tabligh, for example, have had a long presence in Ambon and local accounts concerning the Islamic quality of customary practice sometimes refer directly to the views of such groups. One young Qur'anic reading instructor (*guru mengaji*) from negeri Asilulu spoke of such groups as misunderstanding adat, maintaining that it constitutes an applied form of moral instruction inherited from religiously-informed Muslim ancestors encoding valuable social guidelines for everyday life (*peraturan hidup*). He explained that adat, inter alia, involves identifying certain behaviours as undesirable for a range of legitimate moral and ethical reasons consistent with Islam, and which are forbidden (*dilarang*). In that sense he justified his assertion—one which elicited nods from the several other people present—that local adat acts to strengthen the religious precepts contained in the Qur'an (*memperkuatkan al Qur'an*). On a different occasion a penghulu from Negeri Lima offered an especially cogent formulation in insisting: "custom without religion is crippled; religion without custom is crippled" (*adat tanpa agama pincang; agama tanpa adat pincang*).

It is of concern to some that aspects of ceremonial practice, in particular those surrounding the tiang alif, might be construed by outsiders as a form of non-Islamic object-worship. During a large ceremony marking the removal of a deteriorated tiang alif pole as part of renovating a mosque dome, I watched a *negeri raja* (whom I knew was well-read in contemporary Islamic reformist thought) address a sizeable crowd of attendees, including regional government officials. As the newly removed tiang alif was momentarily held suspended above the roof several negeri residents gathered within the mosque directly below began to collapse in states of spirit possession. At the same time, the *raja* carefully differentiated the respectful acknowledgement of ancestral contributions to the local development of Islam from any form of idolatry (*syirik*). As with others occupying formal administrative positions in Leihitu negeri, he was quick to refer to "the value of local cultural heritage" (*nilai warisan budaya lokal*) in relation to ritual events of this sort—a discourse linked in turn to a resurgence of official interest in distinctive local traditions that has been supported by political decentralisation. It is a perspective that provides ready refuge for distinctively local expressions of Muslim religiosity through implied government endorsement. Whatever the future of ritual action surrounding elements of mosque roofs in Leihitu, interpretive responses to their significance will certainly continue as Ambonese Muslims maintain an enduring and active engagement with the ever-shifting mosaic of ideas, perspectives and values in relation to Islam in Indonesia and the wider Muslim world.

Notes

1. This study was funded by Australian Research Council Discovery Project DP00881464 "Being Muslim in Eastern Indonesia: Practice, Politics and Cultural Diversity", Chief Investigators Kathryn Robinson and Andrew McWilliam, Department of Anthropology, ANU College of Asia and the

Pacific. The author was the Senior Research Associate on this project. Research for this chapter was conducted over a three-month period in 2009, which corresponded with the Islamic festival of Idul Adha. During this period the author resided in Leihitu and visited all *negeri*, conducting interviews in Kaitetu, Negeri Lima, Seit, Asilulu and Wakal.

2. Birgit Bräuchler (2010) mentions this feature in relation to a mosque on Haruku Island near Ambon, but does not elaborate on its significance in local terms.
3. In one Leihitu community experiencing a dispute concerning proper genealogical descent of the local imam, a familial branch involved proffered an aged tiang alif held in their care as evidence of the truth of their claims to the position.
4. Refining UU 22/1999, UU 32/2004 differentiated between genealogical and administrative villages (*desa geneologis* and *desa administratif*), and gave villages a choice in this regard. This status has potentially important implications for arrangements of local governance, notably in regulations surrounding the conduct of village elections. These were still taking shape at the time of fieldwork in 2009, with a great deal of contested opinion concerning the role of resident non-Ambonese populations within Leihitu negeri as well as in local thinking about the inclusive character of democratic practice.
5. A longstanding cluster of Christian households in Hila village was displaced during the years of serious sectarian intercommunal conflict in Ambon between 1999 and 2003; at the time of fieldwork no arrangements were in place for this population to return.
6. Wawané and Kapahaha refer to two different mountain locales in Leihitu, each of which are linked historically to fortified defensive strongholds associated with coalitions or loose federations of local settlements known as *uli* (see also Knaap 2003).
7. A more informal role that involves minor duties such as cleaning, sweeping and generally tidying the mosque tends to be included under this label also—that of the *marbut*.
8. This language is known to linguists as Seit-Kaitetu; it exists in everyday use alongside Ambonese Malay and, to a much lesser extent, Indonesian.
9. Note that the mosque is not claimed by Negeri Kaitetu to be the *first* mosque in Leihitu—though it is sometimes referred to in this manner elsewhere—but rather as the *oldest* of such structures still extant. The occasional instance of official materials erroneously associating the mosque with Hila aggravates tensions between the two negeri linked to longstanding land disputes; the Kaitetu view is that Hila emerged as a settlement during the colonial period, with the Dutch unlawfully excising land from Kaitetu territory for the purpose.

10. The occasion of Maulid (Muhammad's birthday) features distinctly different gendered spatial arrangements—see Winn 2012. Increasingly a second, upper storey for the use of women is becoming a feature of newly-built or renovated mosques (for example, at Negeri Asilulu).
11. At Lebaran (Idul Fitri) and Lebaran Haji (Idul Adha)—the two largest festivals of the Islamic calendar in Indonesia—members of the *orang tua-tua adat* in some *negeri* will fetch the *bapak raja* at salat time and escort him to the *mesjid* which he will then enter first, followed by others. Most opt not to exercise this prerogative and instead arrive early at the mosque by themselves.
12. The Ambonese Malay term *bikin* has a broadly causative character (to create/construct something or make something happen), here combined with the standard Indonesian passive marking affix *di-*.
13. See for example, "Tiang Alif Mesjid Asykin Lako Akediri, Dipancang". *Suara Sesadu.* http://halbarkab.com/suara-sasadu/tiang-alif-mesjid-asykin-lako-akediri-dipancang.html (accessed February 2013). For an interesting example of the potential politicising of such traditions, see "Nama Mesjid Agung Kota Masohi Dirubah, KNPI Demo". *Siwalima.* http://www.siwalimanews.com/post/nama_mesjid_agung_kota_masohi_dirubah_knpi_demo (accessed December 2012).
14. In this context *'ada* (Ar.) should be considered alongside a complimentary concept *'urf* (Ar.). The latter refers to general opinion, longstanding and commonly accepted conventions, or, simply established custom; *'ada* is generally translated as "customary or habitual practice". The two concepts are often viewed by Islamic scholars (in Indonesia and elsewhere) as practically synonymous, despite a subtly different emphasis: custom [*al-'urf* (Ar.)] versus usage [*al-'ada* (Ar.)] (see for example, Prawiro 2016: 60–5).

References

Azra, Azyumardi. 2004. *The Origins of Islamic Reformism in Southeast Asia: Networks of Malay-Indonesian and Middle Eastern 'Ulam' in the Seventeenth and Eighteenth Centuries.* Crows Nest, Australia: Allen & Unwin.

———. 2006. *Islam in the Indonesian World: An Account of Institutional Formation.* Bandung: Mizan.

Bräucher, Birgit. 2010. "Integration and Exclusion: Islam Adat in Central Moluccas." *Indonesia and The Malay World* 38 (110): 65–93.

———. 2011. "Kings on Stage: Local Leadership in Post-Suharto Moluccas." *Asian Journal of Social Science* 39 (2): 196–218.

———. 2015. *The Cultural Dimension of Peace: Decentralization and Reconciliation in Indonesia.* Basingstoke: Palgrave Macmillan.

Bruckmayr, Philipp. 2017. "The šarḥ/ḥāšiya Phenomenon in Southeast Asia. From al-Sanūsī's Umm al-Barāhīn to Malay Sifat Dua Puluh Literature." *Mélanges de l'Institut dominicain d'études orientales* 32: 27–52.

Calder, Norman. 2010. *Islamic Jurisprudence in the Classical Era*, ed. Colin Imber. Cambridge: Cambridge University Press.

Faruq, Umar Abd-Allah. 2006. "Islam and the Cultural Imperative." *Cross-currents* 56 (3): 357–75.

Fox, James J. 2006. "Comparative Perspectives on Austronesian Houses: An Introductory Essay." In *Inside Austronesian Houses: Perspectives on Domestic Designs for Living*, ed. James J. Fox, 1–30. Canberra: ANU E Press.

Frisman, Martin. 2002. "Islam and the Form of the Mosque." In *The Mosque: History, Architectural Development & Regional Diversity*, ed. Martin Frishman and Hasan-Uddin Khan, 1–23. London: Thames & Hudson.

Hannemann, Tilman. 2006. "Customary Law." In *Medieval Islamic Civilisation*, ed. Josef W Meri, 187–8. London: Routledge.

Hassan, Ahmad Sanusi and Spahic Omer. 2013. *From Anatolia to Bosnia: Perspectives on Pendentive Dome Mosque Architecture*. Pulau Pinang, Malaysia: Penerbit Universiti Sains Malaysia.

Hillenbrand, Robert. 1992. *Islamic Architecture: Form, Function & Meaning*. New York: Columbia University Press.

Al-Jasmi, Abdullah and Michael H. Mitias. 2004. "Does an Islamic Architecture Exist?" *Revista Portuguesa de Filosofia* 60: 197–214.

Kersten, Carool. 2015. *Islam in Indonesia: The Contest for Society, Ideas and Values*. New York: Oxford University Press.

Knaap, Gerrit. 2003. "Headhunting, Carnage and Armed Peace in Amboina, 1500–1700." *Journal of the Economic and Social History of the Orient* 46 (2): 165–92.

Lisbon, Gideon. 2003. *Jewish and Islamic Law: A Comparative Study of Custom during the Geonic Period*. Cambridge: Harvard University Press.

Pannell, Sandra. 1999. "Did the Earth Move for You? The Social Seismology of a Natural Disaster in Maluku, Eastern Indonesia." *The Australian Journal of Anthropology* 10 (2): 129–43.

Prawiro, Abdurrahman Misno Bambang. 2016. *Reception Through Selection-Modification: Antropologi Hukum Islam di Indonesia*. Yogyakarta: Deepublish.

Riddell, Peter G. 2001. *Islam and the Malay–Indonesian World: Transmission and Responses*. Honolulu: University of Hawai'i Press.

Shabana, Ayman. 2010. *Custom in Islamic law and Legal Theory: The Development of the Concepts of 'Urf and -Adah in the Islamic Legal Tradition*. New York: Palgrave Macmillan.

Sliwoski, Amelia Helena. 2007. "Islamic Ideology and Ritual: Architectural and Spatial Manifestations." Master's diss., State University of New York at Buffalo.

Vel, J.Y. Zakaria and A. Bedner. 2017. "Creating Indonesia's Village Law." *Asian Journal of Law and Society* 4 (2): 447–72.

von Benda-Beckmann, Franz and Keebet von Benda-Beckmann. 1988. "Adat and Religion in Minangkabau and Ambon." In *Time Past, Time Present, Time Future: Perspectives on Indonesian Culture: Essays in Honour of Professor P.E. de Josselin de Jong*, ed. H.J.M. Claessen, 195–212. Dordrecht, Netherlands: Koninklijk Instituut voor Taal-, Land- en Volkenkunde.

Winn, Phillip. 2012. "Women's Majelis Taklim and Gendered Religious Practice in Northern Ambon." *Intersections: Gender and Sexualty in Asia and the Pacific*, Issue 30. http://intersections.anu.edu.au/issue30/winn.htm.

8

Haji Badar Daeng Pawero

A Bugis Imam and His Roles in Maintaining Islamic Law and Bugis Adat in Kupang

Stella Aleida Hutagalung[1]

Introduction

Bugis as Migrants

The presence of the Bugis in Kupang on Timor island, can be traced back to the 17th century. The Dutch defeated the maritime power, Makassar in 1669, which then lost its control of Timor's waters. Bugis people—who were rivals of the Makassarese—began to trade and settle there (Widiyatmika 2004).[2] Bugis people travelled as far as north Australia in search of *trepang* (*holothurians*, known as sea cucumbers) and many of them settled on Timor (Farram 2010: 41–2). Following Indonesian independence, the presence of Bugis people on Timor increased.[3] An important development that induced migration was the Islamic rebellion of Kahar Muzakkar in South Sulawesi (from 1951 to 1965) where many Bugis left their homeland in search of safer places (Juhannis 2006).

What is the pattern of Bugis migration? First, it is primarily driven by effort to search for a better life. Economic migration is a way of pursuing a more respectable "social location", and a means by which a successful Bugis migrant can demonstrate his ability to pay a high amount of bridewealth and obtain a higher social status through marriage with a noble in the natal village (Lineton 1975; Millar 1989). An economically successful Bugis person considers undertaking the haj pilgrimage a major goal symbolising their personal achievement and higher status; becoming haji ensures a respected position in the community. Like economic success in migration, haji status can bring a high degree of status honour to someone low born (Robinson 2002).

Secondly, migrants maintain contact with relatives in their natal village, who take care of their property. Migrants often return to marry. If a married man is engaged in temporary migration, the wife will stay in the homeland and take responsibility for managing their wealth. While the wife will join her husband if he migrates permanently, sometimes it may take years before the husband is ready to bring his family.

Thirdly, the Bugis maintain chain migration and a patronage system. A common pattern involves a patron in the new destination facilitating migration of followers, as well as chain migration through horizontal ties of kinship (Acciaioli 2000). A patron (Bug. *tau matoa*) is usually an elderly person who has the personality, knowledge and resources to protect and guide followers. The relationship can be based on familial relations, common village membership, or occupational ties. The patronage system is hierarchical, wherein a patron may in turn be a follower of a stronger and more influential patron (Pelras 2000). Patrons are expected to lend support to their followers in matters like finding jobs, providing accommodation or land to cultivate, and assisting in issues related to crimes or disputes. By way of exchange, a follower provides his labour, other services and loyalty.

Fourthly, as Jacqueline Lineton (1975) observed, Bugis have tended to settle in coastal areas and prefer unpopulated places. These "quickly assumed the aspect of purely Bugis districts, in which many of the features of Bugis society in Sulawesi could be recreated" (Lineton 1975: 196). Their dominance in the economic and religious fields often allowed the Bugis migrants to act as "agents of assimilation", where their domination and influence over the local people by way of economic and cultural practices was exercised (Ammarell 2002).

Lastly, being Muslim is an important identity for a Bugis, at home and as sojourners and settlers.[4] Being Bugis and being Muslim are synonymous (Pelras 1996; Said 2004). Christian Pelras (1993) states that there is an obligation for the Bugis to fully accept Islam as an inseparable part of custom. The concept of *adat* (custom; Bug. *panggaderreng*) comprises four interlinked values, namely *rapang* (Bug. good social behaviour), *bicara* (Bug. law/jurisprudence), *wari'* (Bug. rules of descent and hierarchy), and *sara'* (Bug. Islamic law and institutions). Bugis society in new settlements maintains the practice of Islam and customs in ceremonies related to life cycle and Islamic festivals.

Bugis as Aswaja Muslim

Bugis, at home and in their migration destinations, are renown for their strict adherence to Islam.[5] In the conduct of life cycle rituals and Islamic festivals they observe the Ahli Sunnah Wal-Jamaah ("Aswaja"), which literally means the followers of the Prophet's tradition and the consensus of the *ulama* (Islamic scholars).

The main feature of Bugis Aswaja tradition is the public reading from *barzanji* texts. Barzanji are a group of biographical literary works in Arabic on the life of the Prophet Muhammad that have become widespread as devotional texts for recitation (Kaptein 1993). Barzanji texts are used for the birthday of the Prophet Muhammad (Maulid); commemoration of the Prophet's nocturnal journey (Isra Miraj); the anniversary of a death; the ceremonial shaving of the first hair of a newborn baby; the ceremonial gathering at a circumcision; and wedding ceremonies (Kaptein 1993: 126).[6]

The public reading from barzanji texts is especially characteristic of Muslim communities in eastern Indonesia, even though it also occurs in Java and is widespread throughout the Muslim world (Gade 2004; Sila 1998; Alimi 2009). Anna Gade (2004) observed that there are regional variations in barzanji practices with respect to melodies used and the relative participations of men and women.

In the Aswaja tradition among the Bugis people, it is also crucial to chant *selawat* (praise songs to the Prophet Muhammad), *doa selamat* (prayers for safety and wellbeing), and *doa arwah* (prayers for the dead) in life cycle rituals. *Selawat* is usually chanted at the celebration of Maulid. *Doa selamat* and *doa arwah* begin with the recitation of Surah Al Fatiha, the first chapter of the Qur'an. While uttering these *doa* (prayers), the attendees sit on a mat with their legs crossed and raise their arms to place their palms in front of their faces. In *doa selamat,* Al Fatiha is followed by prayers for the living, asking for protection and wellbeing. In *doa arwah,* Al Fatiha is followed by prayers for the dead, primarily asking for forgiveness and a decent place for their spirits in the afterlife.

These aspects of Bugis Aswaja tradition are investigated in this chapter in the Bugis migrant community of Oesapa in Kupang, West Timor. I particularly focus on the important role of the mosque imam Haji Badar Daeng Pawero (henceforth shortened to "Imam Pawero") as a community and religious leader.[7]

Kampung Oesapa and Al Fitrah Mosque

Muslim settlement in Kampung Oesapa was established as recently as the late 1970s. The kampung is located some 10 kilometres east of the city centre along the coastal road that follows the foreshore of Kupang Bay. Kampung Oesapa, part of the Kelapa Lima sub-district, is well connected to other villages, as it is located along the main road from Kupang to Atambua; the latter is a border town between Indonesia and Timor Leste (see Map 8.1). The main road, Timor Raya Street,

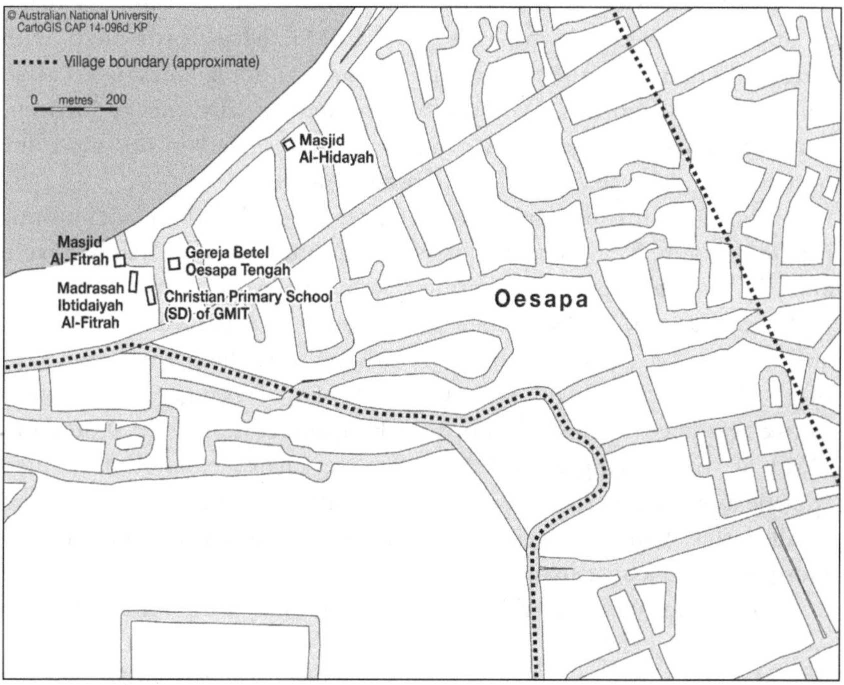

Map 8.1 Kampung Oesapa

is asphalted and in good condition, and is served by public transport such as intra-city public vans (*angkot*) and motorcycle taxis (*ojek*). Along the main road there are many hotels, motels and restaurants.

In the kampung, Muslims are the minority group, representing 15 per cent (around 3,600 people) of the total population of 24,158 (BPS 2011). The kampung represents a Muslim settlement that emerged after independence.[8] Muslims in Oesapa are predominantly commoner Bugis settlers from the Bone district in South Sulawesi.[9] The settlement is often referred to as "Kampung Bugis" (Bugis Quarter).

The kampung has relatively good public facilities. There is one community health centre attended by physicians and midwives. Education facilities are managed by either government or religious organisations (mosque or church). The Al Fitrah Mosque Foundation and GMIT Church[10] each have one kindergarten and one elementary school in the village, while the government also runs junior and senior high schools.

Fishery, cattle and poultry husbandry are important sources of livelihood,[11] as well as non-agricultural forms employment. As many as 800 people work in fisheries (BPS 2011). Many own boats with outboard engines, for their own use or to rent. Some work as artisanal fishers and fish porters. Well-to-do fishermen usually engage in deep-sea fishing using large boats. These can sail as far as the maritime border with Australia, mainly in search of *trepang*.[12]

Bugis Muslims in Kampung Oesapa built Al Fitrah village mosque in 1980 (Figure 8.1). The mosque was built one year after Imam Pawero and the first group of seven Bugis families settled there. According to Imam Pawero, in 1979 they purchased 233 square metres of land and obtained a permit to build a mosque with help from the head of the local religious office, a Catholic named Nanggeang. A committee was then formed, comprising Benyamin Thobias (a Protestant, Head of the Kupang Attorney's Office) as chairperson, Abdurahman Manaje as secretary, and Pawero as a committee member. Imam Pawero recalled that Christian neighbours helped in the construction of the mosque: "The construction of Al Fitrah Mosque was completed in 8 months and 15 days. The first Friday prayers at Al Fitrah Mosque were on 11 July 1980."

Al Fitrah Mosque is the centre of Muslim activities: Islamic learning, religious festivals, life cycles ceremonies and learning for

Figure 8.1 Al Fitrah Mosque. Photo by Stella Aleida Hutagalung.

converts. During fieldwork, I observed that children aged 5–12 years attended *pengajian* (religious instruction including Qur'anic learning) every afternoon (except weekends), while pengajian for women converts (*mualaf*) (Majlis Taklim) was held on Mondays. On Tuesdays and Thursdays Muslim youth conducted the reading of the Qur'an. Women members of the general Majlis Taklim (that is, not the one exclusively for mualaf) met fortnightly for religious instruction. On Fridays, the mosque was packed with members of the congregation for Friday prayers, including university students from nearby campuses.

Celebrations of important days are also held in the mosque, such as Isra Mi'raj (ascension and night journey of the Prophet), gathering for breaking the fast, *tarawih* (Ramadan prayers), and prayers for Idul Fitri (religious festival marking the end of the fasting month) and Idul Adha (The Haj festival). The exception is the Maulid (the birthday of the Prophet Muhammad) celebration, which is held in the open space in front of the *madrasah*, an Islamic school run by the mosque. Life cycle rituals, especially wedding ceremonies, are also held at the mosque.

The mosque is central to the reproduction of the Aswaja traditions discussed above. In Kampung Oesapa, in Kupang city, according to Imam Pawero, the tradition of reading from the barzanji was brought from Bone in South Sulawesi. Al Fitrah Mosque has formed a barzanji reading group comprising ten men including Imam Pawero and the four deputies[13] who were present on important occasions, such as at *akekah* (the first hair cutting), *khitan* (circumcision), and pre-wedding ceremonies (Bug. *mappatemme*, *paccing* and *tudampenni*) (see p. 208).

Public reading from the barzanji is also conducted when Muslims of Oesapa are preparing to undertake the haj pilgrimage. On this occasion, reading from the barzanji along with *doa selamat* (prayers for safety and wellbeing for the living) are undertaken at the mosque every Friday night (for around 40 minutes) before the pilgrims depart and until their return. The intention is to pray for pilgrims' safety in their journey and for their families at home.

Al Fitrah Mosque has a foundation, chaired by the youngest son of Imam Pawero, which is mainly responsible for the financial management of the mosque. It has run a kindergarten since 1983, at which time the foundation signed a partnership with the South Sulawesi Family Association (Keluarga Kerukunan Sulawesi Selatan, KKSS) to establish an elementary Islamic school. In 1994 the school was renamed Madrasah Ibtidaiyah. In 2011, Madrasah Al Fitrah had 431 students, of whom 75 per cent had parents from South Sulawesi and 25 per cent came from Alor, Flores, Java and Kalimantan. The school offered additional courses on Islam after regular hours.

The Imam: Haji Badar Daeng Pawero

Life Story

Imam Pawero is a Bugis commoner from Bone district who pioneered the establishment of the Muslim community in Kampung Oesapa. He was born in 1925 in Cellu village, Barebbo sub-district, in Bone district (South Sulawesi) to J. Mappe Daeng Mekkelo and J. Cabbe. Imam Pawero, completed three years of primary education and joined the Japanese military training for a short period when Japanese troops occupied Sulawesi during World War II.

When Indonesia proclaimed independence in 1945, Imam Pawero joined a paramilitary nationalist group called the village police (*polisi kampung*), serving as a group commander. After the revolution ended in 1949 he married Khatijah Daeng Talumu and found a job on a ship trading in copra. He sailed to various towns in what is now Southeast Sulawesi Province, including Kendari, and went as far as Toli-Toli (Central Sulawesi), and Tawau and other towns in Kalimantan.

In the early 1950s the Kahar Muzakkar Islamic rebellion broke out in Sulawesi and in 1959 Imam Pawero decided to leave his Bone village for Kupang. He settled in Kampung Airmata, where some of his relatives had earlier migrated, and began selling clothes, travelling extensively to the local markets surrounding Kupang. When his business began to pick up, at the end of 1960, he brought his wife and children from Bone. In 1961 he purchased his own mini-van, and was able to make the haj pilgrimage in 1965.

Since his arrival, Imam Pawero has assumed an active role as participant and supporter of the religious activities of the Bugis community. He and his wife organised pengajian for children and market sellers at their house. Later the pengajian was granted assistance from the local religious authority. In 1961, Pawero was appointed to chair the Badan Amil Zakat, which was responsible for organising donation and almsgiving. He has been active in Islamic organisations and between 1994 and 1998 was an elected member of the executive board of the Nahdlatul Ulama of East Nusa Tenggara Province.

Imam Pawero maintained close relationships with other Bugis migrants spread among many urban neighbourhoods in Kupang. In 1968 he helped establish a mosque in Kampung Camplong, one of the oldest Bugis settlements in Kupang. He also began to assist his relatives in South Sulawesi to follow him. Over the course of a few years he had helped as many as 40 members of his extended family to migrate and settle in Kupang.

In 1973 Imam Pawero moved to the predominantly Christian urban village, Kampung Oesapa, and built a house in an uninhabited area. He changed his business from selling clothes to fishing, eventually moving to deep-sea fishing. Migration of Imam Pawero's family opened the way for other Bugis families from Bone in South Sulawesi; many were relatives. He said that the number of families had grown from seven, when he initially moved to Kupang, to hundreds, by the time of my research.

In October 1987 his wife passed away. At the time of my research he was living with one of his daughters, in a house located across from the Al Fitrah Mosque. His youngest child is a government employee at the local office of the Ministry of Religious Affairs.

His Roles

Imam Parewo assumed the role of imam of Al Fitrah Mosque on its establishment. As the founding imam, he served for more than 30 years. Due to his old age and physical frailty, at the time of my research he no longer assumed responsibility for leading daily prayers and was assisted by four deputies—three Bugis and one from Flores—who performed the following tasks: announcing *azan* (call for prayers) and leading prayers (daily and weekly Friday prayers); representing the imam at wedding ceremonies or life cycle rituals; and supervising the organisation of Islamic festivals. Occasionally, they are assigned as *khatib* (preacher) at the Friday prayers when the *khatib* from the Office of Ministry of Religious Affairs is not available.[14]

An *ustad* (Qur'anic teacher) also helped Imam Pawero in the tasks associated with mosque leadership. Religious instruction begins at the age of four or five, when children join daily Qur'anic instruction to train them in reading verses of the Qur'an (pengajian) led by

Ustad Maman. In addition, he also coordinated activities of Remaja Masjid (Muslim Youth) in conducting regular sermons, and organising celebration of important Islamic days.

The following sections describe Imam Pawero's roles in maintaining the integration of Islamic law in Bugis adat through the celebration of Islamic festivals (Maulid, Isra Mi'raj), life cycle rituals such as wedding and *akekah* and through facilitating the conversion process and the establishment of *majlis taklim* for mualaf.

In Islamic Festivals

The Prophet's birthday (*Maulid*): In contrast to other neighbourhoods such as Kampung Solor, Kampung Airmata, and Kampung Bonipoi, Maulid in Oesapa was celebrated as a simple ceremony with no carnival aspects.[15] In the celebration of Maulid, the Imam emphasised three aspects; inclusion of a wide range of Muslims in the celebration, maintenance of Bugis custom, and preservation of relationships with the Christian majority.

I attended the ceremony on 15 February 2011, which was a national holiday. The day before the ceremony, the *masjid* (mosque) youth volunteered to erect the tents, stage and arrange chairs for the guests in front of the *madrasah* (religious school). They erected a banner, decorated the stage with colourful streamers and balloons, and hung decorative eggs. When Imam Pawero was still strong and healthy he would supervise and lead the organisation of the Islamic festivals. But now he leaves it to his deputies and Ustad Maman.

The celebration started at around 10 a.m. Imam Pawero invited the Oesapa village head (a Christian) to attend the ceremony. He delivered a speech in which he expressed his gratitude for being invited, and his appreciation that mutual respect and understanding existed between Muslims and Christians in the kampung.

The celebration comprised a fashion show, dance and musical performances, and a sermon. Children wore Islamic clothes in the fashion show, while South Sulawesi dances were performed by a group of child dancers wearing traditional Bugis costume. Members of the women's Majlis Taklim sang and played music. After the performances, an *ustad* began his sermon about the importance of following the way Prophet Muhammad had lived. At the end of the occasion, all guests received a decorative parcel filled with sticky rice, eggs and fruit.

Imam Pawero explained that Maulid rituals in Oesapa comprise a mix of Bugis tradition from Bone and new elements practised by the Bugis settlers in Kupang. The parcel is a symbol of blessing (*berkat*). Sticky rice symbolises the bond of brotherhood among Muslims, while eggs represent purity of the heart. He said that sticky rice and eggs in the decorative parcels given to the guests were of Bone origin, but Bugis in Oesapa could add new elements such as a variety of fruit and vegetables.

For Imam Pawero the important point was that Maulid was the subject of celebration, even in a modest way. Celebration of Maulid is a way to remember that Muhammad is the Prophet who has called Muslims to obey what Allah commanded and avoid what Allah prohibited. He added, "We celebrate birthdays of our family members, so it would be a pity if we did not celebrate the birthday of Prophet Muhammad. Our children in particular should understand the importance of Maulid."

"*Safar Bath*" (*Mandi Safar*): Another ritual that is important for Bugis people is the performance of the "Safar Bath" on the last Wednesday of the month of Safar. The bathing ritual aims at purifying and seeking protection in the year to come. It derives from Sufi practice and is observed mainly by members of the mystic order, students of religious teachers and people who are sick. It involves praying or writing down a prayer in Arabic words on a piece of paper (Pelras 1996).

I observed Bugis migrants in Kampung Oesapa maintaining this practice. The mosque distributed pieces of paper containing prayers in Arabic words to congregation members who took them home. The bathing ritual is performed in the homes of congregation members, unlike in the older Muslim settlements in Kupang where the Safar bathing ritual was conducted communally in the river or on the beach.

Isra Mi'raj: I had the opportunity to observe the celebration of Isra Mi'raj (Assumption of the Prophet) at the mosque on 29 June 2011. The celebration was comprised mainly of recitation of *selawat*, Qur'anic verses and a sermon. The imam entered the mosque at 8.50 a.m., where members of the congregation waited sitting crossed-legged on the floor. The Remaja Masjid (mosque youth group) members began the occasion by chanting *selawat*. The host of the ceremony then recited several *surah* (chapters) from the Qur'an.

In the sermon, the *ustad* emphasised the importance for Muslims to uphold Prophet Muhammad as the last prophet. The event of Isra Mi'raj was the second biggest miracle (*mukjizat*) given by Allah to Muhammad after the revelation of the holy Qur'an. The primary message of the celebration is for Muslims to obey the obligation to perform daily prayer (*salat*), as it is a way for human beings to worship Allah. The Prophet himself had received the instruction to perform *salat* during the Isra Mi'raj. The *ustad* mentioned Imam Pawero's practice as exemplary: saying that despite his physical constraints, the imam always made the effort to perform obligatory *salat* and recommended (*sunnah*) prayers.

Life Cycle Rituals

The First Hair Cutting (*Akekah*): I attended an *akekah*[16] (hair-shaving and animal sacrifice occasion) for a 2-year-old boy. One day before the ceremony, two goats were slaughtered and the meat distributed to neighbours and orphanages. The parents invited the barzanji group, close neighbours and relatives. The ceremony started at around 11a.m., before the afternoon prayer. Imam Pawero led the ritual. Incense was burning in the living room, where the ritual took place. The barzanji group members gathered inside the room, sitting cross-legged on a carpet, along with the baby boy's father. Women guests sat on the veranda.

Imam Pawero started the ceremony by chanting *doa selamat*. After that, the group recited barzanji. Banana and sticky rice were served on two trays that had been placed beside the burning incense during the recitation. When the barzanji was completed, the congregation stood and performed *selawat*. Meanwhile, an opened young coconut was placed close to Imam Pawero. The father took the baby to Imam Pawero, who placed scissors in the coconut water and then cut a lock of the boy's hair. The young coconut symbolises a healthy and strong character, and expectation of a good life ahead. After the hair was cut, the imam gently uttered a prayer in the boy's ear. Later the father took the boy and presented him to all members of the barzanji group, who took turns to cut his hair. The hair was then weighed, and its weight was equated with gold or silver whose current price became an amount of money that the parents, on behalf of their son, should donate to the poor.

Figure 8.2 *Akekah* ritual. Photo by Stella Aleida Hutagalung.

To conclude the occasion, an *ustad* delivered a sermon. He stressed that *akekah* had the symbolic meaning of parents paying a redemption "fee" (*tebusan*) to Allah to completely claim a child. A child essentially belongs to Allah and will remain so until the parents pay the *tebusan* by performing the *akekah* ceremony. Unless *akekah* has been undertaken, the parents do not "own" the child. Consequently, they will not be able to recognise each other in the afterlife.[17] He added that by completing the *akekah*, the parents symbolically claimed possession of the child which means that when the parents passed away the utterance of *doa arwah* from the child would reach them and help to lighten their sufferings in the afterlife. He stressed that parents who could afford *akekah* should do it at the earliest time possible.

Wedding Ceremonies: For Bugis, marriage within existing kinship networks is regarded as ideal.[18] The most desirable arrangement is marriage between cousins, either parallel or cross cousins (Idrus 2003). Concerning social strata, marriage should be between two persons of equal birth status. However, it is not unusual for a man from a lower status to marry a woman of a higher status. This is justified by the man's personal achievements, such as his position in the bureaucracy, a higher education degree, or wealth (Millar 1989; see Wahyuddin Halim, this volume).

Religion is one of the most important criteria in the selection of a marriage partner, along with kinship, status and personal qualities. A marriage partner should be a Muslim; in their homeland, marriage between Bugis Muslims and non-Muslims is very rare. However, inter-marriage is not an alien practice for Bugis migrants. In such cases, a non-Muslim partner marrying a Bugis is required to convert to Islam. This relates to an expectation that part of a wife's role is to pray for her husband's safety and wellbeing (Bug. *tuling méllauangngi décéng lakkainna*) and to contribute to the household (Idrus 2003: 92).

Personal qualities for male and female marriage partners differ considerably. The desired personal qualities for women are wealth (Bug. *sugi'*), beauty (Bug. *makessi-kessing*), good descent (Bug. *mappa-siabbatireng*) and piety (Bug. *pagama*). These qualities complement each other, but as Nurul Ilmi Idrus (2003: 7) observes, piety is the most important attribute, as it allows a woman to control her behaviour and protect the family's honour (Bug. *siri'*). A prospective husband is ideally brave (Bug. *warani*) to protect the family's honour, clever (Bug. *macca*), wealthy (Bug. *sugi'*) and a religious leader (Bug. *panrita*) so that he can guide his family. Possession of these characteristics is especially important if a man intends to marry a woman of higher status. Of these four qualities, Idrus (2004) notes that the attribute of *panrita* is the most valued. While for a woman, individual piety in everyday life (Bug. *pagaman*) is most important, for a man his knowledge and authority as a religious leader in his community (*panrita*) is most valued (Idrus 2004; Pelras 2000).

In the Bugis tradition, the Islamic ceremony (*akad nikah*) and wedding party are often held on different occasions. *Akad nikah* is the most important step in the entire wedding procedure, as it officially marks the union as legal according to Islam and the state. The *akad* is conducted by an imam and is registered in the Religious Office. The groom signs a marriage contract after repeating marriage vows and paying the bridewealth. Apart from the groom, the presence of the bride's legal guardian and two witnesses from both parties are required in the *akad* for the Islamic marriage ceremony/contract. The wedding festivity, on the other hand, is a requirement of adat.

I attended the ceremonies on the night before the *akad* at a bride's house in Oesapa. The ceremonies comprised four continuous events: the graduation ceremony in Qur'anic reading (Bug. *mappatemme*); a public reading from a barzanji text; a cleansing ceremony (Bug. *paccing*); and a night's vigil (Bug. *tudampenni*). In the graduation ceremony, also known as *khataman*, the bride was required to recite the Qur'an in front of the guests.[19] She was accompanied by four women, comprising her grandmother, mother and aunties.

On this occasion, the presence of the imam (Haji Badar Daeng Pawero) and the barzanji group was required. The bride sat and opened the Qur'an, then read some verses before the imam, witnessed by the members of the barzanji group and close relatives. The imam sometimes helped to correct her pronunciation. After the bride completed the recitation, the barzanji group performed a public reading from the barzanji text. The next step was a cleansing ritual for the bride. Wearing traditional Bugis dress, the bride sat on the floor near a bowl of henna (*innai*) leaves, with her hands upturned. Close family members and relatives took turns to paint her palms with the henna dye. The ritual symbolised love and protection from the family to the bride. The bridewealth in this marriage amounted to a 2-gram gold ring and accoutrements required for worship (*seperangkat alat salat*). In addition to the bridewealth, the groom is required to pay an agreed amount towards the cost of the wedding feast.[20]

After the cleansing ritual, the imam led the chanting of *doa selamat*. The guests were not expected to leave the venue afterwards. Some guests stayed awake at the bride's house all night long (Bug. *tudampenni*). Meals were served and the guests socialised with each other until dawn to show respect for the bride's parents. At the house of the groom, similar rituals were performed for the groom, except for the cleansing ritual with henna dye.

In Conversion

Conversion Rituals. Marital conversion is common in Kampung Oesapa.[21] Many Bugis men marry non-Muslim women who subsequently convert to Islam (and are referred to as mualaf or "the converts").[22] If a person wishes to marry someone of a different religion, one or other partner must convert so the couple professes to the same

Figure 8.3 Bugis pre-wedding ceremony [*mappatemme* (Bug.)]. Photo by Stella Aleida Hutagalung.

Figure 8.4 The newlyweds after the Islamic marriage vows. Photo by Stella Aleida Hutagalung.

religion. Typically, a wife would follow the religion of her husband. There are no official statistics on the new converts in Oesapa, but my informants stated that approximately 20 new converts were registered as members of the Majlis Taklim for *mualaf* at Al Fitrah Mosque. These women mualaf are from different cultural-linguistic groups, including Roti and Flores, and were previously Protestant or Catholic.

Since most conversions were marital, the ritual of conversion usually took place before the Islamic wedding vows. The ritual comprises *mandi bersih* (a symbolic bathing to cleanse the body) and recitation of *syahadat* (testimony of faith). Then a convert is required to take ablutions and perform a *salat*. Before these rituals can be performed, a convert should declare an intention (*niat*) to enter Islam sincerely, only for Allah. The conversion ritual is supervised by an imam and requires the presence of two witnesses. They can be mosque officials or certain figures from the community. Conversion rituals also involve the changing of name and circumcision, but the latter is not obligatory for women.

My informant by the name of Rahma (a Rotenese woman) converted to Islam due to her marriage with Suaib, a grandson of Imam Pawero. Rahma recalled that Imam Pawero conducted a conversion ritual for her one week prior to the wedding ceremony. She performed mandi bersih under the supervision of Imam Pawero and witnessed by close members of the family. Imam Pawero recited prayers and helped her pour the water. Rahma recited the following prayer during the mandi bersih: "I am pouring this first bath water over my body as an intention to convert to Islam. I am washing my body in the hope that Allah will forgive my sins. I hope that Allah takes me out of the dark into the light as if I am a newborn."

The objective of mandi bersih, according to Imam Pawero, was to cleanse the sins and purify the body of the mualaf—from *haram* (forbidden) foods and earthly sins. After undergoing mandi bersih, Rahma was asked to recite *syahadat* witnessed by Imam Pawero, Rahma's husband, and her father-in-law. Rahma then took *wudu* and performed *isya* prayer.

Rahma was very enthusiastic when explaining the conversion process. As part of the conversion, she changed her name from Regina Messakh to the "Islamic name" Rahma. She added: "The word '*rahma*' means blessing. From that moment, I became Rahma. My marriage certificate and ID card bear the name Rahma Suaib. However, old documents such as school certificates still bear my old name Regina Messakh because it was not easy to change it".

In Kampung Oesapa, circumcision is not obligatory for adult females converting to Islam. Of all my informants, only one mualaf was circumcised. A bathing ritual is considered sufficient to cleanse the sins and purify their bodies from *haram* (forbidden) foods and earthly sins.[23] A new convert will also adopt an Islamic name, and change her identity documents accordingly. After legally becoming a Muslim, a process of learning the religion begins. The learning process for these new converts is facilitated by the dedicated Majlis Taklim of Al Fitrah Mosque, which was formed to help these converts.

A marriage between a Bugis man and a female convert can be seen as a process "to make a non-kin into kin" or to make an "outsider" (Bug. *to laing*) into "insider" (Bug. *tennia to laing*) (Idrus 2003). Upon becoming a Muslim, these women are expected to acquire proper knowledge of Islam. They use several sources to learn about their new religion, including their husband, their husband's relatives, and by becoming a member of Majlis Taklim for mualaf in Oesapa. Many express the importance of becoming a good Muslim, by performing obligatory rituals, such as prayers and fasting, and learning to read the Qur'an. I observed that new converts marrying Bugis men put considerable effort into learning Islam. I found that for these new converts, attaining proper knowledge of Islam and being a pious Muslim are considered ways to act befitting a Bugis.

The Majlis Taklim (Religious Study Group) for Converts. At the time of research, Imam Pawero had facilitated conversion of 33 mualaf since 1961—all cases of marital conversion. They came not only from Kampung Oesapa but also from other areas in Kupang. It was because the number of mualaf had been increasing, that Imam Pawero took the initiative in 2000 to form the Majlis Taklim for mualaf women at Al Fitrah Mosque. In its early years, it was run rather poorly and was revitalised only in 2010, when Rahma was chosen as coordinator.

The Majlis Taklim for mualaf women conducts regular pengajian for its members every Monday afternoon for one-and-a-half hours. A councillor from the Office of the Ministry of Religious Affairs is assigned to teach them. At the time of my research, the number of participants varied from 6 to 10 women aged 20–55-years-old and the class took place on the mosque terrace.[24] The Qur'an learning was conducted in stages, starting from the beginner level where they were learning from a reading module called Iqra (little Qur'an). Those who acquired the ability to master Iqra may teach other mualaf. Upon completion the Iqra lessons, a convert could continue to the next stage, referred to as "entering the big Qur'an". This weekly session also offered lectures on various topics about Islam, for instance about morals (*akhlak*), daily prayer and fasting.

Imam Pawero stressed that Islam emphasised the importance of taking care of mualaf, people who will always need guidance in relation to Islam. This is an obligation of every Muslim. The purpose of taking care of mualaf is to prevent them relapsing to the old faith. He added that this is one of the reasons why they are eligible to receive alms (*zakat fitrah*).[25] Imam Pawero emphasised the importance of Majlis Taklim for mualaf, saying:

> It is important to provide guidance for mualaf to show them that they are not alone in learning Islam even though the learning process takes time. The mualaf are similar to kindergarten students, who are just starting to learn basic knowledge. To become a good Muslim, a mualaf should be equipped with the good basics. Majlis Taklim is one of the best ways to guide them and we, as mosque officials, have to encourage them to be involved in activities be that Islamic festivals, discussions and others.

The Majlis Taklim for mualaf received mixed responses from the converts. For some of them, religious learning was difficult. Some were hesistant to attend the weekly session. As coordinator, Rahma spent a lot of time persuading certain mualaf to participate in the activities of the Majlis Taklim. The reason for their hesitation, she asserted, was because they were not practising salat yet, or were still not able to read the Qur'an properly.

Not all of the women were getting the support they needed in learning the new religion. Ideally a husband bears responsibility to teach his mualaf wife. Some were learning Islam from their children, who since childhood had received information about Islam and had skills in reciting the Qur'an from school or pengajian. These converts found the Majlis Taklim provided a good opportunity to learn Islam from *ustad*/*ustazah* and to access books on Islam.

Rosita explained that her husband, a fisherman, never taught her about *salat* or how to read the Qur'an. She felt lucky that she had many mualaf friends in the Majlis Taklim with whom she could learn about Islam and how to read the Qur'an. Rahma on the other hand, preferred to attend short intensive courses on Islam (*pesantren kilat*) organised by Al Fitrah elementary schools, usually during the fasting month.

The learning activities at Majlis Taklim allowed many mualaf to feel more confident in Qur'anic recitation. Gaining confidence is crucial for them because they are expected to be able to help their children in learning the Qur'an as an aspect of the highly-valued role of a Bugis wife to protect the family's honour (Bug. *siri'*).

Conclusion

The *umat* Islam in Kupang displays a hybrid of different Islamic traditions. Each Muslim community is focused on its mosque where religious and ritual practice both preserve traditions brought from places of origin and share influences. This chapter has focused on the Bugis Muslim community in predominantly Christian Kampung Oesapa and the ways in which community members sustain their cultural and religious identities. This is a relatively recent Muslim migrant community in Kupang: the process of migration fits the pattern of Bugis migration, involving chain migration and preservation of Aswaja Islam and Bugis adat. Imam Pawero has been a key figure, acting as patron in facilitating the migration of followers from his home village. But he is also the authority in Kampung Oesapa in regard to both the sharia and Bugis traditions. He performed this role in leading religious observance and guiding community rituals. He anticipated that his replacement, either one of his assistants or his son, will be able to retain this dual role into the future, sustaining the specifically inflected set of religious and ritual practices that express Bugis identity in the diaspora.

Islamisation is an ongoing process in Kupang, and the Bugis migrants of Oesapa reflect influences of other Muslim communities and also contemporary religious organisation—both state and non-state—in their practice of Islam. Despite being a minority, the Bugis Muslim community in Kampung Oesapa has been able to reproduce itself through intermarriage with women from non-Muslim backgrounds and these converts are actively transformed into pious Bugis women. This chapter has demonstrated how conversion through marriage is an important aspect of Islamisation.

The Muslims of Kampung Oesapa exemplify the ways in which Islam has spread through the archipelago, but also the ways that Islam is accommodated to cultural traditions and practices. As members of a Muslim minority in a predominantly Christian part of Indonesia (see also Andrew McWilliam, this volume) they also exemplify the practices of religious harmony achieved through affinal and kinship relations that we find in the eastern archipelago.

Notes

1. This article is based on a chapter of the author's PhD thesis in Anthropology from The Australian National University (ANU) entitled "Being Muslim in a Christian Town: Variety, Practices and Renewal" (2015) for which fieldwork was conducted in Kupang from January 2011 to February 2012.
2. When Timor was under the control of Makassar, Bugis involvement there was restricted but restored after the kingdom was defeated by the Dutch (Widyatmika 2004).
3. Bugis settled in Kampung Alak, Kampung Camplong and also in old Muslim *kampung* such as Airmata and Bonipoi (Widyatmika 2004).
4. According to Pelras (1993), the historical development of Islamic identity among the Bugis occurred in several stages. The first was the introduction of the "five pillars"; circumcision; avoidance of pork; celebration of festivals; and Islamic ways in important life cycle rituals (marriage and funerals). At this stage, Islamic public morality was not emphasised, therefore rent-seeking, gambling, alcohol and opium, and the practice of giving offerings to sacred entities, were tolerated. The second stage was the adoption of Islamic institutions into adat (custom). Pelras (1993) maintains that an important impact of these processes can be seen in the changes in life cycle rituals, which are now characterised by Islamic teachings. For example, in life cycle rituals people read the Qur'an and the barzanji text.
5. Interestingly, pre-Islamic beliefs and practices, including the worship of regalia, and the active role of pagan priests, were also preserved. The religious orientation of Bugis Muslims is divided into orthodox Islam and syncretic forms (marked by mysticism and Sufi orders), albeit this is not a clear-cut distinction (Pelras 1996).

6. Barzanji texts are readily available, commonly purchased, and translated into Indonesian and various regional Indonesian languages including Bugis (Kaptein 1993: 126–7).
7. Haji Badar Daeng Pawero was born in 1925 in Cellu village, South Sulawesi. He passed away in December 2017 at the age 92.
8. The development of Muslim communities in Kupang has taken place in stages since the 1700s. There has been a Muslim minority in Kupang since the city was established by the Dutch. In 2013, Islam is professed by around 16 per cent of the total population of 365,358 (BPS 2013).
9. In their homeland, Bugis society is highly hierarchical. The hierarchy can be seen in the complex division of Bugis people into the different layers of nobles and commoners (Pelras 1996: 152; Millar 1989: 25).
10. GMIT refers to Gereja Masehi Injili Timor (Christian Evangelical Church of Timor) established in the Dutch colonial period.
11. Chicken and pigs are most popular, followed by goats. Chickens are highly valued for both eggs and meat. Like cattle, goats are important for slaughter for Idul Adha (Haj Festival) ceremonial purposes.
12. This enterprise involves substantial capital and risk. While the construction of one of these boats costs Rp50 million (AU$5,000), vessels that have been caught by crossing into Australian territorial waters have usually been confiscated and burned, and the fishermen arrested and jailed.
13. My observations in Kupang were that the number of barzanji groups in other kampung were not limited to ten men. In the other communities, all Muslim men attending Islamic festivals could participate in the public reading a barzanji text. In Kampung Airmata, women also participated in reciting the barzanji even though they were sitting at the back of the mosque behind the men.
14. The selection of the imam and the deputies is based on the ability to read the Qur'an and chant prayers, their knowledge of Islam, and ability to socialise with the community members. Only one of the deputies is a haji.
15. These kampung are older Muslim establishments. For details of Maulid celebration in Kupang, see Hutagalung (2015).
16. *Akekah* is the hair-shaving ceremony for a newborn baby, an important occasion in which to express gratitude to Allah. If the baby is female, one goat is slaughtered, whereas if it is male, two goats are slaughtered. *Akekah* is usually held when a child is 40 days old or less, however, timing is not rigid and it can be done whenever the parents are financially ready. Usually the ritual takes place in the house rather than in a mosque.
17. John Bowen (1993) found that for the Gayo community in Sumatra, *akekah* that they term *kikah* has a symbolic meaning of "redeem the

child from God". The parents are indebted to God and the sacrifice offered in *kikah* aims at cancelling the debt. *Kikah* also establishes ties between the parents and the child.

18. Farid F. Saenong (2012) states that among the nobility, first-cousin marriage is desirable, while among non-nobles marriage between second, third and fourth cousins is preferred. The preference for endogamous marriage is aimed at bringing extended family members closer together. Greg Acciaioli (2000) found that among migrants in Jambi (Sumatra), cousin marriage was still favoured and many young men in Jambi were sent to their natal villages to marry their cousins. Saenong (2012) asserts that cousin marriage has transformed into endogamous marriage on the basis of village, sub-ethnicity and even ethnicity in contemporary Bugis society. In a Bugis migrant village in Bantaeng district South Sulawesi, Saenong (2012: 2) found that while cousin marriage had initially been strictly practised, several generations later endogamy was also practised between Bugis families in the same village, or at least with other Bugis. The notion of *namu to laing napubainé assala' Ugi' mua* (Bug. "It is acceptable to marry 'the Other' as long as s/he is a Bugis") reflects the importance of this principle.
19. Ability to read the Qur'an is essential for Bugis. Children are given religious instruction from kindergarten onwards. Qur'anic learning is usually conducted in stages and is given by an *ustad* at a mosque. Traditionally a celebration is held following a completion of each level (Pelras 1996: 194). The celebration can also be postponed until the pupil is ready to get married.
20. In the Bugis homeland, the system of rank determines how the bridewealth is calculated. The sum varies from one family to another, depending on the hereditary rank, wealth and level of education (Millar 1989). In Bugis custom, the calculation of bridewealth was once quite rigid. For example, a bride of different social status may be worth 22 *riyal*, 44 *riyal*, 88 *riyal* and so forth. In the past, 22 *riyal* was equal to 22 *perak*, probably Rp 22 million at the time of Millar's research (Millar 1989).
21. In Indonesia, marriage between Muslims and Christians is a controversial topic due to the matter of spousal conversion. The prohibition of interfaith marriage is stipulated in the Law of Marriage No.1/1974 (Ropi 2013). If a Muslim wishes to engage in interfaith marriage with a non-Muslim, the marriage can be neither conducted nor registered in the KUA (Office of Islamic Affairs), but rather in Kantor Catatan Sipil (KCS, Civil Registration Office), which is authorised to register marriages of non-Muslim Indonesians. To my knowledge only certain KCS in Indonesia are willing to register an interfaith marriage.

22. In Kupang, he or she will still be called *mualaf* even years after conversion. *Mualaf* implies that his/her heart is attracted to Islam.
23. Notions of cleanliness are important in Islam. In his study of the Banda Islands (Maluku), Phillip Winn (2002) noted that "being Muslim" in Lonthoir equated to *bikin bersih* (that is, being/doing [what is] clean), including ritual cleansing in the context of washing before prayer (ablution), circumcision and restrictions related to menstruation, as well as acting with good intention and behaving morally.
24. I went almost every Monday to this Majlis Taklim and saw how passionate all these mualaf were to learn to read the Qur'an. They would refer to the Indonesian translation of the Qur'an when they needed to understand the meanings of certain verses.
25. The other seven categories of people who are eligible to receive *zakat fitrah* are the poor, the needy, *zakat* collectors, those who are enslaved, those who are in debt, those who work for the cause of Allah, and the wayfarer.

References

Acciaioli, Greg. 2000. "Kinship and Debt: The Social Organization of Bugis Migration and Fish Marketing at Lake Lindu, Central Sulawesi." *Bijdragen tot de Taal-, Land-en Volkenkunde* 156 (3): 588–617.

Alimi, Moh Yasir. 2009. "Inculcating Islam: The Public Sphere and the Islamic Traditions of South Sulawesi." PhD diss., The Australian National University.

Ammarell, Gene. 2002. "Bugis Migration and Modes of Adaptation to Local Situations." *Ethnology* 41(1): 51–67.

BPS (Badan Pusat Statistic) Kota Kupang. 2011. *Kota Kupang dalam Angka 2011* [Kupang Municipality in Figures 2011]. Kupang: BPS Kota Kupang.

———. 2012. *Kota Kupang dalam Angka 2012* [Kupang Municipality in Figures 2012]. Kupang: BPS Kota Kupang.

———. 2013. *Kota Kupang dalam Angka 2013* [Kupang Municipality in Figures 2013]. Kupang: BPS Kota Kupang.

Bowen, John R. 1993. *Muslims through Discourse: Religion and Ritual in Gayo Society*. Princeton: Princeton University Press.

Farram, Steven. 2010. *A Political History of West Timor 1901–1967*. Saarbrücken: Lambert Academic Publishing.

Gade, Anna M. 2004. *Perfection Makes Practice. Learning, Emotion and the Recited Qur'an in Indonesia*. Honolulu: University of Hawai'i Press.

Hutagalung, Stella Aleida. 2015. "Being Muslim in a Christian Town: Variety, Practices and Renewal." PhD diss., The Australian National University.

Idrus, Nurul Ilmi. 2003. "'To Take Each Other': Bugis Practices of Gender, Sexuality and Marriage." PhD diss., The Australian National University.

———. 2004. "Behind the Notion of *Siala*: Marriage, *Adat* and Islam among the Bugis in South Sulawesi." *Intersections: Gender and Sexuality In Asia and the Pacific*, Issue 10. http://intersections.anu.edu.au/issue10/idrus.html.

Juhannis, Hamdan. 2006. "The Struggle for Formalist Islam in South Sulawesi: from Darul Islam (DI) to Komite Persiapan Penegakan Syariat Islam (KPPSI)." PhD diss., The Australian National University.

Kaptein, Nico J.G. 1993. "The Berdiri Mawlid Issue among Indonesian Muslims in the Period from Circa 1875 to 1930." *Bijdragen tot de Taal-, Land- en Volkenkunde* 149: 124–53.

Lineton, Jacqueline. 1975. "*'Pasompe' Ugi'*: Bugis Migrants and Wanderers." *Archipel* 10: 173–201.

Millar, Susan Bolyard. 1989. *Bugis Weddings: Rituals of Social Location in Modern Indonesia*. California: Center for South and Southeast Asia Studies, University of California.

Pelras, Christian. 1993. "Religion, Tradition, and the Dynamics Of Islamization in South Sulawesi." *Indonesia* 57: 133–54.

———. 1996. *The Bugis*. Cambridge: Blackwell Publishers.

———. 2000. "Patron–Client Ties among the Bugis and Makassarese of South Sulawesi." *Bijdragen tot de Taal-, Land- en Volkenkunde* 156 (3): 393–432.

Robinson, Kathryn. 2002. "Inter-Ethnic Violence: The Bugis and the Problem of Explanation." In *Beyond Jakarta: Regional Autonomy and Local Society in Indonesia,* ed. Minako Sakai, 145–72. Adelaide: Crawford House Publishing.

Ropi, Ismatu. 2013. "The Politics of Regulating Religion: State, Civil Society and the Quest for Religious Freedom in Modern Indonesia." PhD diss., The Australian National University.

Saenong, Faried F. 2012. "Kindred Endogamy in a Bugis Migrant Community." *Intersections: Gender and Sexuality In Asia and the Pacific*, Issue 30. http://intersections.anu.edu.au/issue30/saenong1.htm.

Said, Nurman. 2004. "Religion and Cultural Identity among the Bugis." *Inter-Religio* 45: 12–20.

Sila, Muhammad Adlin. 1998. "Ma'rifatullah, in Search of Union with Allah: The Sayyid of Cikoang, South Sulawesi." Master's diss., The Australian National University.

Widyatmika, Munandjar. 2004. *Sejarah Islam Di Nusa Tenggara Timur* [The History of Islam in East Nusa Tenggara]. Kupang: Pusat Pengembangan Madrasah and Kantor Wilayah Departemen Agama Propinsi Nusa Tenggara Timur.

Winn, Phillip. 2002. "Banda the Blessed Land: Local Identification and Morality in a Maluku Muslim Community." PhD diss., The Australian National University.

9

Being Muslim in Eastern Indonesia
Contemporary Patterns of Islamic Practice

Andrew McWilliam[1]

Introduction

Studies of Muslim faith and worship across eastern Indonesia highlight the continuing dynamic relationships between local traditions reproduced over generations of practice. These patterns include ongoing processes of Islamisation; challenges to orthodoxy brought about by influences associated with new forms of *dakwah* (proselytisation); and the "reformist" influences flowing from global Islam. One of the objectives of the "Being Muslim in Eastern Indonesia" project has been to develop a deeper understanding of the comparative dynamics of this interactive field of contemporary Islamic practice, principally through nuanced ethnographic case studies of different Muslim communities across the region. This chapter directs its ethnographic focus to the vibrant, Muslim community of Kupang city in West Timor, the capital of Nusa Tenggara Timur Province. I situate Kupang Muslim identities and practice within four influential themes or shared comparative elements of Islamisation across eastern Indonesia, each of which have contributed significantly to its living forms and expression (see also Hutagalung 2016).

These four themes are those of trade and economic migration (*merantau*); conflict and co-residence with Christian communities; processes of Muslim conversion and expansion; and finally, what I describe as "tensions of tradition". As a broadly comparative framework, these thematic elements contribute to the enduring shape and character of Islamic faith expression across the region and to the specific ethnographic forms that Islam takes among Kupang Muslims.

Theme 1: Trade and Migration

It is well accepted that the maritime spread of Islam, especially from the 15th century, has been critical to the history of the region including representations (often mythic) of the origins of many island settlements and their subsequent development (Meilink-Roelofsz 1962: 144; di Meglio 1970: 116). Muslim Sultanates in eastern Indonesia (Ternate, Tidore, Gowa and Buton among others) and their far-flung allies and dependencies were the inheritors of the earlier Muslim legacy brought by Indian[2] and Arab traders (Andaya 1991; Ellen 2003; Goodman 1998; Reid 1993).

The history of this trade and its Islamic-inflected alliances has informed distinctive and contrastive settlement patterns across eastern Indonesia. Typically, this is expressed geographically as predominantly Islamic, coastal (*pesisir*) populations with long histories as trading entrepôts (see for example, Ellen 2003), and a Christianised, agriculturally-oriented hinterland with Church-based settlements linked into commodity chains to the coasts. This pattern is found inter alia across much of Maluku, Sulawesi Tengah, coastal settlements of West Papua and Nusa Tenggara Timur among other areas (but cf. Phillip Winn, this volume). The maritime history of trade has also contributed to the flourishing of local Islamic religious practice, and intermarriage of local women with mobile traders. Subsequently, religious practice and local organisations developed further through the arrival of learned Muslim scholars (*ulama*), qualified teachers (*ustad*) and other influential figures who provided advice and appreciation of Islamic foundations. Their learned contributions provided many communities with new understandings and knowledge of Islam that had previously resided for the most part, with lightly-trained resident (and often hereditary) imams (see chapters in this volume).

One enduring feature of eastern Indonesia and its maritime history is the widespread and prominent presence of Sulawesi-origin language communities (especially Bugis, Buton and Makassar [BBM]),[3] all of which strongly identify with Islam. They all have their "homelands" in southern regions of Sulawesi, maintain high levels of population mobility and trade links with eastern island ports, and disseminate their own culturally-inflected Islamic traditions.[4] To give a sense of the numbers involved, the Indonesian Population Census 2000 which now records ethnonyms and residence, highlighted the distribution of Buton Island peoples in the eastern islands, and indeed in significant areas of western Indonesia.

Table 9.1 Butonese populations in selected regions of eastern Indonesia (Indonesian Population Census 2000)

Ethnic group	*Sulawesi Tenggara*	*Nusa Tenggara Timur*	*Maluku*	*Maluku Utara*	*West Papua*	*Total*
Buton	414,520	8,539	121,579	41,122	22,585	609,345

Of note in these figures is the comparatively large number of self-identifying, Buton populations living outside their homeland province in Sulawesi Tenggara. The migrant or expatriate populations in Table 9.1 represent 32 per cent of the total population represented here and highlights the continuing importance of *merantau* (sojourning) traditions and economic migration as a livelihood choice for these contemporary trading groups. These patterns of migration histories are built on sponsorship and familial networks of archipelagic scale that facilitate mobility and settlement in distant island settlements while remaining connected to origin communities (see Wahyuddin Halim; Farid F. Saenong, this volume). The currency of connection in most cases is trade and the trans-shipment of diverse commodities back and forward across the tropical waters of the Java and Banda Seas. Michael Southon's study of Butonese maritime trade gives a sense of the diversity of the consignments that are traded in the distinctive, now motorised, Buton Perahu Lambo boats including asphalt, roof shingles, palm thatch, cement, junk iron, empty bottles, cloves, dried fish, bananas, maize, rice, cashew nuts, copra, general merchandise and, of course, passengers (1995: 39–71).

The historical and contemporary role of maritime economic migration and trade in eastern Indonesia contributes to a continuing flow of ideas and influential religious knowledge across the archipelago with impacts in both destination settlements and in the homeland villages and towns of source communities, which often remain in contact with their far flung members and kin (Palmer 2010).

Kupang, the fast-growing capital of Nusa Tenggara Timur (NTT) Province and located in the far west of Timor island overlooking a broad shallow bay of the same name, reflects its diverse maritime origins in terms of demography and religious diversity. The urban population has a thriving, cosmopolitan, Muslim population that includes established communities of Bugis–Makassar and Buton settlers in its multi-cultural mix. But for generations they have lived and thrived in a city and wider region where historically Protestant and Catholic Christianity has predominated and constituted the majority population.

The origins of Islam on Timor are poorly documented and oral traditions reflect considerable variation. Certainly by the early 17th century, Timor had come within the sphere of trade influences of the Sultanate of Ternate and also those of Gowa and Tallo in Makassar, South Sulawesi. But the generally accepted view is that Islam initially arrived in Kupang via Dutch colonial connections with Solor Island on the eastern edge of Flores to the north. A Solorese, Lamakera man, originally from Ternate (Maluku) and known as Atu Laganama (aka Sultan Syarif Syahar or Badaduddin) reputedly established the first Muslim settlement near the spring, Oe Ba, at a site known as Watu Besi on the edge of Kupang Bay and, at the time, a nascent Dutch settlement (Goro 1977). According to oral traditions, Atu Laganama was an *ulama* or religious scholar but appointed by the Dutch as a war leader to fight against the Portuguese who were then rivals in the control of the sandalwood trade. Just when that appointment occurred is unclear, but may be related to participation in the famous rout of the so-called "black Portuguese"[5] forces at Penfui now on the outskirts of Kupang in 1749 (Widyatmika 2004: 48; Goro 1977: 84, 85). Local sources also record that Atu Laganama was later supported in his teaching of Islam by other figures from Solor including Sengadji Susang, who assumed the role of imam or prayer leader at the Batu Besi complex. Later he helped establish the religious community at

Kampung Solor along with the first mosque, when the Dutch moved the community from Batu Besi to the old business district of Kupang.

The subsequent shape and character of Islam in Kupang, however, expresses influences from a wide range of subsequent settlers and Muslim practitioners who have all contributed in different ways to its development in Kupang over the last 200 years. They include people like Abdul Kadir Bin Jailani (from Bima, Sumbawa), and Syaban bin Sanga (Sultan Menanga) who, with his reported 80 followers from Solor, established a mosque in Airmata in 1806 and became the founding imam (Widyatmika 2004: 4). There were also numerous influential Muslim figures who were said to have been exiled (*diasingkan*) to Kupang by the Dutch colonial authorities for their involvement in rebellions or dissent elsewhere in the Dutch East Indies. They included Prince Surya Mataram from Central Java (exiled in 1830 following his involvement in the war of Dipenogoro), Kiai Haji Mohamad Arsyad bin Alwan, Haji Mansyur and Haji Abdul Salam who were involved in a failed rebellion in Banten (Kartodirdjo 1966), and Depati Amir Bahren and Depati Hamzah Bahren of Bangka Island (Hutagalung 2015: 139).

The Hadhrami trader, Sheik Syarif Abubakar bin Abdurrachman Algadri,[6] was another influential exile. Initially deported from Pontianak in Borneo island in 1836, he developed a horse trading business in Sumba, and subsequently formed the vanguard of a strong Hadhrami entrepreneurial group (*pembuka jalan*) initially trading slaves out of Kupang, but subsequently settling in Airmata in 1877 and developing a range of business interests (see Widyatmika 2004, 2008). Hadhrami families were reportedly particularly important in the early expansion of Islam in Kupang through their efforts as religious teachers, *guru pengajian* (teacher of Qur'anic recitation) and *guru madrasah* (teachers in religious schools) (see Goro 1977: 95–8). Their influence and presence provide the alternative name by which Airmata has long been known, namely, Kampung Arab.

Islam in Kupang has also been enriched by numerous migrant groups and settlers from all parts of the Indonesian archipelago. These diverse groups have established Muslim communities along the beachfronts and constituent settlements (*kampung*) that spread out from the old Dutch Fort Concordia overlooking the Bay. They include ethnic Bugis (in Oesapa) (see Hutagalung, this volume), Bugis-Mandar and

Buton (in Namusaen), Buton/Arab (Kelapa Lima) and Alorese (in Kampung Alor) among others. This diversity means that Muslim tradition in Kupang is inevitably a lively and complex amalgam of contributions over time; each drawing on their respective sources, teachings and understandings of ritual and religious orthodoxy and cultural histories. The result is a culture of Islam that remains dynamic and subject to pressures for reform and acceptance of new approaches and practices. Imams from the respective *masjid* (mosque) lead from the centre of these processes through the conduct and guidance of prayer practices and leadership of the worshipful community of faith (*umat*). Imams have been highly influential in shaping and perpetuating the forms and expression of Muslim ritual and spiritual practice in local contexts over time. This is especially so given that the position of imam was frequently an inherited one over generations of practice. While certainly the case in Kupang, the practice has had wide historical application across eastern Indonesia (see chapters by Robinson, Saenong and Hutagalung, this volume).

Theme 2: Conflict and Co-Residence

The history of eastern Indonesia since the 15th century reflects two apparently contradictory patterns among prominent religious communities. The first is an underlying sectarian tension between co-resident or neighbouring Muslim and Christian settlements that has on numerous occasions over the sweep of history, erupted into violence and murderous conflict. At the same time the region reflects a long parallel history of peaceful interaction and engagement, where inter-religious cooperation and mutual respect have accommodated difference and allowed neighbouring communities to live in comparative harmony. This pattern of Muslim and Christian settlements across the region in places like West Papua, Maluku, NTT and Central Sulawesi, is an enduring feature of eastern Indonesia. It reflects a history of long-term accommodation and negotiated modes of engagement in the name of religion; one where conversion and inter-marriage across religious boundaries have helped to shape inter-communal relations and understandings over time.

The latent potential of inter-communal violence has been graphically illustrated in recent times following the demise of the repressive

New Order government, effectively from 1998. The destructive ramifying conflict in northern Maluku (1999–2000) that spread across the province (Wilson 2005), and the phases of vicious inter-communal violence between Bugis Muslims and Pamona Christians centred on Poso, Central Sulawesi (from late 1998) are cases in point. In both areas—also somewhat characteristically perhaps—the outbreaks of violence have their origins in longer term, socio-economic grievances and the politics of favouritism, combined with provocation by external agents and agitators seeking to ferment division in the name of sectarian intolerance and political advantage (see Aragon 2001; McCrae 2013).[7]

But religious conflict in eastern Indonesia is nothing new. Brett Baker (2012) in an ANU thesis exploring Christianity and conversion in 16th-century Maluku provides rich archival analyses of the formative period of the spread and adoption of both Islam and Christianity. Conflict and reprisals were frequent and bloody. In one example, based on reports from a Portuguese priest, Fr Jerome de Olmedo, waves of attacks on Ambon were initiated from Ternate following the assassination of Sultan Hairun in 1570 during a visit to the Portuguese fort at Hitu, Ambon (Baker 2012: 186). In one attack, an armada of ships from the Sultanate launched a surprise assault on two Christian villages on Ambon, and "burnt them and the crosses which were in them, and took whatever they had from them with around 150 captives, most of them women and children". The Ternatans then scoured the surrounding area for those who had fled the assault, "killing and capturing those whom they found" (Baker 2012: 187).[8]

There were two general and immediate responses to the attacks. According to Olmedo, some villages surrendered quickly and renounced their Christianity, and some of these even joined the Ternatans in attacking their neighbours. Other Christian villages seeking protection from the Muslim attacks, united to defend themselves. Olmedo was subsequently able to join a "small armada that the Portuguese had managed to muster in order to assist the Christian villages" and view some of the "damage" up close. "The Christians", he commented, "came to receive us with much joy, bringing the heads which that day they had cut off, of which they are very proud" (cited in Baker 2012: 187).

This historical episode exemplifies that violence and intense enmity have been part and parcel of the historical legacy of Muslim (and

Christian) communities and the spread of these world religions in eastern Indonesia. According to Baker's assessment the corrosive sectarian rivalries of the 16th century contributed to the varying segregation of the religious communities where once they were evidently much more intertwined and co-resident (Baker 2012).[9] A similar view might be expressed in contemporary Maluku following the communal violence that erupted at the turn of the 21st century (1999–2000) where over many years preceding these events, harmonious residential integration had been widely enjoyed. This is the flip side of religiously motivated violence, one distinguished over a much longer period by "peaceful" co-existence and the mutual tolerance of difference that has greater continuity in the history of the region. Arguably it is not the outbreaks of violence and reprisal that demand explanation, but the extended periods of peace, accommodation and tolerance.

In this respect Kupang provides an illustrative example. The history of Muslim–Christian relations in Kupang is generally one of long-standing acceptance and mutual tolerance since at least the early part of the 19th century when Muslim communities consolidated their presence in what has long been and remains a stronghold of both Protestantism and Catholicism. The only significant variation in this pattern occurred in 1998 when a series of targeted attacks were initiated against Bugis mosques and infrastructure in the settlement area of Oesapa, over a period of three days and nights (Sihbudi and Nursahim 2001: 53–4). In a remarkably short period of time however, the incipient conflict was brought under control through swift intervention which included activating existing inter-faith arrangements of mutual cooperation and assistance among religious leaders, who were mobilised to urge calm and commit to rebuilding the damaged mosques and associated facilities (Robinson 2002). Blame for the destruction was directed to outside provocation[10] that had inflamed jealousies and emotions among a radicalised Christian youth. The events were seen as part of a wider process of destabilisation, pursued in the wake of the political demise of the Suharto New Order government, but thought to be ultimately founded in jealousies and rivalry due to the commercial success and expanding visibility of Bugis traders.

This event was unique at the time in the history of Kupang communal relations and should be seen as an exception that proves the long-standing rule of "religious tolerance". Even when sectarian tensions were raised over the proposed construction of a new mosque at Batuplat in 2011—motivated in part due to attacks on Christian Churches in Java and mutual suspicions over the proselytising intentions on both sides—outbreaks of violence did not occur (Hutagalung 2016: 447–8). In the case of Kupang and its multi-religious and multi-ethnic populations drawn from the constituent islands of NTT and beyond, there are two strong thematic elements that contribute to these comparatively harmonious relations. Firstly, the role of inter-religious communication and cooperation is a significant buffer against communal violence or conflict. This cooperation is achieved through such institutions as the Religious Community Communication Forum (Forum Komunikasi Umat Beragama—Propinsi) promoting interfaith dialogue, and the general practice of the city government inviting all religious leaders to represent their faith communities in formal government and civic events. Kupang imams are active participants in this ecumenical grouping that is charged by the mayor (*wali kota*) with maintaining religious harmony and mutual respect among the different religious practitioners.

More importantly perhaps, people point to the role of inter-marriage and the intermingling of Christian and Muslim practitioners in extended family networks as a key mechanism for ensuring good relations between religious groups. If the religious "other" is part of your family or relation, this tends to reduce the prospects for conflict while fostering respect and mutual tolerance of difference. In Kupang these familial ties encourage regular, reciprocal participation of Muslims and Christians in their respective religious events and life cycle rituals. As an historical and continuing feature of social and religious life in Kupang, inter-marriage facilitates an accommodative approach to religious difference in ways that are distinctive of this and other regions of eastern Indonesia. In this context local imams play a key role in facilitating the conduct of marriage and in managing the induction of Christian converts (*mualaf*) into the Muslim umat. They are also active in constructive cooperation and mutual assistance for the celebration of opposing religious celebrations; Idul Fitri and Christmas being two cases in point. This level of tolerance and, indeed mutual participation, is all the more striking given the broader 1991 Muhammadiyah *fatwa* (injunction) against Muslims wishing Christians "Merry Christmas".

Kupang however, as in all other areas of eastern Indonesia, is not immune from less tolerant even subversive outside influences. The rapid spread of telecommunications and social media networks across Indonesia provide increasing opportunities for the dissemination of alternative theologies and fundamentalist agendas. Such mechanisms have already been clearly implicated in the mobilisation of protagonists and gangs during the Muslim–Christian violence in Maluku (Bräuchler 2003). In Kupang the rise of social media combined with the well-known susceptibility of Kupang locals to rumour and misinformation, based on my own experience of the city, adds to the potential at least for social disruption. This concern was well illustrated at the 2012 Idul Adha commemoration at the Al-Baitul Qadim Mosque in Airmata (Kupang). Here a government representative of the city, the (Christian) deputy mayor (*wakil wali kota*) presented a brief formal speech of acknowledgement where he included specific mention of these disruptive possibilities and urged the umat to be vigilant against the "seeds of fracture" (*benih benih pemecahan*) that may be carried via SMS communications. His presence and his point reinforced the continuing commitment by the local government to maintain interfaith harmony and respect (see additional perspectives in Hutagalung 2016).

Theme 3: Muslim Conversion and Expansion

Merle Ricklefs (1979) has depicted the acceptance of Islam in Java as neither a step nor an event but as an ongoing journey over six centuries of Islamisation. His point is also highly relevant to eastern Indonesia where Islam arrived late and did so in the context of dynamic military and commercial contests with Portuguese and Spanish Christianity. According to Baker (2012) initial conversion to Christianity or Islam was readily relinquished in the shifting politics of trade and alliance, and periods of conversion and apostasy occurred quite readily. He argues that during this crucial period of the 16th century, the choice of religion remained a personal and local act, resulting in a shifting, religiously diverse landscape. People of Tolo in Central Sulawesi for example "on at least two different occasions with identical circumstances, made very different choices, some maintaining their Christian identity, others abandoning it and still others adopting a different identity as Muslims" (2012: 131–2). Anthony Reid has argued that between 1540 and 1640 the boundary of Islam gradually became clearer and acceptance of Islam came to be seen as a test of political loyalty to Muslim leaders where non-Muslim groups were seen, not simply as latent Muslims, but as actual or potential enemies (Reid 1999: 338). To facilitate this boundary-marking process, again according to Reid, the initial threshold of entry into the house of Islam in Maluku was set deliberately low, namely to recite the confession of faith (*syahadat*—there is no God but Allah and Muhammad is his prophet), agree to submit to circumcision and to abandon the consumption of pork. Understanding of the message of Islam could proceed later (Reid 1999: 336), and in this sense we can appreciate how the establishment and subsequent development of Muslim faith communities in the region, the process of "becoming Muslim", was a protracted one informed by diverse religious and cultural practices. In many areas it continued in the context of potentially rival forms of religious faith, especially forms of Christianity that simultaneously offered a potentially plentiful source of converts (*mualaf*) to Islam in addition to the expansion of the umat by natural growth, conversion through interfaith marriage and incorporation of migrant Muslim allies and relatives.

One of the striking and obvious characteristics of eastern Indonesian provinces like Nusa Tenggara Timor, and its capital Kupang, is that the Muslim community lives and is reproduced within a large majority Christian context. Recent figures for Kupang highlight these relativities where Protestants and Catholics make up some 85.8 per cent of the 390,877 population and Muslims just 12.3 per cent or around 52,995 people (Badan Pusat Statistik 2016). However, the present Muslim population represents a significant increase over time, both in terms of raw numbers and in percentage terms. In 1977 for example, it was estimated that there were just 6,000 Muslims resident in Kupang representing 8.8 per cent of the population (Goro 1977). But current figures arguably under-estimate the actual numbers of Muslims due to the transient or mobile nature of many Muslim residents based in the coastal settlements and port area of Kupang bay but retaining their official residential status in home settlements of Sulawesi.

A sense of the growth and expansion of Islam in Kupang can also be gauged from the spread of mosques over a similar period. In the late 1960s, for example, there were still only five established mosques in Kupang city. These *tempat ibadah* (places of worship) included the old centres at Bonipoi, Airmata, Kampung Solor and Namusaen with a newly-constructed mosque at Oepura within the regional government precinct in the hills several kilometres inland. Today this number has mushroomed to around 56 established mosques within the city boundaries, each with its complement of religious leaders (Hutagalung 2015). A comparable rate of increase can also be seen in rural districts of West Timor. In Kabupaten South Central Timor (TTS), for instance, from modest beginnings in the capital So'e and the establishment of the Al-Ikhlas Mesjid, there are now 32 mosques throughout the district including one operating a *pesantren* in Oe Ekam, eastern TTS which boasts 2,000 local *mualaf* Islam (converts) (pers. comm. Haji Hasan Kia 2012). One of the mechanisms encouraging the spread of Islam is the role of Bugis traders and retailers who follow the market circuits around rural areas of TTS and establish fledgling centres of Islamic worship. Over time conversion through marriage with local non-Muslim women from NTT communities provides another source of growth of the umat.

The processes of development and expansion of Muslim households and communities across Timor, is one that inevitably populates and extends into what are essentially Christian spheres of practice. It indicates that cities like Kupang and eastern Indonesia more generally, will continue to represent an opportunistic domain for expanding processes of Islamisation in ways that contrast with western Indonesia or Java where Islam and Islamic communities have for many years constituted the overwhelming majority.

Through a combination of natural population increase, in-migration and inter-marriage, where typically spouses convert to Islam and not the other way around, there is considerable scope for a gradual increase in the Muslim presence in eastern Indonesia. In addition, the Muslim population of Kupang and NTT Province more broadly, remains a minority religion within a Christian-dominated social field. But in a recursive sense they represent the majority religion of the nation and this balance tends to offset their minority local status in ways that permit a more assertive stance in relation to the Christian majority than might otherwise be the case. In such areas aggressive forms of proselytising and the continuous construction of Islamic places of worship are combined with the entry of more globally-oriented Islamic organisations such as Jemaah Tabligh and Hizbut Tahrir, to expand the appeal and reach of Islam (Hutagalung 2015; Nisa, this volume).

The religious affiliation to a majority national Indonesian Islamic identity also allows Islamic umat to benefit from state-based support for a range of religious activities and institutional development programs such as the construction of mosques, the expansion of religious education (via *madrasah* and other institutions) and in the general deployment of Muslim civil servants and security forces throughout the region. Commenting on this trend, a Catholic acquaintance commented ruefully that Christianity in NTT was like a great elephant that was slowly being brought down by the march of (Muslim) ants incessantly chewing away and hollowing out its strength. His view illustrates some of the latent suspicions and hostility that can underlay the overt public sentiments expressed towards peaceful, inter-religious relations and dialogue.

Theme 4: Tensions between Tradition and Reform

The fourth and final theme of my assessment is the much-considered relationship between old and new, between tradition and reform, conservation and renewal. Eastern Indonesia has, for some decades, been a key region for the study of Austronesian language communities and cultural comparison (for example, Fox 1980; Fox and Sather 1996; Reuter 2006; Vischer 2009). It is evident that the early history of religious conversion to Islam across the region was accomplished via an integration and adaptation to diverse and vibrant local traditions. One of the achievements of the present project is to pursue comparative explorations of this relationship between local cultural traditions and the expressions of Islam in daily life. In this respect, current researchers Adlin Sila (2015; this volume) in relation to Sumbawa, Faried S. Saenong (this volume) in Bantaeng (South Sulawesi), Stella Hutagalung (this volume) in Kupang and Wahyuddin Halim (this volume) in South Sulawesi all report on the rich diversity of adaptations that have shaped a common set of core Islamic beliefs and practice.

Among the various permutations of expression of pre-existing *custom* and *belief* in local Islamic traditions, we can identify a general pattern distinguished along a continuum of stronger and weaker forms of *adat* (tradition) expression or integration. The former gives a more explicit role to adat practice and Austronesian preferences as distinct but complementary forms within Islam; the latter reflects adaptive traditions that are integral and commensurate within a local set of Islamic practices.

By way of example, this distinction may be seen in the contrasting examples of Muslim traditions in Wabula, Buton Island, Southeast Sulawesi, and those of Kupang NTT. In Wabula for example, formal Islam has long been enacted and articulated in a context of assertive, adat-based, complementary ritual practices. In one sense social life is regulated by the rhythm of the Islamic calendar (Maulid Nabi Muhammad/the Prophet's birthday), Idul Fitri (end of Ramadan), Idul Adha (feast of sacrifice) with mutual gift giving and commensality among households highlighted at this time. But Cia-Cia speaking communities in Buton are socially and religiously focused on the twin structures of local tradition—the mosque (*mesjid*) and the central meeting house (*galampa*) (Cia-Cia language, henceforth CC)—which provide the locus for a range of adat ceremonies and ritual cycles that link both institutions to the origins of settlement. In Wabula the ritual centre of community is constituted symbolically by these two structures, separated with a cleared space (*kalia* [CC], the field or yard) and defended, also symbolically, by an old Dutch cannon that points seaward. The structural relationship between the *mesjid* and the *galampa* (CC) is understood as a gendered unity, one in which both the *galampa* and its formal leader, the *parabela* (CC), are symbolically male (*mo ane* [CC]), and the mosque (*mesjid*) and the resident *moji* (CC) or imam are symbolically female (*mo vine* [CC]). Ironically, according to Wabula local tradition, there is—and may only be—one mosque in the settlement because it symbolises the monogamous "marriage" between religion and adat. The generative metaphor of conjugal union alludes to the importance placed on the life-giving significance of the marital household to the reproduction of community (McWilliam 2009). It is also recognisably Austronesian in its classificatory intent.

An example of the latter form of adaptive Islam may be seen in the traditional Islamic rituals and practice sustained by the established Muslim umat in Kupang. Here there are no overtly or distinctive pre-Islamic traditions that retain a complementary distinctive form, but rather, we see a set of Islamic traditions of worship and ritual that reflect several centuries of in-situ tradition that has shaped current practice. Examples include the festivities of Maulid Nabi at the old Airmata mosque that feature elaborate displays of fruit baskets and the central decorated banana stem construction known as Siripuang, symbolic of fertility and new life. The use of such visual symbols of fertility as the Siripuang are widely criticised within purifying agendas of reforming currents of contemporary Islam, but the religious leaders and participating umat of the old Airmata mosque, find in the performance of the Siripuang, the celebration of a distinctive Islamic identity that has subsumed or integrated its Austronesian origins.

The umat community of Airmata also retains elements of a reciprocal relationship that reflects its origins and early relationships. This comprises a division of the community into two parts, Kampung Imam and Kampung Raja. This division is founded on a distinction between the descendants of the first Imam of Airmata, Solorese migrant Syaban bin Sanga (1800), and a highly-regarded teacher of Islam, Mohammad Badaruddin, and other Muslim settlers. The groupings reflect different historical, complementary responsibilities designed to facilitate the smooth running of mosque activities and relations within the umat.

In explaining the operation of this traditional system, Imam Abdul Rachim Mustafa, current head of Kampung Imam, compared the division with the central concern in Islam to maintain "good relations with God, and good relations between people" (*ḥabl min Allaah, ḥabl min al-naas* [Ar.]). However he cautioned that the Kampung Imam and Kampung Raja are not ends in themselves, but simply mechanisms to ensure that these two objectives of Islam are met and well managed (Goro 1977: 91–2). Having said this, he acknowledged that traditionally the division translated into different tasks and responsibilities. The Kampung Imam by definition, provided the Imam Mesjid, and Kampung Raja the *khatib*, who delivers the sermon (*khotbah*) including during Ramadan. During the fasting month, Kampung Imam is responsible for refreshments after the *tarawih* prayers and the *khataman* (Qur'anic recitation) for the first 15 days of Ramadan, then the responsibility is handed over to the Kampung Raja group. These elements have less prominence these days, which is to say there is less emphasis accorded strict adherence to the old division of duties, but the dual structure and the sense of reciprocal or mutual obligations within the community remain important values of traditionalist Islam in Airmata. These are values that are distinctively Austronesian in their symbolism and complementarity, and highlight one example of the way that cultural traditions across eastern Indonesia have been organically integrated into what are now regarded as orthodox expressions of regional Muslim faith worship. Sila (this volume) in his exemplary study of the Bima Sultanate in Sumbawa, offers a comparable example of an institutionalised diarchic religious structure in the distinction between the Sultan's spiritual authority and the administrative authority of the Raja Bicara (see also Sila 2015).

At a broader level of comparison, this diversity and the richness of local expressions of Muslim practice is characteristic of the Nahdlatul Ulama (NU) aligned "traditionalist" Islam found across the eastern archipelago. But it is also one that is performed and reproduced in the context of an ongoing debate and in the face of sustained criticism from more reformist-minded Muhammadiyah proponents of a "modernist" Islamic practice, cleansed of unacceptable or heretical innovations (*bidah*) and elaborations beyond textual truths. The struggle here is not a new development, but reflects a tension that has a genealogy in the Indonesian archipelago going back to the 19th century. It is also one that has been intensified in recent times through the advent of more puritanical elements of Salafi and Wahhabism movements determined to purge Indonesian Islam of "alien" additions and bring it more into line with practices of Muslims in Arabia. As Martin van Bruinessen has noted, "[t]he struggle against indigenous beliefs and values has been a chief concern of reformists" (1999: 163).

Among these concerns, James J. Fox has noted that "it is largely in the practice of Islam [that is, not in doctrine] that modernists differ from traditionalists". Modernists do not participate in *tarekat*, religious orders that are fundamental to NU, nor do they see Islamic mystical traditions (*tasawuf*—Sufi way) as part of their practice. Indeed "they have little regard for the panoply of rituals that organise the lives of most traditional Muslims" (Fox 2004: 5–6). This panoply of rituals includes a wide range of practices that have long been considered to be the core elements in traditional Islamic practice in Kupang. They include the celebratory forms of Maulid Nabi Mohammed and accompanying *selawat* and *barzanji* recitations; the practice of *tahlil* commemorative prayers for the dead; doctrinal practices such as the recitation of 23 *tarawih rakaat* during Ramadan rather than the abbreviated 8 *rakaat* version; as well as the use of perfumes and incenses (*kemenyan*) to sweeten the air (see also Adlin Sila and Yasir Alimi, this volume).

What I think may have changed somewhat in this contentious field over the last couple of decades, is that the processes and pressures for reform are being extended ever further into remote corners of eastern Indonesia. These influences contribute to a destabilisation of comfortable local orthodoxies creating debates and dissension among local Muslim umat and questioning what should and should not be considered proper forms of Muslim worship and ritual practice. The mechanism of extending and intensifying reformist Muslim principles and practice involves a combination of factors, especially the role of formal religious education and literacy among the younger generation. Muhammadiyah has been especially active in promoting religious education in Kupang. It has meant that, young people pursuing their studies through institutions like *madrasah* and *pesantren*,[11] sometimes distant from their home communities, return with specialised knowledge of Muslim philosophy and practice, and with views that are often at variance with what they come to see as unacceptable elaborations undertaken in the name of Islam. Their literate views and learning on Islam offer increasingly influential voices in home communities including Kupang where these kinds of internal debates are also being canvassed. An example is the mixed acceptance among the Kampung Solor umat of the appointment of two "deputy" imams who were educated outside Kupang, are aligned with Muhammadiyah and oppose elements of the Al-Fatah mosque traditions that they regard as expressing unacceptable "Hindu" influences.[12] Their positions reflect a political push for change among a group of younger people and influential imams in the community. However, as my journalist colleague, Abbas Abdul Manan Ndoen[13] from Kampung Solor observed, this debate around religious practice is one that the resident majority has lost (*mengalah*), but has not accepted, and that these issues are not based on differences of belief, simply different versions of the same thing. The "true" imam remains Haji Hamzah Iyang, a descendant of the Solorese ancestor Atulaganama and with Imam Tahir Zen seeks to maintain the orientation to older, original forms of practice.

Although reformist Muhammadiyah-based ideas are influencing aspects of the well-established Islamic traditions of Al-Fatah Mosque, there remains a majoritarian view among the four central historical umat in Kupang, namely, Airmata, Bonipoi, Kampung Solor and Namusaen, that the old Muslim traditions remain valued and relevant. Imam Abdulrachim Mustafa of the Ai Baitul Qadim Mosque in Airmata, for example, described their position as having built a *benteng* (fortress) around the old traditions, to ensure that they are not undermined and subject to the revisionism of new ways of thinking.[14]

Ambarrak Bahzier, a Hadhrami Arab resident of Airmata, also expressed criticism of the push for modernist renderings of Islam as narrow and constrained views of Islam from educated people who do not understand Islam. He felt that experienced imams know that aspects of adat which generate Islamic tradition are part of the experience of Islam in particular places and serve to honour the faith worship of their Muslim ancestors. His comments, I think, highlight the continuing influential role of the imam in both preserving and reproducing traditionalist forms of Islam, but also as an influential source of change and modernisation as the Al-Fatah example demonstrates. In other words, the more persuasive influence at work here shadowing everyday practices is the informal leadership of the imam rather than learning through varieties of formal religious education.

Debates and attention accorded appropriate forms of Islamic worship and devotional acts form part of a more general trend towards what might be termed the intensification of Islam across Indonesia. The increasing use of Islamic symbols such as Islamic dress, Islamic greetings, and mosques have become a much more visible feature of public life (Fealy 2008). Greg Fealy has also observed increases in Islamic consumption and commodification around religio-economic transactions, where the symbols of faith are used to market Islam-associated products (2008: 17). By focusing on the popularity of the emergent Islamic product market, he argues that Islamic consumption is driven by the pursuit of "moral certainty, spiritual enrichment and pietistic identity" (Fealy 2008: 16). One can think of numerous examples where this kind of engagement with visible Islamic symbolism and piety is also evident throughout eastern Indonesia including consumption-inspired lifestyles with strong Islamic associations, and for new cars and comfortable homes in gated communities. Popular media programmes often give substantial space to Islamic ceremonial events and lessons from esteemed invited religious scholars (*ustad*) or prominent imams and other religious figures, usually preaching to groups of devout followers sitting in pious submission. Similarly, the extensive redevelopment of that core symbol of Muslim iconography, the mosque (*masjid*) is a favoured site for channeling substantial investments and projecting the modern face of Islam in a grander style. Substantial financial gifts and contributions to local mosques and associated organisations by wealthy benefactors are increasingly common and viewed as expressions of *zakat* (alms/gift) piety and community-mindedness. This includes the provision of private land for the construction of mosques which, in places like Kupang, has also included gifts of land by community-minded Christian owners. These and other patterns of Muslim expression reflect both a growing prosperity among eastern Indonesian middle-class Muslims, as well as a reflection of the wider concerns with religiosity, of becoming better Muslim in terms of public devotion and in personal piety (Fealy and White 2008).

Conclusion

One conclusion that might be drawn from this brief chapter is that, "Being Muslim in eastern Indonesia" is a more complicated field of practice and worship these days, than might have been the case in earlier times when Islamic practice tended to be much more local in its understanding and performative expression. Processes of globalisation and the expansion of social media, mass travel and exposure to new ideas and modernist aspirations are changing the face of Muslim practice across the eastern archipelago. These influential drivers of change will undoubtedly contribute to continuing debates around what constitutes correct Muslim practice. Trends towards more formal religious education and greater religious literacy among the Muslim populations may lead to a greater acceptance of "reformist" practice. But there remain strong and enduring local values that will resist changes to local traditions that have served communities well for generations and form part of cultural identity politics that has been much empowered in recent years through decentralisation and regional autonomy. Central to these struggles are local imams who, as spiritual leaders, represent and lead their respective umat. They remain, in most cases, conservative centres of spiritual assurance and knowledge to whom most of the umat will continue to depend on for life cycle ritual services, religious guidance and community wellbeing.

Notes

1. This study was funded by Australian Research Council Discovery Project DP00881464 "Being Muslim in Eastern Indonesia: Practice, Politics and Cultural Diversity", Chief Investigators Kathryn Robinson and Andrew McWilliam, Department of Anthropology, ANU College of Asia and the Pacific.

2. Especially Bengali, Gujurati and Calicut traders (see di Meglio 1970: 119).
3. The collective term BBM, in reference to the Sulawesi-based language groups, Bugis, Buton, Makassar, became a widely used and somewhat derogatory term, used especially during inter-ethnic tensions around 1998, to refer to these identities who tend to dominate regional trade in the many parts of the archipelago.
4. Another important ethno-linguistic community with both extensive trade links and a strong orientation to Islam, are the Hadhrami Arab traders who are found in settlements throughout the region (see Mobini-Kesheh 1999).
5. This is the name accorded the part-Portuguese freelance traders and de facto rulers of much of Timor during the late 17th and mid-18th centuries, described by G.C. Gunn (1999: 94) as having a "testy loyalty to the [Portuguese] Crown often amounting to economic independence". The battle at Penfui signalled a turning point in their fortunes and reach of their power.
6. The grave of Algadri has subsequently become a site of veneration by people of Hadhrami descent and other members of the Airmata mosque.
7. Lorraine Aragon argues that the different conflict phases in Poso were events involving patronage politics that mobilised groups who harboured pre-existing resentments about ethnic disparities in land and political control, and who subscribed to ideologies divided along 21st-century religious currents (2001: 77).
8. Quotes from a letter, "Fr Jerónimo de Olmedo SJ, by order of Fr Rector Luís de Góis, to the Jesuits in Goa. Ambon, June 2, 1570" (Baker 2012: 187).
9. Baker writes that hints do exist in the contemporary literature (of the time) which suggest that Muslim villages, exactly like their Christian counterparts, were far from religiously homogenous (2012: 218).
10. The term "*provokator*" that was popularised at this time was often directed at the disruptive participation of certain un-uniformed Indonesian military in the provocation who, nevertheless, were recognised by their military boots.
11. *Pesantren* are more commonly found in Java and other areas of western Indonesia and in South Sulawesi.
12. The term "Hindu" is often used to describe practices that are considered unorthodox and dismissed as accretions from an imagined pre-Islamic, Hindu past.
13. The surname, Ndoen, identifies Abbas as a man of Rotenese descent, which is usually associated with Christianity but in this case his grandfather grew up in Kampung Solor and served as an imam in the mosque.
14. The tensions and reformist efforts in the Al-Fatah mosque in Kampung Solor notwithstanding.

References

Andaya, Leonard. 1991. "Local Trade Networks in Maluku in the 16th, 17th, and 18th Centuries." *Cakalele: Maluku Research Journal* 2 (2): 84.

Aragon, L. 2001. "Communal Violence in Central Sulawesi: Where People Eat Fish and Fish Eat People." *Indonesia* 72 (October 2001): 45–79.

———. 2012. "Development Strategies, Religious Relations, and Communal Violence in Central Sulawesi, Indonesia: A Cautionary Tale." In *Development Strategies, Identities, and Violence in Asia*, ed. William Ascher and Natalia Mirovitskaya, 153–82. New York: Palgrave MacMillan.

Badan Pusat Statistik. 2016. *Kupang Dalam Angka, 2016*. Pemerintah Kota Kupang: Kupang Indonesia.

Baker, B. 2012. "Indigenous-Driven Mission, Reconstructing Religious Change in Sixteenth Century Maluku." PhD diss., The Australian National University.

Bräuchler, B. 2003. "Cyberidentities at War: Religion, Identity, and the Internet in the Moluccan Conflict." *Indonesia* 75 (April 2003): 123–51.

Buehler, M. 2008. "The Rise of Shari'a By-laws in Indonesian Districts: An Indication for Changing Patterns of Power Accumulation and Political Corruption." *South East Asia Research* 16 (2): 255–85.

di Meglio R.R. 1970. "Arab Trade with Indonesia and the Malay Peninsula from the 8th to the 16th Century." In *Islam and the Trade of Asia: A Colloquium*, ed. D.S. Richards, 105–35. Pennsylvania: University of Pennsylvania Press.

Duncan, C.R., ed. 2004. *Civilizing the Margins*. Ithaca, NY: Cornell University Press.

———. 2005a. "The Other Maluku: Chronologies of Conflict in North Maluku." *Indonesia* 80: 54–80.

———. 2005b. "Unwelcome Guests: Relations between Internally Displaced Persons and their Hosts in North Sulawesi Indonesia." *Journal of Refugee Studies* 18 (1): 25–46.

———. 2008. "Where do we go from here? The Politics of Ending Displacement in Post-Conflict North Maluku." In *Conflict, Violence, and Displacement in Indonesia*, ed. Eva-Lotta E. Hedman, 207–30. Ithaca, NY: Cornell University Southeast Asia Program Publications.

Ellen, R. 1983. "Social Theory, Ethnography and the Understanding of Practical Islam in Southeast Asia." In *Islam in Southeast Asia*, ed. M.B. Hooker, 51–91. Leiden: Brill.

Ellen, R. 2003. *On the Edge of the Banda Zone. Past and Present in the Social Organization of a Moluccan Trading Network*. Honolulu, HI: University of Hawai'i Press.

Fealy, G. 2008. "Consuming Islam: Commodified Religion and Aspirational Pietism in Contemporary Indonesia." In *Expressing Islam: Religious Life and Politics in Indonesia*, ed. G. Fealy and S. White, 15–39. Singapore: Institute of Southeast Asian Studies.

Fealy, G. and S. White, eds. 2008. *Expressing Islam: Religious Life and Politics in Indonesia*. Singapore: Institute of Southeast Asian Studies.

Fox J.J., ed. 1980. *The Flow of Life, Essays on Eastern Indonesia*. Harvard: Harvard University Press.

Fox, J.J. 2004. "Islam and Asia: Currents in Contemporary Islam in Indonesia." Paper presented at Harvard Asia Vision 21, 29 April–1 May 2004, Cambridge, Mass.

Fox J.J. and Sather C., eds. 1996. *Origins, Ancestors and Alliance: Explorations in Austronesian Ethnography*. Canberra: ANU Press.

Goodman, T. 1998. "The Sosolot Exchange Network of Eastern Indonesia." In *Perspectives on the Bird's Head of Irian Jaya*, Proceedings of the Conference, Leiden, 13–17 October 1997, ed. J. Miedema, C. Ode and R.A.C. Dam, 421–54. Amsterdam: Editions Rodopi B.V.

Goro, A.K.G. 1977. "Sejarah Perkembangan Agama Islam di Kabupaten Kupang" [The History of the Growth of Islam in Kupang District]. BA diss., Universitas Nusa Cendana, Kupang.

Gunn, G.C. 1999. *Timor Loro Sae: 500 years*. Macau: Livros do Oriente.

Hutagalung S. 2015. "Being Muslim in a Christian Town: Variety, Practices, and Renewal." PhD diss., Canberra: The Australian National University.

______. 2016. "Muslim-Christian Relations in Kupang: Negotiating Space and Maintaining Peace." *The Asia Pacific Journal of Anthropology* 17 (5): 439–59.

Kartodirdjo, S. 1966. *The Peasants Revolt of Banten in 1888: Its Conditions, Course and Sequel: A Case Study of Social Movements in Indonesia*. 's-Gravenhage: Martinus Nijhoff.

Klinken, G. van. 2007. *Communal Violence and Democratization in Indonesia: Small Town Wars*. London: Routledge.

McRae, D. 2013. *A Few Poorly Organized Men: Interreligious Violence in Poso, Indonesia*. Power and Place in Southeast Asia Series. Amsterdam: Brill.

McWilliam, A.R. 2009. "The Spiritual Commons: Some Immaterial Aspects of Community Economies in Eastern Indonesia." *TAJA* 20: 163–77.

Meilink-Roelofsz, M.A.P. 1962. *Asian Trade and European Influence in the Indonesian Archipelago between 1500 and 1630*. The Hague: Martinus Nijhoff.

Mobini-Kesheh, N. 1999. *The Hadrami Awakening: Community and Identity in the Netherlands East Indies 1900–1942*. Ithaca: Cornell Southeast Asia Program.

Palmer, B. 2010. "Migration and Sukses in Boneoge, South Sulawesi." PhD diss., The Australian National University.

Parsons, N. and M. Mietzner. 2009. "Sharia By-Laws in Indonesia: A Legal and Political Analysis." *Asian Law Journal* 11: 190–217.

Reid, A., ed. 1993. *Southeast Asia in the Early Modern Era: Trade, Power, and Belief.* Cornell: Cornell University Press.

Reid, A. 1995. "Continuity and Change in the Austronesian Transition to Islam and Christianity." In *The Austronesians: Historical and Comparative Perspectives*, ed. Peter Bellwood, James J. Fox and Darrell Tryon, 333–50. Canberra: The Australian National University.

———. 1999 [1988]. *Southeast Asia in the Age of Commerce 1450–1680*, vol. I *The Lands Below the Winds*, 7th printing. New Haven and London: Yale University Press.

Reuter, T. 2006. *Sharing the Earth, Dividing the Land: Land and Territory in the Austronesian World.* Canberra: ANU E Press.

Ricklefs, M.C. 1979. "Six Centuries of Islamization in Java." In *Conversion to Islam*, ed. Nehemia Levtzion, 100–28. New York: Holmes & Meier.

———. 2007. *Polarising Javanese Society: Islamic and Other Visions, c. 1830–1930.* Singapore: NUS Press.

Robinson, K. 2002. "Inter-Ethnic Violence: The Bugis and the Problem of Explanation." In *Beyond Jakarta: Regional Autonomy and Local Society in Indonesia*, ed. Minako Sakai, 145–72. Adelaide: Crawford House Publishing.

Sakai, M. 2010. "Performing Fasting in Indonesia: Social Meanings of Fasting among Muslims." ANRC Paper presented at the Workshop on Human Security and Religious Certainty in Southeast Asia, Chiang Mai University, Thailand, 15–17 January 2010.

Sihbudi, R. and M. Nurhasim, eds. 2001. *Kerusuhan Sosial Di Indonesia: Studi Kasus Kupang, Mataram dan Sambas* [Social Violence in Indonesia: Study Cases of Kupang, Mataram and Sambas]. Jakarta: Grasindo, Kantor Menteri Negara Riset dan Teknologi RI, Lembaga Ilmu Pengetahuan Indonesia.

Sila, A. 2015. "Being Muslim in Bima of Sumbawa, Indonesia: Practice, Politics and Cultural Diversity." PhD diss., The Australian National University.

Southon, M. 1995. *The Navel of the Perahu: Meaning and Values in the Maritime Trading Economy of a Butonese Village.* Canberra: Research School of Pacific and Asian Studies, The Australian National University with the Australian Centre for International Agricultural Research.

Spyer, P. 2002. "Fire without Smoke and Other Phantoms of Ambon's Violence: Media Effects, Agency, and the Work of Imagination." *Indonesia*, no. 74: 21–36.

Statistics Indonesia (BPS) Population Census 2000; analysis of data by Phillip Winn.

van Bruinessen, M. 1999. "Global and Local in Indonesian Islam." *Southeast Asian Studies* 37 (2): 157–75.

Vischer M.P., ed. 2009. *Precedence: Social Differentiation in the Austronesian World*. Canberra: ANU Press.

Widyatmika, M. 2004. *Sejarah Islam Di Nusa Tenggara Timur* [The History of Islam in East Nusa Tenggara]. Kupang: Pusat Pengembangan Madrasah and Kantor Wilayah Departemen Agama Propinsi Nusa Tenggara Timur.

______. 2008. *Menyulasuri Jejak Islam di Bumi Cendana* [Searching for the Imprint of Islam in the Land of Cendana]. Kupang: Pusat Pengembangan Madrasah.

Wilson, C. 2005. "The Ethnic Origins of Religious Conflict in North Maluku Province, Indonesia 1999–2000." *Indonesia* 79: 69–91.

Glossary

The glossary has standardised Indonesian and Arabic spellings based on the following sources:

Balai Pustaka. 1995. *Kamus Besar Bahasa Indonesia*, Edisi Kedua. Jakarta: Departemen Pendidikan dan Kebudayaan.

Echols, J.M. and H. Shadily. 1965. *An Indonesian–English Dictionary*, second edition. Ithaca, NY: Cornell University Press.

Fealy, Greg and Virginia Hooker (comp. and eds.). 2006. *Voices of Islam in Southeast Asia. A Contemporay Sourcebook*. Singapore: ISEAS Publishing.

Federspiel, Howard M. 1995. *A Dictionary of Indonesian Islam*. Athens, OH: Ohio University Centre for International Studies.

adat [Ind.]: custom, tradition

Ahli Sunnah Wal-Jamaah [Ind.; Ar. *ahl al-sunna wa al-jamaa'a*]: followers of the Prophet's tradition and the consensus of the *ulama* (Islamic scholars)

akad nikah, *akad* [Ind.]: marriage contract

akekah [Ind.; Ar. *'aqiiqah*]: birth ritual involving the shaving of a baby's head and animal sacrifice

akhlak [Ind; Ar. *akhlaaq*]: morals, morality, ethics; used for individual behaviour and for codes of ideal behaviour for all Muslims as laid down in the Qur'an and *hadis*

As'adiyah: influential Islamic learning institution in South Sulawesi comprising *pesantren*, *madrasah* and training of *ulama*

Aswaja: refers to Ahli Sunnah Wal-Jamaah (commonly understood to refer to traditionalist Islam in Indonesia)

azan [Ind.; Ar. *adhaan*]: call to prayer

baca baca [Ind.]: recitation of prayers and mantras

barzanji: popular literary genre, poems recounting the life of the Prophet recited at life cycle rituals and thanksgiving, named for its author, Al Barzanji; special prayers given on the birthday of the Prophet (see Maulid Nabi)

BBM [Bugis, Buton and Makassar]: pejorative acronym for Sulawesi-origin language communities, a word play on the acronym for oil based fuels (Bahan Bakar Mesin)

berkat/berkah [also *barkat*, *barakat*, *barakah* [Ind.]; Ar. *baaraka*; Bug. *barekka'*]: God's blessing

bidah [Ind.; Ar. *bid'ah*]: heresy or innovations in religion

bilal [Ind.; Ar. *bilaal*]: name of an Ethiopian member of the Prophet's community who had the duty of uttering the call to prayer to summon worshippers to the mosque for each of the five daily prayers; name referring to the *muezzin* whose duty is to make the call to prayer

bismillah [Ind.; Ar. *Bismillaah*]: In the name of God

buku nikah [Ind.]: marriage certificate

bupati [Ind.]: district head

busana Muslim [Ind.]: Muslim dress

dakwah [Ind.; Ar. *da'wah*]: Islamic proselytisation

Darul Islam/DI [Ind.; Ar. *daar al-Islaam*]: Abode of Islam; place where Islamic law and teachings are upheld; in Indonesia this refers to the Islamic-inspired rebellion against the newly formed government of Indonesia, aimed at establishing the new republic as an Islamic state. It was led by the charismatic figures Kartosoewirjo, in West Java; Daud Beureuh in Aceh, and Kahar Muzakkar in southern Sulawesi. It continues to exist as a non-violent political movement.

desa [Ind.]: village

doa [Ind.; Ar. *du'aa'*]: prayer, usually in the sense of supplication to God, as opposed to liturgical prayer

duduk bersanding [Ind.]: bride and groom sit next to each other in the marriage ceremony

dukun [Ind.]: indigenous healer and/or ritual practitioner; *dukun pesta* [Ind.] ritual expert for festivals, especially weddings

dikir/zikir [Ind.; Ar. *dhikr*]*:* repetition of the names of Allah and other religious formulae as a way of demonstrating piety, or to induce a trance; devotional prayer for the remembrance of God

fatwa [Ind.; Ar. *fatwaa*]: ruling on a point of law or dogma issued by an authorised scholar

fikih [Ind.; Ar. *fiqh*]: Islamic jurisprudence

fitnah [Ind.; Ar. *fitna*]: slander, calumny, sexual temptation which can lead men to sin

hadis [Ind.; Ar. *ḥadith*]: report or account of the words or deeds of the Prophet Muhammad; Hadis form a basic source of Islamic law

Hadhrami/Hadrami [Ind.]: people from the Hadhramaut region of Yemen and their diasporic communities.

hafiz [Ind.; Ar. *ḥaafiẓ*]: "preserver"; those who memorise the Qur'an in its entirety (30 chapters)

haj [Ind.; Ar. *ḥajj*]: annual pilgrimage to Mecca during the month of Dhu al-Hijjah

haji [Ind.]: one who has made the *haj* pilgrimage; title and term of address for a male who has performed the *haj* (female *hajjah*)

halal [Ind.; Ar. *ḥalaal*]: allowed, permitted (under Islamic law)

halaqah [Ind.; Ar. *ḥalqah*]: religious gatherings and study circles

haram [Ind.; Ar. *ḥaraam*]: forbidden, proscribed (under Islamic law)

hijrah [Ind.; Ar.]: the "flight" of Muhammad and his followers from Mecca to Medina to avoid persecution; to avoid, withdrawal (from a threatening environment)

Himpunan Mahasiswa Islam/HMI: The Muslim Students' Association, one of the largest students' associations in Indonesia

Hizbut Tahrir Indonesia/HTI: Liberation Party founded in Jerusalem in 1953 with the central aim of reviving the caliphate; Indonesian branch active from 1982

hukum [Ind.; Ar. *ḥukm*]: law

Idul Adha [Ind.; Ar. 'Iid al-Aḍḥa]: "the feast of the sacrifice"; held on the tenth day of Dhu al-Hijja after the conclusion of the *haj* rituals to remember Abraham's willingness to sacrifice his son when tested by God; unblemished animals are slaughtered and their meat distributed to the poor

Idul Fitri [Ind.; Ar. 'Iid al-Fiṭr]: "festival of breaking the fast" is an important religious holiday celebrated by Muslims worldwide to mark the end of Ramadan. The holiday celebrates the conclusion of the 29 or 30 days of dawn-to-sunset fasting (*ṣawm*) during the month of Ramadan. The day of 'Iid falls on the first day of the month of Shawwal (the tenth month in the Islamic calendar)

ikhlas [Ind.; Ar. *ikhlaaṣ*]: sincere; absolute devotion to God in religious faith, practice and action

ikhtilat [Ind.; Ar. *ikhtilaaṭ*]: prohibition of social mixing between men and women

imam: "model", "exemplar", the spiritual leader of a Muslim community or group; the leader of prayers in a mosque; in this volume the term refers to a local religious authority

imam besar [Ind.]: grand imam such as the grand imam of Istiqlal Mosque, central Jakarta; official title for an imam in charge of leading congregational prayers religious rites in a Grand Mosque (Mesjid Raya)

imam desa [Ind.]: village imam

imam pembantu [Ind.]: assistant imam

imam rawatib [Ind.]: imams assigned to take turns to lead optional prayers in the mosque, for example the *tarawih* prayers in the fasting month of Ramadan *imam tetap* [Ind.]: permanent or professional leader of the five congregational prayers

imam salat [Ind.]: leaders of congregational prayer in mosques

imam tarawih: a seasonal leader of congregational prayer during Ramadan

Inco: Inco (International Nickel) was a Canadian mining company and the world's leading producer of nickel; in 2006 it was purchased by the Brazilian mining company Vale; the Indonesian subsidiary was called PT Inco, but is now called PT Vale

iqra [Ind.]: reading module used at the beginner level of Qur'anic learning

Islamist [Eng.] term for social and religious activism that asserts that public and political life should be guided by Islamic principles; also used to refer to movements that want the formal implementation of *sharia*

Isra Mi'raj [Ind.]: Ascension and Night Journey of the Prophet

Istiqamah: school founded by a religious cleric (KH. Muzdakir Ali) in Kahar Muzakkar's Islamic state, dedicated to purifying Islam in South Sulawesi after the latter's dissatisfaction with Muhammadiyah

isya [Ind.; Ar. *'ishaa'*]: night-time daily prayer

jemaah, *jamaat* [Ind.; Ar. *jamaa'ah*]: congregation, assembly

Jemaah Tabligh/Tablighi Jamaat: an Islamic organisation founded in India in 1927 by Muhammad Ilyas al-Kandahlawi in India

jilbab [Ind.]: tight veil, head covering that exposes face but not hair, neck or ears

juz [Ind.; Ar. *juz'*]: section of the Qur'an

kabupaten [Ind.]: district

kadi [Bug.; Mak.; Ar. *qaadiy*]: judge in religious court; an official appointed by Bugis and Makassar polities responsible for the administration of Islam

kafir [Ind.; Ar. *kaafir*]: infidel, non-believer (in Islam)

mengaji [Ind.]: recite Qur'anic verses; learn to read the Qur'an

kalesunrang [Mak.]: rank price

kawin [Ind.]: to be married, marriage/wedding

kawin kontrak [Ind.]: contract marriage

kawin Islam [Ind.]: Islamic marriage, sometimes referring to unregistered marriage which has been conducted according to Islamic law

kawin lari [Ind.]: elopement

kecamatan [Ind.]: sub-district

kelurahan [Ind.]: political district administered by a *lurah*; suburb/neighbourhood in urban area

kenduri [Ind.]: ritual communal meal (held on any number of occasions; often including Islamic prayers and blessings)

kepala desa [Ind.]: village head

Kesatuan Aksi Mahasiswa Muslim Indonesia/KAMMI: The Indonesian Muslim Student Action Union, founded by activists of Jemaah Tarbiyah in 1998

Khalwatiah: a Sufi *tarekat* organisation

khatib [Ind.; Ar. *khaaṭib*]: mosque official (who gives the sermon at the Friday communal worship)

khutbah/*khotbah* [Ind.; Ar. *khuṭbah*]: sermon (especially during Friday communal prayers)

kiai or *kyai* [Ind.]: "lofty", "noble": title of religious scholar/s or leader/s

KUA/Kantor Urusan Agama: Office for Religious Affairs

KUHP: Kitab Undang-Undang Hukum Pidana, Indonesian Criminal Law

kunut [Ind.]: a special recitation made at the second cycle of the morning prayer

La Galigo: a textual corpus/religious tradition with roots in pre-Islamic South Sulawesi societies

langgar [Ind.; Ar. *muṣalla*]: small prayer house

lebe [Bim.]: Islamic cleric or person in charge of leading the ritual prayer in a mosque

Lembaga Dakwah Kampus/LDK: Islamic Campus Predication; refers to diverse university based-movements, particularly Jemaah Tarbiyah, Hizbut Tahrir and Jama'ah Tabligh or Tablighi Jama'at

liqo [Ind.; Ar. *liqaa'*]: used by followers of Jemaah Tarbiyah to refer to their weekly religious circles

madrasah [Ind.; Ar.]: "place of study"; Islamic school administered by the Indonesian Ministry of Religion (not the Ministry of Education), and offering a curriculum focused on Islamic religion and secular subjects

magrib [Ind.]: sunset; the evening prayer

majlis taklim [Ind.; Ar. *majlis al-ta'liim*]: Islamic religious circle

Majelis Tabligh (MT): a section within Muhammadiyah concerned with *tabligh*: the deepening of understanding among Muslims concerning Islamic teaching through instruction

makole [Sor./Mori]: customary ruler

mandi bersih [Ind.]: symbolic bathing to cleanse the body before taking the Islamic wedding vows

marbut [Ind.]: caretaker of mosque, primarily responsible for cleaning

masjid/mesjid [Ind.; Ar. *masjid*]: mosque

masjid agung [Ind.]: grand mosque indicates either a newly built, bigger and better architecturally designed mosque in the district capital or a newly renovated longstanding great mosque/*masjid raya*

masjid raya [Ind.]: "official" or state mosque located in the district or subdistrict capital

Maulid Nabi [Ind.]: birthday of the Prophet Muhammad celebrated on the twelfth day of the month Rabiulawal *mazhab* [Ind.; Ar. *madhhab*]: ("direction"; school of legal thought; the four main schools in Sunni Islam are Shafi'i, Maliki, Hanafi and Hanbali/Hambali distinguished by their different methods of jurisprudential reasoning

mayat/mayit [Ind.] human corpse

mantri sawah [Ind.]: agricultural extension officer

merantau [Ind.]: sojourning, economic migration

mihrab [Ind.; Ar. *miḥraab*]: niche in the centre of one wall of the mosque denoting the direction of the Kaaba in Mecca (*kiblat*); place where the imam stands to lead congregational prayer

mimbar [Ind.; Ar. *minbar*]: the pulpit, speakers podium in the mosque from which the Friday sermon is given

Modernist: Term denoting a religious strand that puts emphasis on teaching purely derived from the Qur'an and Hadis. Inspired by reforming movements in Saudi Arabia in the late 19th and early 20th century. In Indonesia it has given rise to movements such as Muhammadiyah, Persis and more recently Jemaah Tarbiyah, and is distinguished from Traditionalist Islam (represented by NU) which upholds the distinctive modes of Islam that have developed through accommodation to local practices.

modin [Ind.; Ar. *mu'adhdhin*]: religious functionary/mosque official who calls the congregation to prayer (*azan*) (synonym *muazin/ muezzin*)

mualaf [Ind.; Ar. *mu'allaf*]: a person who has newly converted to Islam

mubalig (m)/*mubaligah* (f) [Ar.; Bug. *pattabellek* or *padda'wa*]: preacher

mudarris [Ar.]: teacher

Muhammadiyah: A socio-religious organisation in Indonesia founded in 1912 by Ahmad Dahlan. It has a modernist or reformist inclination; and is often distinguished from, or even opposed to, more traditionalist religious organisations such as Nahdlatul Ulama (NU) and As'adiyah.

musholla [Ind.; Ar. *muṣalla*]: prayer house or room for performance of religious duties, smaller than a mosque

MTQ/Musabaqah Tilawatil Qur'an: Indonesian religious festival which focuses reading of the Qur'an in a beautiful manner

Muslimah Dakwah Kampus: Proselytising group for young women on university campuses run by Wahdah Islamiyah

NTT (Nusa Tenggara Timor): East Nusa Tenggara (Province)

Nahdlatul Ulama/NU: "renaissance of the religious scholars"; Indonesia's largest Islamic Organisation established in 1926 to promote traditionalist Islam

negeri [Ind.]: local socio-political entity, Maluku

New Order: self-ascribed title of the Suharto regime (1966–98)

Normalisasi Kehidupan Kampus/NKK: "Normalisation of Campus Life": policy issued by Suharto regime in 1979 aimed at controlling student political activity

Orang Asli Sorowako OAS [Ind.]: "original" or Indigenous people of Sorowako

Pancasila [Ind.]: "Five Principles"; the ideological foundation of Indonesia: Belief in One God, Humanitarianism, National Unity, Democracy as expressed through Representatives of the People, and Social Justice

panrita [Bug.]: a man with knowledge and authority including as a religious leader in his community

pengajian [Ind.]: Qur'anic recitation; religious studies group

penghulu [Ind.]: term for mosque officials; also term for civil servants dealing with religious matters

pengkaderan [Ind.]: caderisation programme, creating cadres

Pengkaderan Muhammadiyah: Muhammadiyah caderisation called DAD/Darul Arqam Dasar

peraturan daerah [Ind.]: district regulation

perda syariah [Ind.]: district regulation influenced by sharia

Persis: Persatuan Islam (Islamic Association); reformist Islamic organisation founded in 1923, belonging to the modernist stream (and expressing an early view of fundamentalism)

pesantren [Ind.]: place of the *santri*; traditional Islamic school where most students are boarders

pesantren kilat [Ind.]: short intensive courses on Islam usually held in *pesantren*

Qur'an [Ind.; Ar. al-Qur'aan]: God's word as revealed to the Prophet Muhammad; the primary scripture of Islam; believed by Muslims to be a miracle revealed through the medium of the angel Gibrail, and serving as a guide for human conduct

Qur'an kecil [Ind.]: "little Qur'an"; the 30th part of the Qur'an, usually printed separately from the whole Qur'an

raja bicara [Ind./Bim.]: prime minister; secular authority subordinate to the sultan

rakaat [Ind.]: essential unit of prayer cycle of postures in the ritual prayer consisting of standing, sitting, bowing and prostrating a prescribed number of times

Ramadan [Ind.]: ninth month of the Islamic lunar calendar; the fasting month

rukun Islam [Ind.; Ar. *rukn al-Islaam*]: pillar, essential principle. There are five "pillars" or foundational principles of Islam: the confession of faith, prayer, fasting, pilgrimage and giving alms to the poor.

sajadah [Ind.]: prayer mat

Salafi [Ind.; Ar. Salafiyyun]: a term for those who seek to emulate the practice of the Pious Ancestors; to return to the teaching and example of the earliest Muslims at the time of the Prophet

Salafism [Ind.]: Term used to describe movements that seek to return to the early teachings and practice of Islam; used to denote the strictest and most puritanical of religious movements *salam* [Ind.; Ar. *salaam*]: "peace", used in greeting and in concluding the prayer

salat [Ind.; Ar. *ṣalaat*]: the prescribed ritual prayer to be performed five times a day: dawn prayer/*salat subuh* [Ind.], early afternoon/*salat zuhur* [Ind.], late afternoon/*salat asar* [Ind.], sunset/*salat magrib* [Ind.], and evening/*salat isya* [Ind.]

salat Jumat [Ind.]: Friday congregational prayer

sara' [Bug.]: Islamic law and institutions

selamatan [Ind.]: a ceremonial meal to commemorate important events in an individual's life

selawat [Ind.] *ṣalawaat* [Ar.]: a prayer to God containing salutation upon the Prophet Muhammad

Shafi'i [Ind.; Ar. Shaafi'ī]: one of the four main Sunni law schools; dominant in Southeast Asia

sharia [Eng.]: Islamic law, the holy law of God

sigi/masigi [Mak.]: mosque

silariang [Bug./Mak.]: both man and woman agree to leave or run away

siri' [Bug.]: honour

soa [Amb.]: a territorial/social grouping of a number of lineages

subuh [Ind.]: dawn, time the early morning obligatory prayer

sujud [Ind.]: bow from a kneeling position to touch forehead to floor; prostrate oneself in the act of prayer

sunnah [Ind.; Ar.]: established custom and normative precedent in Islam based on the precedent of the Prophet Muhammad

surah [Ind.]: a chapter of the Qur'an

syahadat [Ind.]: the profession of faith, that there is no god but God and Muhammad is His messenger *tabligh* [Ind.]: sermon at a religious meeting; Islamic concept concerning the deepening of understanding through instruction

tafsir [Ind.; Ar. *tafsiir*]: explanation of passages of al Qur'an by supplying additional information; the genre of religious literature that provides commentary on the structure, language and usage of the Qur'an

tahfiz [Ind.; Ar. *taḥfiiẓ*]: "know by heart"; referring to Qur'an memorisation

tahfiz al-Qur'an [Ind.]: Qur'an memorisation programme of the religious organisation As'adiyah

tahiyat [Ind.]: welcoming prayer upon entering the mosque; consisting of two cycles

tahlil [Ind.; Ar. *tahliil*]: repeated recitation of the confession of faith, "There is no god but God"

tahlilan [Ind.]: ritual prayers to commemorate the deceased

tajwid [Ind., Ar. *tajwiid*]: rigorous system of vocalisation for correct recitation of Al Qur'an

tarawih [Ind.; Ar. *taraawiiḥ*]: non obligatory special prayer performed in the evening in the month of Ramadan

tarbiah/tarbiyah [Ind., Ar.]: Islamic education

tarekat [Ind.; Ar. *ṭariiqah*]: methods used by mystics to come into the presence of God; a Sufi group or order

tasbih [Ind.]: prayer beads

TPA/Taman Pendidikan Al-Qur'an: informal school where students are instructed in religious practice, often by young professional *ustadz*

tiang alif [Ind.]: pole; structural element at the highest point of the mosque roof. *Alif* is the first letter of the Arabic alphabet

tilawah [Ind.; Ar. *tilaawah*]: the recitation of the Qur'an

Traditionalist (Islam): The forms of Islamic practice identifying with long-held beliefs and practices as laid down by the schools of jurisprudence (*mazhab*) especially the Shafi'i school in Indonesia. In the Indonesian context, it most commonly refers to the practices endorsed by Nahdlatul Ulama which upholds the distinctive modes of Islam that have developed through accommodation to local practices.

UIN/Universitas Islam Negeri: State Islamic University

ulama [Ind.]: religious scholar; from Arabic, plural of *alim* meaning "learned"; Islamic scholar/s

umat [Ind.; Ar. *'ummah*]: community of believers, usually used for Muslims

UMI/Universitas Muslim Indonesia: Muslim University of Indonesia

umrah/umroh [Ind.; Ar. *'umrah*]: the "lesser pilgrimage"; to perform pilgrimage to Mecca outside of the haj season (between the eight and thirteenth days of the twelfth month Dhul-Hijjah)

undang undang [Ind.]: law

UNISMUH/Universitas Muhammadiyah Makassar: Muhammadiyah University of Makassar

UNM/Universitas Negeri Makassar: Makassar State University

usrah [Ind.; Ar. *'usrah*]: Arabic word for family, used interchangeably with "*halaqah*", meaning the method of religious instruction based on a small group. Associated with the Egyptian Muslim Brotherhood

ustad/ustadz [Ind.; Ar. *'ustaadhun*]: religious teacher

ustazah [Ind.]: female preacher

Wahdah Islamiyah: Makassar-based Salafi movement

Wahhabi: Saudi-based religious purification and social reform movement founded in the late 18th century by Muhammad ibn 'Abd al-Wahhab; used for some contemporary reformist groups

wakaf [Ind.; Ar. *waqf*]: property donated for religious purposes; perpetual charitable trust for religious purposes

wali [Ind.; Ar. *waliy*]: male relative, guardian

wali kota [Ind.]: mayor

wudu: ritual ablution before prayers

YASIM/Yayasan Islam: Islamic organisation founded in 1968 to represent the royal family in appointing mosque officials in Bima

zakat [Ind.; Ar. *zakaah*]: "purification"—wealth tax, alms; one of the five pillars of Islam

zakat fitrah [Ind.; Ar. *zakt al-fiṭr*]: payment, often in the form of food, to those in need; marks the end of the fasting month

zikir/dzikir [Ind.; Ar. *dhikr*]: Repetition of the names of Allah and other religious formulae as a way of demonstrating piety, or to induce a trance; devotional prayer for the remembrance of God

List of Contributors

Wahyuddin Halim is Senior Lecturer in Anthropology and former Director, Center for the Study of Islam, Science and Technology (PuKISTek), Alauddin State Islamic University of Makassar.

Stella Aleida Hutagalung is an independent researcher in Jakarta focusing on gender, social inclusion and interfaith issues.

Andrew McWilliam is Foundation Professor of Anthropology, University of Western Sydney.

Eva F. Nisa is Senior Lecturer, Anthropology, College of Asia and the Pacific, The Australian National University.

Kathryn M. Robinson is Emeritus Professor, Anthropology, College of Asia and the Pacific, The Australian National University.

Faried F. Saenong is Researcher, School of Humanities and Social Sciences, the University of New South Wales (UNSW) Canberra-Australia, and Institute of Perguruan Tinggi Ilmu Al-Qur'an (PTIQ) Jakarta.

Muhammad Adlin Sila is Research Professor, Research and Development Agency, Indonesian Ministry of Religious Affairs (MORA) and Lecturer at the Faculty of Social and Political Sciences, Syarif Hidayatullah State Islamic University, Jakarta.

Phillip Winn is former Senior Research Associate, Anthropology, College of Asia and the Pacific, Australian National University.

Moh Yasir Alimi lectures on the anthropology of religion in the Department of Sociology and Anthropology, Semarang State University.

Index

(The definite article "al" in names is ignored in sorting. Page numbers containing "n", such as "60n2", indicate page number and note number.)